Playing with Balance

Playing with Balance: Game Economy Design is your guide to understanding why games are unlike any other medium: they are built on verbs, not nouns. Players don't just watch or read – they do. Every choice, action, and interaction forms part of a living system designed to engage, challenge, and reward.

Great game economies are about far more than numbers or virtual currencies. They are intricately designed systems that blend anticipation, frustration, fear of missing out, and the relief of success. Through systems thinking, we can create experiences that keep players coming back – not through manipulation, but by balancing curiosity, challenge, frustration, and satisfaction across days, weeks, and months of play.

Oscar introduces the three loops of engagement – **Core, Context,** and **Culture** – showing how they build authentically on intrinsic player motivations to create value loops that feel desirable, meaningful, and fair. These foundations provide a framework for designing progression, difficulty, and rewards that truly resonate with different kinds of players. You'll discover why ethical design isn't just the right thing to do, but a commercial necessity – and why short-term exploitative tactics inevitably undermine long-term loyalty and success.

Drawing on deep industry experience and insights from leading designers, this book combines diverse perspectives with practical tools to help you calculate value, balance economies, and adapt from launch through LiveOps.

Whether you're building a small indie project or running a massive live game, *Playing with Balance: Game Economy Design* gives you the tools to craft mechanics that feel alive.

Oscar Clark is a pioneer in mobile and connected games. He has been working with online games since 1998 running British Telecom's online games platform, Wireplay. Since then, he has been the global lead for games for Hutchison Whampoa and their mobile operator Three in the

UK, the most successful mobile games platform in terms of revenue per user in the world in 2005. In 2006, he headed mobile strategy at Nvidia, where he led efforts to bring 3D gaming to mobile phones. He was also Home Architect for Sony's Online Virtual World, PlayStation Home, and Evangelist for Ads at Unity Technologies. He is currently CSO of Arcanix (BV), who are developing a LiveOps Strategy Platform initially for game development teams. Additionally, he works with the team at SteelMedia as a Contributing Editor.

Playing with Balance
Game Economy Design

Oscar Clark

CRC Press
Taylor & Francis Group
Boca Raton London New York

CRC Press is an imprint of the
Taylor & Francis Group, an **informa** business

Designed cover image: Oscar Clark

First edition published 2026
by CRC Press
2385 NW Executive Center Drive, Suite 320, Boca Raton FL 33431

and by CRC Press
4 Park Square, Milton Park, Abingdon, Oxon, OX14 4RN

CRC Press is an imprint of Taylor & Francis Group, LLC

ISBN: 9781032971605 (hbk)
ISBN: 9781032971599 (pbk)
ISBN: 9781003592471 (ebk)

DOI: 10.1201/9781003592471

Typeset in Minion Pro
by codeMantra

Contents

CHAPTER 1

Introduction

DOI: 10.1201/9781003592471-1

WHAT IS THIS BOOK ABOUT?

Games design is an art form with an identity crisis. Ask anyone and they will 'know' what a game designer is. But get them to explain what a designer does? Or the purpose of game design? Let alone what game design is? You will find a huge range of answers. Too many people will fixate on the visual art of a game, or the game code rather than exploring the mental magic when we connect a physical action to a mental problem. Even that core experience is just touching the surface, and in this book we will explore how simple mechanics can build into complex, compelling systems. We plan to unlock how we can create systems which can sustain player engagement with challenges, resolutions, rewards, purpose, progression, optimisation, and narrative in the context of collaboration and competition to create something which can create a cultural zeitgeist. Whether you are making a simple indie game, a huge liveops experience or want to see how the unique alchemy that goes into games can apply to your own endeavours please read on. This book is all about how we can play with balance to create sustainable delight for players.

DO GAMES MATTER?

Despite play being an integral human activity across all cultures throughout history, as well as observed in a wide variety of animals, including crocodiles,[1] we still too often dismiss games as being trivial or 'for kids.' Despite that, the explosion of, in particular, mobile games since the introduction of the iPhone App Store in 2008 has transformed almost everyone into game-players to some level.

But it's not just because games are the single largest form of digital entertainment on the planet[2] that they are important, they also provide a unique form of media which combines problem-solving, physical interaction, and narrative with expression and personal agency. Games are verbs, unlike any other media. We "Do".

The consequences of this mean that games provide an amazing framework to safely explore human nature at a personal level, through experiencing the narrative personally and within our own perspectives and decisions, the medium allows us to explore motivation and engagement at a deep level. Indeed, according to a meta-analysis in *Contemporary Educational Psychology*[3] "...narrative video games are able to affect players' attitudes towards the topics depicted in these games. This effect is present in studies focused on both implicit and explicit changes in attitude."

In turn, as we have learned more about this relatively young form of entertainment[4] (compared to Movies/Novels/etc.), video games have evolved into living, 'breathing' ecosystems that increasingly need to simulate expected experiences from the real world, which includes providing reactions and consequences for decisions made within the game. Some of this comes through in terms of the physics in the interactions; apply a force on an object and it should move in ways which appear consistent with the game context (often not the same as the real – Mario can jump five times his height[5]!). Other considerations come from the relationship between effort, reward, and engagement. This can be thought of in terms of Flow, as defined by psychologist Mihaly Csikszentmihalyi,[6] which explored the balance between anxiety and boredom in creating sustained engagement states of mind. Then there are the behavioural factors, especially when it comes to competitive and collaborative effort. This is not just a theoretical application of what can be found in Game Theory founded by John von Neumann[7] in 1928, further explored in the pivotal *Theory of Games and Economic Behavior*. Games have to balance entertainment, engagement, suspension of disbelief, and in the end are not based solely on the principles of 'Zero-Sum-Game.'

Commercial games introduce real money into the entertainment equation as well. The implicit effect of 'real-world' stakes on a format which, according to the definition in Homo Ludens by Johan Huizinga,[8] should be "connected with no material interest, and no profit can be gained from it." However, we also acknowledge that the craft and production of games are valuable and are happy to exchange our hard-earned money for those experiences.

This book will explore the core concept of balance at the heart of all games, but with particular attention to how this affects commercial models of gameplay. This includes games we pay for upfront, including those which have sequels and additional downloadable paid content as well as those with In-App Purchases, Subscriptions, and of course Ad-Funded models.

A lot of focus will be on 'pay in game' models, commonly referred to as free-to-play, because these provide some of the best examples of the implementation of best practice and indeed include many of the most commercially successful games of all time.

However, these games, as we will endeavour to demonstrate, are usually delivered as a 'Service,' success is measured by lifetime value. This means that it is essential to understand what players are getting from playing your game and how you can continue to delight them over days, months, and years.

This book is about crafting balanced, thriving game economies that boost both engagement and retention – core elements that will help your game thrive in today's competitive landscape.

The focus here is not just on theoretical ideas but on real, validated game strategies based on data, player personas, and the ability to pivot. Whether you're an indie developer or part of a larger studio, mastering these principles is crucial for ensuring a game's long-term success.

HOW "GAME THINKING" CAN HELP ANY SERVICE ENGAGE THEIR AUDIENCE

At the time of writing, the games industry is just coming out of a difficult period, but even now remains the largest form of digital entertainment because games are generally not just 'consumed and done' in a couple of hours. Play often takes place over multiple sessions with many hours of play, throughout which we have a sense of a personal stake in the outcome. The level of immersion this delivers inherently engages players with something that becomes a personal life experience and one which can be shared with other players. This means that in games, especially services, the experience is not just in the media itself, but in the shared social context in which the audience engages, as well as the specifics of the mechanics. The common moments, the shared understanding, the chance to tell stories about our perspectives that can help us understand each other. This is something truly human. The emotions are, of course, shared by most other forms of media, even non-entertainment experiences; but only in games can that connection be intrinsic to the medium.

Building a common and shared social component helps us create a sustainable audience that has become critical to so many aspects of modern life, including commercial ones. Even high-street retail stores have recognised the benefits of adding a 'service' and community experience to survive and succeed. For example, in the UK, the historic music, video, and fan merchandise retailer, HMV, has bands perform live in their store venues to attract engagement.[9]

If we want to create a sustained, repeatable service experience, we need to have an understanding of the motivation of our audience and how we can sustain that engagement. This means we have to start out with an understanding of who and where that audience is. We face the challenge of understanding what will attract their interest when looking for something to play, and how our game provides anticipation, and delivers a satisfying experience. We need our audience to feel the immersion and delight in the pay-off from play as well as, ideally, leaving enough anticipation for them to want to do that again, and again, and again.

In game design terms, we can break this down into four stages:

- Start Condition
- Challenge
- Resolution
- Reward

We will explore how to use "game design thinking" in ways which specifically support the creation of great playing and social experiences in games. But we will also try to point out the common lessons that can be applied in other service-based industries. In this way, even if your focus is not specific to making a game, you can consider what these techniques can do for building better shared commercial experiences for your audience. This means exploring the ways you balance incentives, rewards, and forms of exchange in ways that keep your audience motivated to return again and again.

For game designers, we will also attempt to address the intricacies of managing in-game rewards against difficulty, and progression in ways which drive deep engagement and inspire players to explore the optimisation of their activity and resources. This will include currencies, power-ups, abilities, game modes, and cosmetic options inherent to play, and explore where commercial models and monetisation strategies can complement the overall experience. We intend to demonstrate that game economy design is a field of expertise that combines creativity, psychology, and data-driven precision; but that at its heart has to be about delivering satisfying experiences that make players feel good. We hopefully will also encourage you to look at other services' experiences, and what makes those great so you can apply the relevant concepts in your games too.

Whether you are managing a loyalty programme in retail, running a fitness app, or designing a learning management platform, the foundational concepts of game economy design can transform how you approach audience engagement, retention, and, of course, monetisation.

Ultimately, this book is a guide to understanding how incentives, progression, and balance shape human behaviour in complex systems. Whether you're a game developer or someone managing user engagement in another field, the tools and principles outlined here will help you design experiences that keep people invested and coming back for more.

Interview

SYSTEMS THINKING AND GAME DESIGN – AN INTERVIEW WITH EDWARD CASTRONOVA

One of the central factors of game economy design is the necessity to be able to think in systems rather than just linear interactions. Edward 'Ted' Castronova,[10] author and professor of media at Indiana University, has spent his career studying virtual economies and the complex systems that underpin them.

Systems thinking contrasts sharply with linear thinking. While linear thinking follows a straight cause-and-effect path, systems thinking seeks to understand how interconnected parts interact within a whole. As Castronova states:

> With systems thinking, there's causation, but it's so complex. It forces you to go into this vibrant electric ball of things that can happen. And then you get an outcome later, but perhaps more interesting than some outcomes from beginning to end.

One way to look at this type of complexity is to view the systems as a "black box." For example, if you had to prepare a bath without a plug: with separate hot and cold taps (common in the UK) which have to be adjusted separately, you can't test the temperature or see the water level only when the water comes out of the waste or overflow pipes. Getting the balance right would be extremely complicated due to the unpredictable nature of interconnected systems. Castronova expands on this,

> The frustrating thing is you can open the black box and you can walk around inside of it and look at everything and know absolutely everything inside the black box. But you can't really understand what it's doing until you step away and see the whole to see the emergent part.

This aspect of systems thinking (emergent properties) is an almost unquantifiable essence of a new thing that can't be traced to any of the particles.

"So when you're doing systems thinking, you're recognizing that an engine exists. …but you can't trace it to the spark plug and the fuel injector and the pistons. Just all of those things working together," Castronova continues.

Balance doesn't mean stasis.

"Systems thinking brings up this wonderful idea of equilibrium," says Castronova. He uses an analogy "Water is always running downhill [but] there are lakes. There are lakes on mountaintops."

This happens because of the unseen processes of evaporation and the water cycle, combined with the storage capacity of the lakes and the constraints on the flow rates. The apparent stability of water levels is a reflection of the dynamic nature of these phenomena working in equilibrium.

Dynamic equilibrium, where forces push and pull in opposite directions, creating apparent stability, is a useful model for game designers. The structures in our design and the forms and rates of exchange allow us to modify the outcome, but as Castronova states, this is "just sort of nudging the outcome over in this direction."

However, balance also creates engaging challenges. Players often seek the sweet spot between balance and imbalance, where their actions have meaningful consequences. As Castranova states:

It's not always about balancing all of the moments and the pieces of the puzzle. In fact, in some ways, creating the space in which we can act.

A common way to explore equilibriums and flow in game design lies in the management of exchange, often in the form of in-game currencies. Castronova describes the need for "faucets" (sources) that introduce currency and "drains" (sinks) that remove it, ensuring economic balance.

One of the key challenges in game design is accounting for emergent behaviour – unexpected player actions that arise from the system. Castronova highlights how a single player's strategy can spread, altering the entire game's dynamics.

"It's like a disease spreading through ideas," he says.

This underscores the importance of designing both global systems (overall game balance) and local incentives (individual player choices) to mitigate unintended consequences. As Castranova explains,

…you have to think holistically about what happens if all of my players do this?

Once one player identifies an exploit, they're all doing it. For example, "You can't have a merchant that sells an apple for one gold and another merchant that buys it for two gold." That would quickly explode and break the game economy.

Castranova also highlighted that, whilst complexity adds depth, excessive complexity can alienate players. Castronova asserts:

> The goal here isn't to have the most intricate economy with the most number of goods, but to have one that just feels so wonderful.

Games like *Faster Than Light* and *Plants vs. Zombies* demonstrate how simplicity, when combined with meaningful choices, can be deeply satisfying. In effective design, every player's decision point matters. Even in games with extensive item catalogs, clarity, and purpose in player choices are vital to maintaining engagement.

Players derive satisfaction not just from mechanics but from the stories and meanings that emerge from their interactions. Castronova draws parallels to music, where expectation and resolution create pleasure. In games, a tool might have an obvious use, but can become unexpectedly valuable, enriching the player's experience through surprise and discovery.

This application of context separates game economy design from economic game theory. Take the example of the Prisoner's Dilemma: for an economist, this is a question of logical maximisation of utility for the players, or indeed, a zero-sum game. As Castranova describes when talking about the Prisoner's Dilemma:

> There's no fairness [in the model]. The numbers in the cells totally and completely describe all of their payoffs… Economists would predict this certain outcome because they assume that everyone would approach this system in a completely faultless hypothetical, whereas, as you point out, when you actually put people through it, they bring in all kinds of assumptions into this situation.

Game designers have to consider how the Prisoner's Dilemma mechanic is profoundly affected by context, emotion, and narrative.

Castranova went on to think about some underexplored areas in game economies, such as public goods and common-pool resources. Introducing mechanics where players collectively manage shared resources (like a communal fishing lake) can foster cooperation and community building, but at the same time, "if we all fish in the lake, all the fish are going to die," a principle known as The Tragedy of the Commons. This was considered inevitable until the Nobel prize-winning work of Elina Ostram[11] which recognised the ability of groups to avoid the tragedy of the commons without requiring top-down regulation.[12] As Castronova asserts:

> "If you have an incredibly important common-pool resource, you'll get a community where people are going to say, stop fishing. You have to get away from that. Right. We all get to fish for 10 minutes a day and nobody gets to fish any more than that. And it would all be enforced through, you know, social stigma and norms". He went on to explore how they can be leveraged in game by allowing the development of nations/factions who fight against one another for control of those resources – something we see come to life in games like EVE Online. Castronova commented on how important it was that EVE "brought out all of the very realistic actions, including fraud and theft. That's a real thing."

This speculation takes us beyond just basic currencies, to consider other interesting types of resource/goods, like the airwaves (broadcast frequencies) which are less tangible but can have a profound impact on a game economy.

One of the techniques outlined in this book is the concept of the 'Anchor Currency,' and Castronova went on to explain: "I think, [an Anchor currency] unlocks a bunch of stuff about where you start when you launch an economy. Because … it's forcing the players to think about the value of their own time."

The concept of a resource that can only be obtained from play allows us to create a fixed rate against which that player can assign a value to their own time spent in the game, compared to that in the real world.

> "Now you have something firm and you can just internally say, okay, I want an orange to cost a half an hour of someone's time," Castronova states. "And then that tells you how to price it."

Ultimately, systems thinking in game design aims to create satisfying, sustainable experiences. As Castronova concludes:

"The economy exists to make people happy, not rich." By focusing on how systems interact, predicting emergent behaviours, and valuing player time, designers can craft engaging economies that stand the test of time.

NOTES

1 https://www.sciencenews.org/blog/wild-things/five-surprising-animals-play
2 https://www.forbes.com/councils/forbesagencycouncil/2023/11/17/the-gaming-industry-a-behemoth-with-unprecedented-global-reach/
3 https://www.sciencedirect.com/journal/contemporary-educational-psychology
4 https://www.history.com/topics/inventions/history-of-video-games
5 https://www.techradar.com/news/the-real-life-physics-of-super-mario-how-could-a-portly-plumber-jump-that-high
6 https://en.wikipedia.org/wiki/Mihaly_Csikszentmihalyi
7 https://en.wikipedia.org/wiki/John_von_Neumann
8 https://en.wikipedia.org/wiki/Johan_Huizinga
9 https://hmv.com/live
10 linkedin.com/in/edward-castronova-951a8a8a
11 https://evonomics.com/tragedy-of-the-commons-elinor-ostrom/
12 https://youtu.be/s4Z1SNhYs18?si=yURAvmvN9jhshMC7

CHAPTER 2

Defining an Economy

DOI: 10.1201/9781003592471-2

BASIC ECONOMIC CONCEPTS

Economics is the study of how societies use limited resources to satisfy the wants and needs of people, often defined as 'Utility' – the quality or condition of being useful. In essence, it considers the concept that resources such as land, labour, and capital are finite, while human desires are essentially infinite. This foundational real-world problem affects the allocation of resources, forcing individuals, businesses, and governments to make choices. Economists seek to understand these choices and the trade-offs involved, and the consequences of those decisions, either in the scale of a specific market or form of transaction, Microeconomics, or Macroeconomics that describes the scale of the whole economy, considering national (even international) income, inflation, unemployment, and economic growth. Game designers benefit from trying to understand both of these perspectives of economics as a foundation for building sustainable experiences in their games.

Scarcity and Choice

Scarcity is the most fundamental problem in economics. The balance in terms of supply (i.e., both quantity and availability) of necessary commodities is generally lower than the demands for those goods, sometimes referred to as a 'Need State,' which just refers to a moment of need expressed by an individual or group of individuals at any particular time. The imbalance between the Need State and Supply at any time is what forces people and societies to make choices about ways to allocate the available resources. This translates into how we apply a measure of value and/or opportunity cost to that category of items. What are we willing to exchange for those resources? In economics terms, it comes down to the exchange of Capital (owned wealth) or Labour (applied effort and skills) mediated via some form of barter or currency (usually Money).

In economics, capital refers to the ownership of assets, infrastructure, or resources, often financial, used to produce goods and services, while labour refers to the effort exerted by individuals in the production of those resources, and its value is affected by skills, experience, and motivation. In games, the systems we create need to simulate the environment for this exchange, with the act of play generally replacing the role of labour, motivated by narrative, rewards, and progression.

With any exchange, we need to consider the opportunity cost of the transaction. Our labour is finite, and we need to decide how the value we produce will be allocated in exchange for what resources.

For instance, in the real world, is it better for a government to allocate resources to build a transport route, or instead build hospitals or a school? The opportunity cost of one is not just the specific deliverables but also requires us to comprehend the longer-term consequences. For example, the road might lead to increased commercial activity leading to larger taxable income and an improvement in living standards for those who use it, but the hospital or school could provide for the health and welfare of the citizens and potentially increase their productivity in the longer term. Understanding opportunity cost is crucial for comprehending the trade-offs involved in virtually every economic decision. In games, understanding the dilemma associated with these kinds of opportunity costs can add depth and engagement, and help create emergent forms of play for the player to explore how to optimise their rewards. As an illustration of this, let's say we have two enemies in a game we can target, a Rat or a Spider:

Is the player better off taking on the riskier monster, the Spider? This monster does grant more XP and gold, but if the player is willing to take the additional time, they can unlock the same value for less risk. So why bother taking on the Spider? At a basic economics level, the only reason would be the different 'drop' Utility – in other words, to obtain the commodity Silk, rather than Hide. But in practice, there are other factors at play such as 'challenge', personal narrative, novelty, availability of each monster type, player skills, and how much time the player has to sink into

Enemy	Danger	Time To Kill	XP	Gold	Drop
 🐀	Low	90s	10	30	Hide
 🕷	High!	180s	30	90	Silk

FIGURE 2.1   A simplified example of different monster data.

the game. Any of these factors may more directly affect the player's decisions, guided by contextual factors such as challenges or crafting actions the game has assigned to them at the time.

Microeconomics: Supply and Demand

Microeconomics is the study of individual markets where the interaction between buyers (demand) and sellers (supply) determines the price and quantity of goods and services in a market. The 'Law of Demand' states that, all else being equal, the quantity demanded of a good decreases as its price increases. Conversely, the law of supply asserts that the quantity supplied of a good increases as its price rises. The intersection of these two curves – the supply curve and the demand curve – determines the equilibrium price, where the quantity demanded equals the quantity supplied. The following diagram, developed by economist Alfred Marshall in 1892,[1] outlines the principles of the "law of demand" and is still used to this day.

Starting with the thick line on the graph where the supply and demand lines cross, we see the equilibrium point. That places us on both a price and quantity for the items. If there were an increase in demand, shifting the demand line up to the dotted line, we find that there is pressure for the price and quantity sold to change, until buyers and sellers are back in balance. That point is shown by where the new demand level meets the (unchanged) supply level.

Both supply and demand curves can shift due to changes in external factors. For example:

- Demand can shift due to changes in consumer preferences, income levels, or the prices of substitutes or complementary goods. A rise in consumer income can increase the demand for luxury goods, shifting the demand curve to the right. On the other hand, if consumers' preferences change (e.g. a decline in the popularity of a particular type of clothing), the demand curve may shift to the left.

- Supply can shift due to changes in production costs, technology, or the number of suppliers in the market. An improvement in technology may lead to more efficient production, increasing supply,

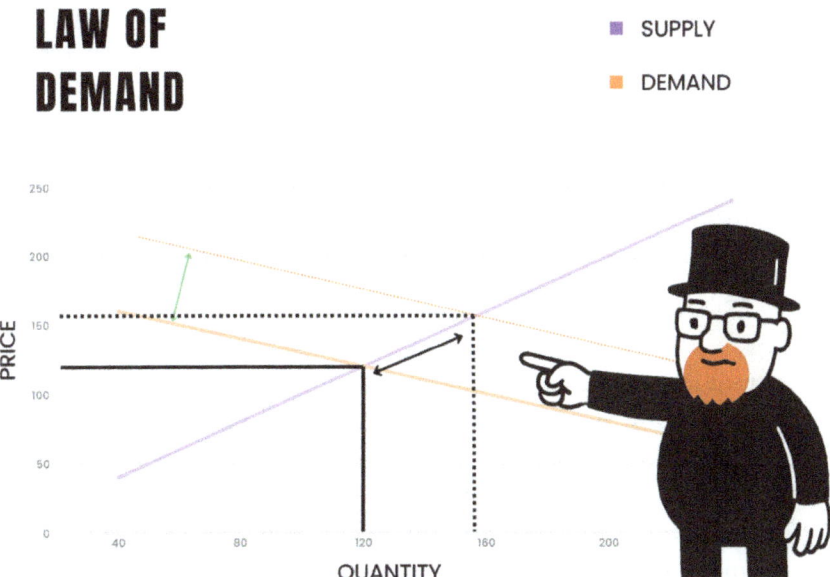

FIGURE 2.2 "Law of Demand" Alfred Marshall 1892.

and shifting the supply curve to the right. Conversely, an increase in the cost of raw materials can reduce supply, shifting the supply curve to the left.

However, in the real world, these lines are rarely flat, as outlined in the graphic. Instead, we see that there are different levels of sensitivity to changes in supply and demand that we refer to as Price Elasticity of Demand, which measures how responsive the quantity demanded of a good is when there is a change in its price. If a small change in price results in a large change in the quantity demanded, demand is said to be elastic. If the quantity demanded changes only slightly in response to a price change, demand is inelastic.

Several factors affect price elasticity:

1. Availability of substitutes: If close substitutes are available, demand tends to be more elastic. For example, if the price of one brand of coffee rises, consumers may switch to a different brand.

2. Necessity vs. luxury: Goods that are necessities (such as basic utilities or medications) tend to have inelastic demand because people need them even when prices rise. Conversely, luxury goods are more likely to have elastic demand.

3. Time period: In the short run, consumers may not be able to find substitutes, making demand less elastic. Over time, however, they may be able to adjust, leading to more elastic demand in the long run.

Understanding price elasticity is crucial for managing 'Pay Upfront' (Premium Games) when setting the initial launch price, as well as when considering sales discounts. If the demand is particularly elastic, setting the price low can dramatically increase total revenue. If demand is inelastic, setting an initially higher price can reinforce the quality of value proposition, maximising revenue.

Ultimately, the 'Law of demand' is more of a guideline and there are many exceptions, often described as 'perverse demand'. These include:

- 'Giffen goods,' which are poor-quality items where demand increases when the price goes up – for example, in the Irish Potato Famine, the necessity of the carbohydrate as such a staple of the diet led to the population cutting back on more expensive food products in order to stock up on more potatoes.

- 'Necessity goods' such as medicines, where demand has no relation to changing price, there is a required quantity of demand regardless of the supply or price.

- 'Hot-hand Fallacy' where stock-market traders will increase their purchasing of commodities when stock prices are trending upward, as a result of purchasing activity rather than any direct changes to supply.

- 'Veblen Goods' which are usually scarce or exclusive items where the price fluctuates based on some level of exclusivity. This is usually derived from some social capital influence separate from their general utility; indeed, the very expense drives up the perceived demand. These can include gold, art, or even just 'snob appeal'.

This matters to us in game design as it allows us to think about the frequency of the drops of each reward type against the effort exhibited by the player through the experience. We can also use the concepts in these exceptions to appreciate that there are different models which can mix up the demand, and in turn, player satisfaction. This also provides us with a set of issues we need to watch out for; after all, if we unintentionally make the player too dependent on a specific currency type or too focused on the scarcity of some cosmetic item that may break the game balance.

System Thinking and Keynesian Economics

While microeconomics deals with individual markets, macroeconomics looks at the broader economy. One of the key areas of macroeconomics is the study of aggregate demand, or the total demand for goods and services in the wider economy. Keynesian economics, developed by John Maynard Keynes during the Great Depression, took a system thinking approach to the concept and emphasised the importance of aggregate demand in determining the overall level of economic activity. There is an irony that his approach to economics has been associated with left-wing politics; however, Keynes was quoted as saying that "The class war will find me on the side of the educated bourgeoisie"[2] in a rejection of Marxism. Whatever your political persuasion, his models provide an essential framework for thinking about systems in the real world and by inference, in games.

Keynes showed how economic systems are not static; they are dynamic and often involve feedback loops – circular processes in which an initial change causes further changes that amplify (positive feedback) or dampen (negative feedback) the initial effect.

- Positive feedback loops occur when an initial change in the economy leads to further changes that reinforce the original effect. For example, an increase in consumer spending can boost business profits, which can lead to higher wages and further spending, creating a self-reinforcing cycle of economic growth. During periods of economic expansion, positive feedback loops can accelerate growth.

- Negative feedback loops, on the other hand, occur when changes in the economy lead to adjustments that counteract the initial change.

For example, rising inflation might lead to higher interest rates, which could reduce borrowing and slow down economic growth, mitigating the initial inflationary pressure. Negative feedback loops are essential for stabilising economic systems and preventing runaway inflation or deflation.

The interplay between positive and negative feedback loops is central to understanding business cycles and economic stability. In practice, these feedback mechanisms can either amplify or dampen economic shocks, depending on the underlying conditions and the actions taken by governments, businesses, and consumers.

It was through this thinking that Keynes argued that economies could experience prolonged periods of low output and high unemployment if aggregate demand falls short of the economy's potential output. This situation could result from a variety of factors, such as reduced consumer spending, business investment, or government expenditure. This analysis led to an understanding that government intervention through fiscal policy (e.g. increased public spending or tax cuts) could help stimulate aggregate demand, boost economic activity, and restore full employment.

Game economies can themselves also be viewed as non-static systems. and we can deliberately leverage positive and negative feedback loops to direct and regulate longer-term player behaviour.

In this highly superficial introduction to core economic tenets, we have so far just scratched the surface of some of the core ways of thinking which most directly influence the author's approach to game design. We encourage further study on this extremely deep topic, as, for any game designer, we think it provides foundational concepts.

BEHAVIOURAL ECONOMICS

One of the criticisms of economic thinking is that it generally assumes two key things:

- Everyone has complete information.
- Everyone acts solely to optimise their value exchange.

Of course, this is not accurate for real world assessment and especially when it comes to player behaviour, we will intentionally subvert these two principles.

Behavioural economics attempts to consider the ethical, cognitive, social, and personal motivations behind the decisions people make. Whilst concepts such as 'loss aversion' have been explored even as far back as Adam Smith's 1759 'Theory of Modern Sentiments,'[3] it has only been relatively recently that there has been a resurgence of interest in behavioural economics in popular culture. There are multiple models available which can help a game designer when thinking about how players may react to the design of economic systems. These include:

- Reference dependence: When evaluating outcomes, the decision maker considers a "reference level." Outcomes are then compared to the reference point and classified as "gains" if greater than the reference point and "losses" if less than the reference point.

- Loss aversion: The risk of a loss is something people try to avoid much more than any equivalent gains that will be sought out. In their 1992 paper, Kahneman and Tversky[4] found the median coefficient of loss aversion to be about 2.25, i.e., losses hurt about 2.25 times more than equivalent gains reward.

- Non-linear probability weighting: Decision makers overweigh small probabilities and underweight large probabilities – in general humans are poor at conceptualising probabilities.

- Diminishing sensitivity to gains and losses: As the size of the gains and losses relative to the reference point increase in absolute value, the marginal effect on the decision maker's utility or satisfaction falls.

- Hot–Cold Empathy Gap: When in an emotional state, we often underestimate the influences of visceral drives on our own attitudes, preferences, and behaviours. This makes us more likely to spend more than we want on items we don't need. This is a key risk we need to be aware of as game economy designers, as it can lead to significant 'buyer's remorse.'

These are just a sample of some of the factors we need to consider when exploring player engagement with the economy of a game. They provide us with both an opportunity to create vectors for the player to engage with the game's economy, as well as warning systems for us to avoid or mitigate against to avoid player frustration and making the mistake of falling into 'Dark Patterns.'[5]

Interview

DESIGNING GAME ECONOMIES FOR COMMERCIAL SUCCESS – A CONVERSATION WITH CHARLES LEES-CZERKAWSKI

Game economies are a fundamental part of creating engaging and sustainable games, yet they are often an afterthought in development. To gain deeper insight into what makes an economy successful and what leads to failure, I explored this with Charles Lees-Czerkawski,[6] an experienced game economy designer and author of *Game Economy Design: Metagame, Monetization and Live Operations*,[7] with a career spanning multiple international studios. Our conversation explored economy design principles, progression systems, balancing challenges, and monetisation strategies in live-service games.

We talked about the role of economy design in game development, and Czerkawski emphasised the importance of incorporating economy design from the very beginning of game development:

> I've had experience working on projects that were pretty much in the form of a PowerPoint presentation at the time. And I've also joined projects that are closer to the end.

He noted that while he could contribute value at any stage, integrating economy design early on made a significant difference:

> I personally find it a bit more relaxed when you're coming in at it from the start because I have a methodology, which I talk about in the book, a method of thinking about the design.

Czerkawski highlighted the importance of respecting existing work when joining a project late but acknowledged the benefits of having autonomy from the outset to shape an economy that aligns naturally with gameplay.

When approaching game economy modelling, Czerkawski takes a structured, top-down approach:

> When I like to start, first of all, I'm looking at it from a very top-down perspective in terms of... what things are the player doing? Essentially, what's their actions? And then what's the weight of them? What's the focus?

He emphasised the importance of mapping out resource flows early on:

> What resources are exchanging hands and moving? So it's a really, really, you can imagine if you're modelling it, you know, you've got your basic diagram with a flow chart or something along those lines.

A core part of this process is understanding how actions and resources interact over time, ensuring a coherent and engaging progression system.

Balancing reward structures and difficulty progression is a key challenge in economy design. Czerkawski discussed how randomness and skill-based rewards share similarities in modelling:

> You can't sort of simulate human behaviour as such, but you can get the... I think the whole point of the spreadsheet we're trying to get at is you're just getting the outliers or... an average.

Understanding how different player types interact with rewards is crucial:

> What I'm typically doing is I want to find out from a spreadsheet the extremes. So let's say we've got an unskilled player who's engaged... an unskilled player who's not engaged... a highly skilled player who isn't engaged and then one who is engaged. So you've got four archetypes of players.

Czerkawski stressed that spreadsheets provide a baseline but must be complemented with real-world playtesting:

> Spreadsheets get you so far. They can show you the outliers, the extreme cases. And then, you know, typically what I would do is if I build something, you know, it's randomly generated, I simulate it a bunch of times... but it kind of stresses the importance of also being able to get away from that and shift to seeing how something plays as well.

Live-service games introduce unique economy challenges, particularly when developers are looking to develop long-term economic sustainability. This is often an issue in games which tend to focus on content and how they avoid the "content treadmill."

> "I've often thought that there are, I guess, tricks for the content treadmill, pushing players back into existing areas so they can grind for new things." Said Czerkawski

He pointed out the importance of structured long-term engagement:

> If you solidly plan your user journey from the start, where you've got players that are sustained for a long time, we need an end-game, and it needs to be different from what normal, like, a beginning player is playing.

Czerkawski also discussed the role of competitive mechanics in sustaining engagement:

> Tying into that competitive nature is something that just inherently will hold more attention for longer.

When discussing monetisation and economic balance, Czerkawski distinguished between different types of in-game purchases:

> When I've been in monetization design for live operations, I do believe that when you're selling pure cosmetic content... it's more of a classical sales [approach]. You cannot, you know, just find what people want and sell it to them. It's very, very hard to say what people want. You just have to see what works.

Managing in-game stores and inventory is more complex than it seems:

> Building a live store... it should have been simple, but it just became a nightmare to manage. So that's, to me, the biggest challenge in running live.

He also emphasised the importance of player-driven engagement in monetisation strategies:

> I think we're actually creating something which makes the game meaningful for the long term... at the end of the day, players won't spend money in the game if we don't get our job right.

Game Economy as a Pillar of Engagement

Czerkawski summarised his perspective on economy design as the backbone of long-term player engagement:

> If the guy next to me is building the weapon systems and he's interested in making the shooting fun, I'm interested in making, why is that fun to keep coming back to six months later?

In essence, a well-designed economy is more than numbers – it provides the framework for sustained engagement, meaningful choices, and commercial success. By integrating economy design from the outset, balancing progression and difficulty, and leveraging data-informed adjustments, developers can create experiences that keep players engaged for years to come.

NOTES

1 https://archive.org/details/elementsofeconom00marsuoft/page/8/mode/2up
2 https://foreignpolicy.com/2019/12/05/keynes-keynesian-socialism-biggest-hero-bourgeois-british-capitalist/
3 https://en.wikipedia.org/wiki/The_Theory_of_Moral_Sentiments
4 Tversky, Amos; Kahneman, Daniel (1992). "Advances in Prospect Theory: Cumulative Representation of Uncertainty". *Journal of Risk and Uncertainty* 5(4), 297–323
5 https://core.ac.uk/download/pdf/301007767.pdf
6 https://www.linkedin.com/in/charles-lees-czerkawski-46293524
7 https://amzn.eu/d/iyXllA4

CHAPTER 3

Defining a Game Economy

DOI: 10.1201/9781003592471-3

WHY DOES A GAME NEED AN ECONOMY?

At its core, game economy design is about creating systems that motivate, sustain, and engage players over time. This only works when it serves an experience that the player cares about. We need to start with a clear vision of how we serve players a meaningful experience.

Once we have that vision, we can then use systems to build great mechanics and interaction methods that are intrinsically enjoyable. Great game designers will leverage both the intrinsic motivation to play (again) and extrinsic reward systems that communicate and regulate our progress through the game. That is essentially what game economy design is all about.

It would be easy to fall into the trap that playing a game is all about 'the pursuit of happiness,' but being 'happy' is questionable as a useful goal in and of itself. Rather, it can be argued that as players we are more engaged by 'the pursuit of meaning' as defined by Viktor Frankl[1] in his 1946 work, in which he states, "What man actually needs is not a tensionless state but rather the striving and struggling for some goal worthy of him."[2] This implies that satisfaction is about the ongoing tension inherent in working towards attainable goals where our actions and decisions actually matter.

Games can overtly channel this principle and have the capacity to provide a degree of meaning through play. It is directly through economy design that this process is regulated – at least as much as any associated narrative arc – as it allows us to deliver consequences and impact based on effort, performance, and choice, which importantly can be accumulated over time.

Of course, this is not to imply that games are a substitute for meaning in a player's life. However, raising this perspective of meaning allows us to think beyond the simplified view that games are simple Skinner box-like[3] 'operant conditioning' dopamine engines – stimulating our reward processes. There is value in understanding Skinner's results, but of course there is much more to it and understanding our ability to impact human behaviour is more complicated and nuanced. Not least that game rewards are not the same as 'food' and our responses to sustenance needs are different from our response to 'novelty' when it comes to the brain's reward process. As neuroscience has evolved we have come to understand that dopamine has more to do with driving the pursuit of novelty rather than being the reward for finding it.

This impacts how we need to interpret how game designs impact player behaviour and remains an under-researched area. Games and their complex role in our mental health is a much wider subject that we won't be covering in this book, but it's worth noting that whilst the World Health Organization decided to include "gaming disorder" in the 11th edition of the International Classification of Diseases in 2018, this was not universally accepted and objectors question the evidence base for why this is any different from other vectors related to underlying behavioural addictions.[4] Indeed the author gave a talk on this subject at GDC (Game Developer Conference in San Francisco) in 2015.[5]

The controversy around the WHO classification, however, does serve to highlight just how connected with human behaviour and motivational thinking game economy design is and how, as designers of any kind of service, we can learn from different disciplines such as psychology, neurology, and marketing to behavioural economics. This makes the study of game economic design a fascinating window into understanding how to model and observe human behaviour, and given the scale of game audiences, with some titles such as Subway Surfers reaching over 4 billion all-time worldwide downloads in 2023, 10 years after its release.

The impact a game economy has goes even deeper when we include monetisation design aspects. Building on a well-designed game economy is a necessary aspect of all games, regardless of business models. However, the function of adding commercial motivations as well as 'play' motivations changes the framing of decision-making within the game. Done well, this magnifies the sense of commitment and engagement, even as far as a sense of personal ownership. However, done badly, this alienates the player from their experience and undermines their decision-making processes – potentially even the very reasons why they wanted to play in the first place. The commercial imperative is generally necessary in order to fund the development of content, but we will argue that understanding the role of monetary elements in a fine-tuned, balanced experience can indeed create deeper and more profound experiences that keep players feeling invested.

We aim to show how, whilst there are patterns and techniques, it's necessary to understand that games are dynamic systems which need to evolve with the player and support a sense of progression and the pursuit of future satisfaction. That comes only from focusing on what your audience truly values – something that can be difficult to accurately diagnose. Players' explanations of what drives them often translate badly into game design as they won't always understand the complex drivers behind the game systems. Usually, we need a combination of Qualitative (opinions) feedback and Quantitative (data) analysis in order to uncover the best options to sustainably improve the game. That requires a unique combination of artistic, craft, and data-driven analysis which has not always been fully realised.

The need to take the player 'with you' in terms of design and our focus on long-term player value means that in this book we aim to demonstrate the importance of an ethical approach to monetisation. It is the author's view that this is not simply the right thing to do, but it is actually critical to long-term value for any game – especially those delivered as services. Authenticity and trust are the most effective ways to consistently and sustainably deliver the bottom line – way more than any short-term deceptive special offer or "Dark Pattern." We intend to demonstrate that bad commercial experiences such as poorly designed 'Loot Crates,' 'Kompu Gatcha,' and cynically engineered battle passes are in the end counterproductive damaging Lifetime Value and general consumer trust in games. However, we will also show how many of these so-called 'Dark Patterns' are the result of a failure in delivery of techniques that in context, ethically delivered, can indeed provide genuinely satisfying player experiences. More often it is the failure to identify the 'unintended consequences' due to pressures on delivery rather than a deliberate effort to mislead or manipulate. A 'Good Loot Crate' is capable of being a delightful "predictable surprise," a 'Good Gatcha' can package collective excitement and indeed that a 'Good Battle pass' is the most powerful way to create amazing motivations to play more. Unfortunately, it's almost impossible to differentiate the mistakes from actual bad actors – and the games industry has seen many of those! When those implementations show strong short-term gains in one game, they quickly inevitably get reused by other designers in other games, and especially where those designers lack the understanding or data to demonstrate the longer-term consequences, it can lead to damage not just to that one game but the wider adoption and perception of games as a whole.

Building 'authenticity' can only happen when we get the non-commercial aspects of the game economy right first. This is crucial to monetisation regardless of the chosen commercial model of your game.

Obviously, for free-to-play and live-service models there is a direct correlation between player retention and revenue. However, even for games where there is a clear beginning, middle, and end (e.g. narrative game), therefore requiring an upfront payment model (that many call premium), it's still vital to understand that the value benefit for the player matters when it comes to initial pricing, sales management, and other upsold elements such as DownLoadable Content (DLC).

As we have already said, any environment where long-term engagement is essential requires a deep understanding of what motivates the audience to return. The 'economy' design of effort versus reward still applies in the way retailers design loyalty programmes to encourage repeat purchases, educational platforms track progression systems to motivate learners, and fitness apps amplify health goals to keep users committed. Game economy design provides a blueprint for how to do just that.

A SHIFT IN THINKING: GAMES AS SERVICES

One of the most important shifts in the games industry has been the move toward the service approach or Games as a Service (GaaS). This approach isn't just a label you can slap on your game; it requires a complete change of delivery mindset. GaaS games are not static products, they require consistent, sustained, predictable updates, and where community engagement is a central component of the experience. Each game will have different levels of cadence, quantity, and player expectations that range from hosted multiplayer experiences to full-blown MMOs with new daily challenges and monthly narrative updates. Even studios with portfolios of one-off narrative games benefit from service thinking with bug-fix updates, sales promotions, community events, and other activity to sustain hype and anticipation for the next title. What is common between GaaS and a portfolio of products is that there needs to be a level of predictability to the life of the brand/community, supporting reasons for players to continue to engage with the game(s) and the team. This generally takes the form of continuous updates to playing challenges, new content releases, narrative progression, and improving features, as well as sales promotions and the essential technical support and management of hosted servers. When done right, we get more players, doing more things, more often and for longer.

This shift has brought with it a new way of thinking about game design – about what progression means, about narrative, and game lore.

Games are no longer just created, sold, and forgotten; instead, they are seen as ongoing experiences that must be nurtured to maintain player interest over the long term. And if we aren't careful, this extra work can quickly become unsustainable for the creators. We will explore some elements of this, but our focus in this book is on building the game economy. Check out Games as a Service: How Free To Play Design Can Make Better Games[6] (also from Taylor & Francis and this author).

In this new era of GaaS, the game economy serves as a foundation upon which long-term engaging experiences must be built. The in-game economy defines the rules by which players interact with the game world and with each other, and it determines how value is distributed within the game. That definition of value is also critical to understanding the optimal commercialisation of the game. For a game to be successful in the GaaS model, its economy must be carefully designed and continually adjusted based on player feedback and data. Unlike many early sandbox games we can't ignore 'broken' game economies... Yes, even beloved games like Skyrim are lessons in what not to do, as the failure to properly balance the in-game economy meant a lot of enjoyable systems quickly become irrelevant (despite this it still remains one of my all-time favourite games!).

UNDERSTANDING THE ROLE OF THE GAME ECONOMY

In this book, we define the role of the game's economy to provide the systems which regulate play mechanics, rewards, and progression; including the commercial elements. These can include currencies, resources, narrative, cosmetics, blueprints, recipes, and other methods of progression of items and difficulty that underpin the gameplay experience. Balance, in this context, relates to the relationships between effort, scarcity, difficulty, and progression, which is presented through character statistics, levelling up of abilities, unlocking items or upgrades/repairs, as well as the acquisition of both consumable and permanent in-game assets. Each economic element represents a form of exchange or utility for the player that serves some benefit for the player experience. But despite that, what delivers value is not the 'benefit' that the player actually receives, but instead their expectation of that value. This way, whilst scarcity and the effort required to unlock an item (e.g. a purely cosmetic item), do provide a starting point for understanding the value of that item, other cultural factors such as 'cool,' 'status,' and 'ability to show off' can play significant multiplying factors. This 'social capital' factor means that the received value and cost/effort-over-time calculation is always subjective and weighted towards motivation to act, rather than a post-play assessment of what was received. Real-money transactions add additional nuance to the value a game economy delivers for the player, but by understanding the utility a player gains from the underlying economy, we can optimise the value of any offers, bundles, and content sales.

You don't create a great commercial game by slapping on a couple of currencies and capping the flow of play with a cluster of ads. Great game economy design is irrevocably tied to the flow of play, and when done well, it delivers such a satisfying experience that the player is happy in later reflection with the time and money they have invested in the game.

Take a look at the way 'Gold' can be used in a game as a form of exchange, often required as a partial payment towards different forms of character or equipment progression. To an extent, it is a representation of your experience development, but you don't just accumulate it; you also spend it. It is commonly a 'Soft' currency meaning you can earn it readily through play, but perhaps you may want a boost and buy additional 'gold' in bundles for real money. This would be very different from a 'Hard' currency, a common example being 'Gems.' These generally are much harder and slower to accumulate through play – if it's even possible at all! Gems, as an alternative currency are usually 'flavoured' so they can only be used for certain types of purchase. We will get into much greater detail on this topic later, but the point is that understanding exactly what each item in your economy does in play, and how the player accesses that item, is vital to understanding its value, impact, and therefore real-world verse in-game cost.

For example, in a mobile game, players might be able to earn Gold as a Soft currency by completing daily challenges or progressing through levels. This makes Gold a positive reward for that interaction as well as a form of currency to exchange for upgrade items. This in turn transforms otherwise repetitive activities into challenges worth completing and sets a baseline of value for the associated upgrades and rewards. Let's say there is a Hard currency that can be used to speed up the progress of those actions or acquire exclusive items; establishing a value only accessible from using this premium asset. Providing a small volume of that Hard currency as part of rewards will establish their value beyond a simple 'real-money' exchange rate, and form part of the players understanding of the balance between these two types of currency. If the Hard currency is overused, players may feel that the game is pay-to-win, which can drive away non-paying players. On the other hand, if that Hard currency isn't valuable enough, players may have little incentive to make the higher-value purchases, which could hurt the game's revenue. This is just one example of the kinds of nuance that develop when we explore these types of economic systems.

In addition to simple currency exchange, the game economy must also take into account other factors that impact player engagement, reward drop-rates, difficulty, and retention. These include understanding the impact of rewards against the player's performance through play, the pacing of content updates, the availability of items and features, and even the ways in which players can interact with each other. A well-designed economy creates a sense of progression and achievement while also providing opportunities for longer-term play, as well as social interaction and even competition.

Direct spend, upfront or in-game is obviously part of the commercial application of a game economy, but since 2012, the role of in-game ads has become an essential component of mobile monetisation. Ads behave differently from real-money exchange, but they can serve as a simple exchange of time for money (when the game has a certain level of scale). But the development of Rewarded Ads (which are optional to watch in return for some – usually – in-game benefit) introduced a range of new techniques which had the potential to affect the underlying game economy and to unblock 'free-players' to engage more deeply in the game than they would otherwise have done, and can even create a better player experience.

Achieving a 'good' experience with ads requires a deep understanding of the placement, function, and exchange – again all requiring a deep understanding of the underlying player utility and the game economy as a whole. It means considering the role, drop rate, and specialist applications of in-game currencies and 'flavoured' resources and how these help the player to unlock new functionality, narrative moments, and general progression. It also includes understanding the role of systems for balancing supply and demand, managing player progression. Ads can even support creating meaningful choices for players, including demonstrating the reasons for those players to invest their own hard-earned money on a power-up or even a full DLC release. Whilst the author is not a fan of forced ads (interstitials), there can be times and placements when this becomes helpful for the overall player experience, providing a 'rest' moment breaking the player from potential burnout.

As we further explore the topic, we will explore the different layers that apply within game economy design. This includes building up from simple mechanics, rewards, currencies, and resources, as well as how we can smoothly integrate commercial elements from microtransactions to complex subscription or advertising-based models without falling into manipulative 'Dark Patterns'. We will show that at its core, a game economy is about creating meaningful value for the players and that good monetisation design must build on this meaningful value to ensure that the game remains financially viable, and that those players will be happy to continue to invest again and again.

ENGAGEMENT AND RETENTION ARE CRITICAL

As we have already stated, the primary goals of a game economy are to drive engagement and retention. Engagement refers to how involved and invested players are in the game, often reflected in their session length and frequency, whilst retention measures how long players stick around and continue to play, usually measured in terms of 'days since initial install'. A successful game economy encourages players to return to the game regularly, provides meaningful rewards for their time and effort, and keeps them motivated to progress.

For games to deliver sustained engagement, they require a strong core underlying mechanic coupled with an effective sense of purpose and progression. This typically involves a strong forward-motivating narrative and personal character development but also sufficient friction that makes the actions, performance, and choices meaningful. We need the payout of rewards versus difficulty and progression to feel grounded, even (perhaps especially) where there is no ultimate end goal. The perception of scope for optimisation can also play a huge factor in understanding the emergent properties which create powerful compelling reasons to play again. The more ambiguous this optimisation is, the more compelling it can be, as long as the player still feels that it was their agency/choices that were key to the outcome.

Retention is partially driven by having a strong foundation of engagement but with reasons for the player to feel they can break from play, with a reason to come back later. We need to create reasons for players to come back in the next 20 minutes, next hour, next day, next week, and to keep coming back for months. Achieving that means understanding both the intrinsic motivations of play as well as using more system-based external motivators that evolve over the longer term. We need to feed the experience through the context of the longer-term game loops as well as by providing regular updates and events. These updates can be as simple as new challenges, missions, narrative moments, but can also include new content, new customisation, and even new features. They also provide opportunities for monetisation. For example, a game might introduce a limited-time event that offers exclusive rewards, encouraging players to log in and participate before the event ends.

By carefully designing the economy to support these events, developers can create a sense of urgency, excitement, and ultimately satisfaction that encourages players to come back time and again.

However, we need to be sensitive to the players' other needs. Our game is their chosen form of entertainment, but we don't get to decide when they have time to play or not. We can present options and motivational reasons to return, even habit-forming behaviour, but creating systems which force the issue can backfire, making the game no longer a safe escape.

Balancing Profit and Player Experience

While engagement and retention are critical to a game's success, for most game developers, we need to address the commercial reality that we also need to optimise revenue as well. This is especially true for free-to-play games, where players are not required to pay upfront to access the game. Instead, developers rely on a variety of monetisation strategies, such as in-game purchases, ads, and subscription models, to generate income.

One of the biggest challenges in game economy design is finding the right balance between profitability and player satisfaction. If a game is too aggressive in its monetisation, players may feel that they are being exploited, which can lead to frustration and churn. On the other hand, if a game is too lenient, it may not generate enough revenue to sustain development.

The key is to design monetisation systems that feel fair and rewarding to players while also providing a steady stream of income for the developers. In future chapters, we will demonstrate that this isn't just about 'pay upfront' versus 'pay in-game', and that there are different pricing models that can be adapted to different games and player segments. We will also explore how even in free-to-play models we have to ensure that both free players and paying players feel valued so everyone can enjoy the game without feeling disadvantaged.

Setting the Stage for Success

The design of a game economy is one of the most critical factors in determining a game's long-term success. A well-balanced economy has to be focused on delivering an experience that players care about and that keeps them engaged and motivated, but also ensures that the game remains financially sustainable. By understanding the core principles of game economy design, developers can create experiences that are both rewarding for players and profitable for studios.

In the chapters that follow, we will dive deeper into the specific components of game economy design, exploring how to create meaningful value for players, how to validate game ideas with data, and how to adapt and pivot when necessary. By the end of this book, you will have the tools and knowledge you need to design game economies that drive engagement, retention, and long-term success.

Interview

LESSONS FROM *DUNGEONS & DRAGONS* – AN INTERVIEW WITH KRISTIAN ROBERTS[7]

The Economics of Game Development

Game balance and economy design are not just about tweaking numbers but about understanding the core principles that govern player engagement, monetisation, and progression. Kristian Roberts,[7] CEO and Managing Partner at Nordicity, has spent years dissecting these principles, and in this discussion, he draws on his love for Dungeons & Dragons (D&D) to illustrate key economic lessons for game developers.

> "I've been spending the last 17 years trying to answer the same question, which is like, how does the economics of the video games industry work? And it's actually taken me 17 years to come up with any answers," said Roberts.

He continued using the classic tabletop roleplaying adventure game, D&D, as a central metaphor. With its mechanics of rolling 20-sided dice, Roberts argues that this provides an ideal framework for discussing game balance. In the game industry, launching a title is akin to rolling a die – you might roll a natural 20 and achieve massive success, or a 1 and see a total failure. The trick lies in minimising the difficulty check (the target number you have to roll on the die), ensuring that even if you roll an average number, your game will still succeed. In the game, we use skills, proficiencies, and other abilities. For game developers, this means player engagement strategies, monetisation models, and game balance all have to come into play.

> When you publish a game, you're essentially rolling a dice to see how the market reacts to that game.
>
> —*Kristian Roberts*

Changing market conditions play a part in this challenge, and development strategies are affected by lessons and trends from other teams. In particular, LiveOps as an approach has transformed from something specific in niche MMO games to a strategy to scale revenues for relatively simple free-to-play mobile games. With 78% of the revenues in 2022 coming from free-to-play live service games[8] and a fundamental requirement across all game genres. Games are no longer static products but evolving services.

> "Now that's every game, right? It's not just limited to the world of free-to-play games," says Roberts.

Even developers who have a portfolio of one-time pay upfront 'Premium' games are increasingly acting as if they are services, with a focus on building sustainable communities. This is because the principles of user acquisition, retention, monetisation apply universally, and reengaging a 'happy' customer is always more effective than finding a new one.

Roberts continued exploring the metaphor by considering how we can think of the long-term success of a studio in the same terms as a long-term campaign. He argues that a game studio's long-term success isn't determined by a single release but by its ability to build and sustain a player base across multiple titles. Just like a Dungeon Master crafts a compelling campaign to keep players engaged across multiple sessions, game developers must create a continuous narrative, brand, or ecosystem that keeps players invested in their games. For example, Supergiant GAmes did a magnificent job of delivering regular, concrete updates on what was happening for Hades II, involving their community at every step.[9]

> "If you think of the long-term evolution of a games company as a *Dungeons & Dragons* campaign… the underlying thesis that brings customers from title to title, that's the sticky thing." Said Roberts.

But what does that mean for the development team themselves? One of the most common pitfalls in game development is assembling an incomplete team. Too often, studios focus exclusively on creative and technical talent but neglect crucial roles like community management, marketing, and business strategy. A successful development team should be balanced, much like a well-rounded D&D party.

"One of them is that you need to gather your party before you venture forth," and this includes "Choosing the subclass that contributes to the story is actually a benefit. It's primarily a benefit to your other players," Roberts argues. You need a balance of skills in the team, and that includes thinking about not just the powerhouse of the group. In D&D terms, this would be the fighters, clerics, and rogues but also the party member who can connect to the wider world, in D&D this is usually the Bard." Roberts says.

Robert's point is that we need to appreciate that it takes a diverse collection of skills to have a truly effective team that can adapt to all the situations the team is likely to face. And in games, increasingly this is as much about building community as it is about design, programming, art, or narrative.

Community is not just a buzzword it's a core mechanic in successful game economies. A strong community can drive user acquisition, retention, and organic growth. Just as D&D players bring others into the campaign, engaged players in a game economy help drive growth through word-of-mouth and social influence.

Taking this thinking further, we can see further parallels as we try to recruit a community to join us on our adventure.

"You're trying to encourage your players to transition from one game to another or to stay within your live service environment." says Roberts.

We go on to talk about the importance of sustaining that community and that retention doesn't just happen through compelling gameplay; it also requires a carefully designed economic loop. Whether it's in-game currency, cosmetic purchases, or battle passes, developers must structure spending opportunities that feel natural and rewarding. Players should feel like they're investing in their progression, much like levelling up a character in D&D.

This isn't just about building more things, according to Roberts.

We quite often overshoot the expectation and we over-deliver on that quality because we're delivering quality for the sake of quality.

A common mistake in game development is over-investing in content that doesn't significantly impact player retention or revenue. Instead, developers should focus on optimising quality based on player expectations and engagement data. This efficiency-first approach ensures that studios allocate resources effectively without diminishing the player experience. Roberts proposes that this emphasis on optimising player experiences has deeper implications, and he went as far as to say that it's also critical to genuine user acquisition.

> "Discoverability is an output of audience development, not an input to audience development," he states.

But we cannot ignore the world-building we exist in. We have constraints on what we can build based on the tools and platforms available to us. But here again we can see the importance of having a party who can understand, adapt, and execute any scenario that might come up. This includes regulatory changes which have the potential to dramatically change the landscape and what path our adventures can take.

For example, regulations like the Digital Markets Act are an attempt to level the playing field for discoverability, Roberts argues that discoverability is ultimately driven by audience engagement. Developers cannot rely on algorithmic placement alone; they must actively cultivate communities and build direct relationships with their player base.

Conclusion: The Ultimate Quest in Game Development

In the ever-evolving game industry, success is not just about rolling high numbers – it's about minimising difficulty checks through strategic planning, community engagement, and efficient resource management. The principles of D&D serve as a powerful analogy for understanding game balance and economy design. Whether you're a small indie studio or a large publisher, assembling the right party and crafting a long-term campaign are essential to sustainable success in the gaming landscape.

> "So once again, we must gather our party before we venture forth," Roberts concludes.

NOTES

1 Viktor Frankl was an Austrian neurologist, psychologist, philosopher, and Holocaust survivor https://en.wikipedia.org/wiki/Viktor_Frankl
2 https://en.wikipedia.org/wiki/Man%27s_Search_for_Meaning
3 https://practicalpie.com/skinners-box-experiment/

4 https://www.psychiatryadvisor.com/features/dont-hate-the-player-controv ersy-over-gaming-as-mental-disorder-levels-up/

5 https://uat.gdcvault.com/play/1022259/Spellbound-Asking-Questions-About-Habit

6 https://www.taylorfrancis.com/books/mono/10.4324/9781315849102/ games-service-oscar-clark

7 https://www.linkedin.com/in/kristianroberts

8 https://www.prnewswire.com/news-releases/new-bain--company-research-finds-global-revenue-for-games-could-grow-by-more-than-50-ov er-the-next-five-years-301648703.html

9 https://www.gfinityesports.com/article/hades-2-is-how-developers-should-do-early-access

CHAPTER 4

Why Do We Play? (And Pay?)

DOI: 10.1201/9781003592471-4

MOTIVATIONS FOR PLAY

Before we start diving into the practical tools of the game economy, we must first get to some basic principles of game design. Why do we play?

This is probably the most fundamental question of game design – in fact, of any game business. It is an essential element we need to understand to resolve the core problem we are trying to solve as game makers... which is "why should the player care?"

Identifying and then understanding the psychology of your player is essential for your game to have any chance of success. The more clarity we have on who they are, how we identify them, and what their needs are the better. Often we will use basic demographic information, but it is always better where we can add additional psychographic and, where possible, more meaningful behavioural characteristics, as well as motivational characteristics and lifestyle concepts such as 'Mode of Use.'

There have been many attempts to provide frameworks for understanding player motivations, famously with the work done by Richard Bartle[1] to assess the user behaviour of players of MUD (the original multi-user-dungeon). He described 'Achievers,' 'Killers,' 'Socialisers,' and 'Explorers' as the four principal archetypes within that game specifically, but this model has been used extensively by designers across other games, despite Richard's protestations against the practice. Other teams have attempted to identify different player archetypes and their associated motivations. In her book 'Game Thinking', Amy Jo Kim[2] built on Bartle's model looking at the same axis of motivation defining users as Competitors, Expressers, Collaborators and Explorers. Other groups have used data to build on these models including Quantic Foundry[3] who built a gamer motivational model based on data from 1.7m players and broke down six pairs of motivational factors when it comes to the reasons we play. These include:

- **Action**: Destruction, Chaos, Mayhem, Guns, Explosives, Excitement, Surprises, Thrills

- **Social**: Play Together, Community, Teams, Chatting, Interacting, Competition, Matches, Ranking, Status

- **Mastery**: Challenge, Practice, Skill, Strategy, Thinking Ahead, Decision-Making, Autonomy, Meritocracy

- **Achievement**: Completion, Collection, Milestones, Power, Unlocking, Maxing Out

- **Immersion**: Fantasy, Story, Roleplay, Escape, Narrative, Character, Hero's Journey
- **Creativity**: What If? Design, Expression, Customisation, Discovery, Tinkering, Experimentation, Emergence

Similarly, NewZoo[4] created their own set of player personas which provides an alternative way to look at the player audience and defined these in terms of the following segments:

- **Ultimate Gamers:** Fully immersed in all aspects: playing, owning, viewing, socialising.
- **All-Round Enthusiasts:** Interested in all areas, but less intensely than Ultimate Gamers.
- **Time Fillers:** Casual players, often on mobile, filling spare time.
- **Bargain Buyers:** Seek quality games, preferably free or discounted, and cost-conscious on hardware.
- **Community Gamers:** Engage in discussion, media, podcasts, and community participation.
- **Hardware Enthusiasts:** Focus on optimised experiences and stay up to date on hardware trends.
- **Popcorn Gamers:** Prefer watching games over playing.
- **Backseat Viewers:** Former gamers are now re-engaging primarily through viewing content.
- **Lapsed Gamers:** Once active, now disengaged due to changing interests or life priorities.

GameRefinery,[5] now part of Liftoff, has a similar approach where they break down the motivational characteristics of each of the motivational drivers from Escapism to Expression, Mastery to Exploration. From this, they defined eight archetypes:

- Expressionist
- King of the Hill

- Networker

- Skill Master

- Strategist

- Thinker

- Thrill Seeker

- Treasure Hunter

Each of these models takes different approaches to how we can frame the motivational needs in our game. In the following example, we looked at a range of motivational types we felt might be expressed in a game, taken from the different models in this case, and mapped where we felt they might be positioned along two dimensions. In this example with Expression to Achievement along our horizontal axis and with Optimisation and Discovery on the vertical axis. This kind of thought experiment can help us consider what motivations are most important for our target players.

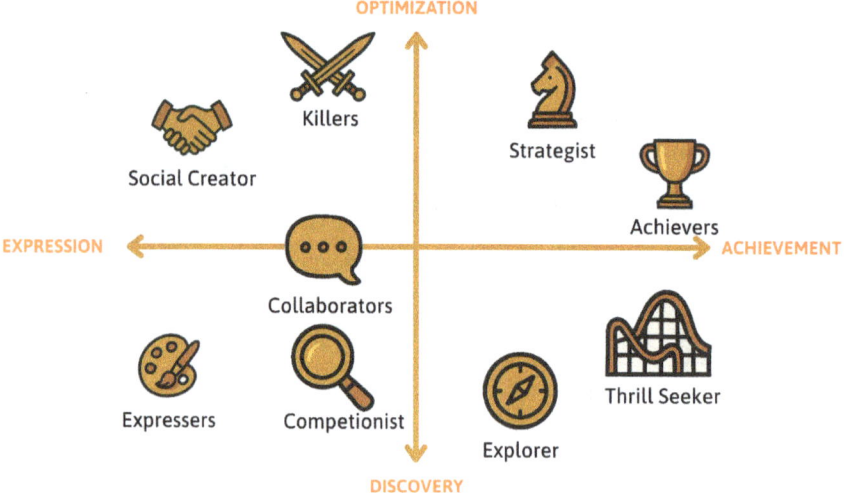

FIGURE 4.1   Player architypes.

As useful as it can be to explore these models, we should try to understand some of the psychological principles that can help us understand what players want. One of the key concepts is called Self-Determination Theory[6], and it explores the basic principles of motivation.

FIGURE 4.2   Self determination theory and motivation.

This model identifies three basic human needs:

- **Competence:** the need to be effective within your environment

- **Autonomy:** the need to have control over the self and your actions

- **Relatedness:** the need to have a meaningful connection with others

These three factors help us understand the core elements which develop internal motivation, but this is further developed by Edward L. Deci and Richard M. Ryan as a subtheory of Self-Determination known as 'Cognitive Evaluation Theory,' which explores the difference between internal and external factors. External factors such as rewards (expected as much as real), social recognition, and general feedback mean the results of our actions and the impact in terms of both social and environmental factors. When well balanced, these external rewards, recognition, and feedback positively reinforce further actions. Tangible rewards can reinforce behaviour to a degree, but if they become too overt, this can become detrimental, undermining the sense of autonomy. Similarly, if these are too limited or absent, then that can also be detrimental and create disincentives to continue those actions.

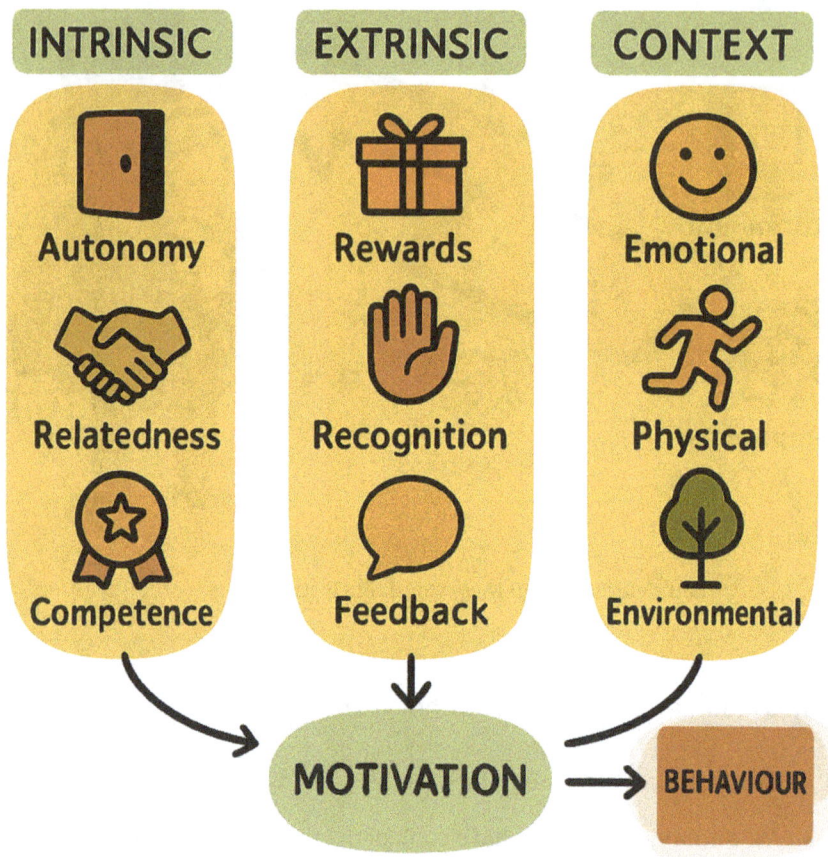

FIGURE 4.3   Intrinsic vs extrinsic motivations and context.

However, humans can't really be reduced to simple reward states. There is always context. This context can be in the form of different states of emotional, physical, or environmental circumstances. This results in what is referred to as the Intention-Behaviour Gap[7] or more simply, why we do things that go against our core intentions.

All these factors are going on behind the scenes in our players and we cannot control (nor should we attempt to) all these elements. However, if we can understand the intrinsic motivations as they apply to our game and balance the extrinsic motivations, whilst sensitive to the player's context (we do at least know they are currently seeking out entertainment in some form), then we can optimise the experience to support a rewarding and meaningful playing experience.

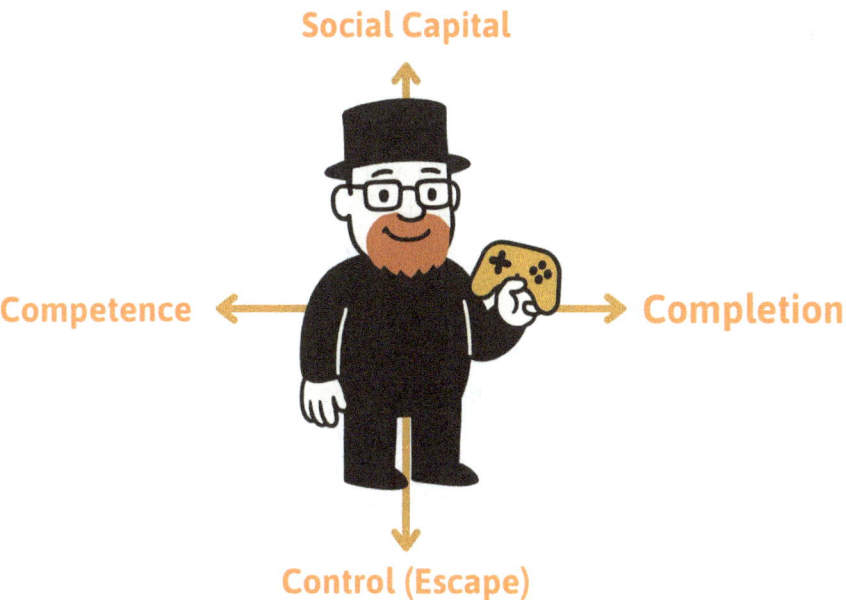

FIGURE 4.4   Core player motivation.

So, if we consider the different player types and the principles of self-determination, we can break the intrinsic motivations into four factors that are useful for play. Each game will offer different levels of each of these factors, but they will all need to consider how they provide extrinsic rewards which reinforce the motivations implicit in these forms. The four forms are:

Competence: I want to be able to both feel and demonstrate my competence at the tasks involved in this game. The process of practice, repetition, and performance mastery is all in service to this ambition. Generally, the emphasis on player skill within the context of the mechanics is paramount – anything which overtly detracts from the absolute application of skill is considered 'cheating' as it undermines the expression of skill.

Completion: I want to resolve every single element of the game in terms of goals, collectables, and missions. Unlike Competence, the emphasis is not on raw skill but instead on persistence and exploration. The rarity of discovery in the game adds to the level of thrill, but anything which prevents the player from tracking this kind of performance damages the derived value for the player.

Control: I want my decisions to matter in terms of the development of my character and the game world. Learning how to optimise core systems and to either create or destroy in the game environment is as important as the choices I make to affect the game's narrative arc. The act of control also provides players with a sense of escape, allowing them access to a sense of 'powerfulness' often missing in their ordinary life. Decisions in the game design which subvert or take away what the player thought they had control over can profoundly undermine the player experience.

Social Capital: I want to show others who I am and what I am capable of, as well as to connect with others of my 'Tribe.' Games, for many players, are as much about the expression of your identity as they are about connecting with groups we consider ourselves to identify with. Social Identity Theory is a key factor in understanding that, as players (and humans generally), we define our identity as much by the Tribes we belong to (and reject) as we do our individual identity. Too many games still underestimate the inherent value in players being able to communicate their skills, values, and creativity through play.

Defining Player Personas

A common tool, and arguably an essential starting point, for product development and marketing more generally is to define your target audience. One of the most common techniques for this is to start with a thought experiment to develop 'Personas.'

These are essentially a set of framing statements that allow us to focus our design thinking on making sure that what we deliver is relevant to suitably large and targetable groups of potential players. This exercise helps us get out of the frame of mind of the game maker, instead considering who the audience will be and what they want from our game, separate from what we would want to make just for ourselves.

We can create a range of persona types to fulfil different roles – but the following are examples of the persona types we might consider for making a game:

- **Primary Audience**: The core player for this game, the people who will be captivated by the essential mechanics of the game and for whom the rewards need only to be purely intrinsic to sustain their longer-term engagement.

- **Secondary Audience**: A wider group of players who, whilst finding the mechanic enjoyable require a context in which to engage more deeply with the game. This context is usually delivered through a sense of purpose, progression and optimisation of play, especially where that creates a sense of personal narrative within the experience.

- **Tertiary Audience**: The widest addressable audience who will not actively seek out your game until it becomes part of the wider cultural zeitgeist. Players who often become engaged only after watching others engage with the game. This can often be split into advocates or influencers as much as those affected by such 'second hand' endorsement with the game.

- **Converting Audience**: Players who don't just play the game but who are specifically engaging with spending money (real money or engagement with ads) within the game.

- **Detractor Audience**: Non-Players, including those whose influence and opinions may derail wider adoption of the game. Steam Review Bombers are an example of the types of players who could object and undermine other audiences in the game.

- **Creator Audience**: Players who themselves form a communication channel to other potential players as well as help sustain your game community. These can be major scale 'influencers' with millions of fans across the live streaming or social platforms to smaller 'Micro' (1,000s of subs) or 'Nano' (100s of subs) scale who grant the game exposure through playing, reviewing, and creating related content leveraging your game with their own audiences.

For each of these player personas, we need to come up with a sketch of what we think the typical individual will be like. It's vital that we think broadly; the audience for our game will be international and diverse. If we ignore other cultural influences and context, we risk undermining the potential for the game, unnecessarily excluding potential audiences and markets.

We are looking for clusters of people, 'cohorts' whose behaviour/choices/actions can be generally understood. We are not interested in a specific individual; too closely targeting a single person with data very quickly comes across as creepy and becomes counterproductive. On the other hand, we also need to understand that we can clearly communicate with that audience effectively. When working on a game based on The Rocky Horror Show, we struggled when it turned out that there were no clearly identifying characteristics we could use to define a persona who would like or not like Rocky Horror. The audience wasn't defined by age, social demographics, a love of 1950s sci-fi tropes or other lifestyle factors. It was more about cultural exposure and a connection to the show.

In a typical Persona assessment, we are looking for characteristics to get us into the mindset of an example member of the group. This means making a logical sketch of that example person and even includes us naming them, using a picture, and deciding their typical profession and other lifestyle elements, as well as trying to define their player personality.

The factors include:

- **Name**: Creating a name creates a cognitive shortcut to put ourselves into the mindset of what they will do. We also recommend creating an image for that person, again to more fully connect with them. The site https://thispersondoesnotexist.com/ can be a great tool for accessing AI-generated images, but it is worth reading about the background to that site and its intention to question the use of fake AI-generated images.[8]

- **Background & Location**: A shortcut to their cultural context and biases, as well as a shortcut for understanding how they might respond to game and narrative cues.

- **Age**: Another shortcut to connect us with the generational and cultural context and biases.

- **Demographic Grade**: Originally a UK-specific model based on how the main household income was derived in any given postcode region (and largely debunked in its original form). This is a letter categorisation which helps us further estimate the social cultural context for the persona. These elements are defined by the UK Office of National Statistics[9] and the list below comes from the UK's 2011 Census for all four UK countries.

Social Grade	Description	UK Population
AB	Higher (A) & intermediate (B) managerial, administrative, professional occupations	22.17%
C1	Supervisory, clerical & junior managerial, administrative, professional occupations	30.84%
C2	Skilled manual occupations	20.94%
DE	Semi-skilled (D) & unskilled (E) manual occupations, Unemployed and lowest grade occupations	26.05%

FIGURE 4.5   UK social grade demographics.

- **Salary Income**: An estimate of the financial security of the individual. This is not always as useful as it may seem, as we are often more interested in the proportion of disposable income the player is willing to use within games like ours. Salary is not always a good indication of that as factors such as personal expenditure commitments, including food/rent/mortgage will play a significant factor. In addition, games are often seen as a personal 'escape' luxury item, further complicating how well we can assess the connection between salary and potential games spend.

- **Genre Bias**: Game genres themselves are a terrible methodology for identifying player motivations, but we cannot ignore that players often have their personal taste bias and genre is the only shorthand we have where there is some data – even if only through the game charts from Apple/Google/Steam/etc. Unfortunately, genre is used as a search function and the differences between subgenres can be extreme e.g. players who love match3 games may well have no interest whatsoever in physics-based puzzle games – but they are still classed as puzzles.

- **Example Games**: What other game titles does this persona typically play, and under what circumstances.

- **Mode of Use**: What circumstances do they look for moments to play, and do they have different games for different 'Modes of Use,' such as a mobile game when on the go, a console game for which they have an appointment time of play, and a PC game that they use to escape from the family in their den.

- **Player Motivation**: What are the key in-game player motivations for the style of play that these players engage with? Are they focused on Completion? Competence? Control or Social-Capital? If they are a content creator, what do their audience expect to see through their play? And how do they build that audience?

- **Thinks/Feels/Says/Does**: Given what we know about these players (or at least what we have hypothesised about them), what do they 'really' think about the game, and how does that reflect what they 'feel?' How is that different from what they say about the game and do in the game? These may seem to be the same thing, but they rarely ever are. The gap between understanding what players say and what they do can be massive.

- **Channels**: What are the principal media platforms that these players engage with? Is that through social media such as Instagram or Bluesky? Is it through video content such as Twitch, YouTube, or TikTok? Community platforms such as Reddit? Or perhaps more consumer platforms such as mainstream TV, newspapers or even specialist media sites such as Pocket Gamer or GameIndustry.biz.

Once we have these thought experiments, we can use them to help us direct the initial design of game experiments we can test, e.g. through game trailers or playtest sessions or even in the form of more open surveys. Further, we can use our testing to check the validity of our personas themselves, as after all, these are simply a set of hypotheses in themselves.

The following is a very simplified example of a personal thought experiment:

PERSONA 1: Primary Audience

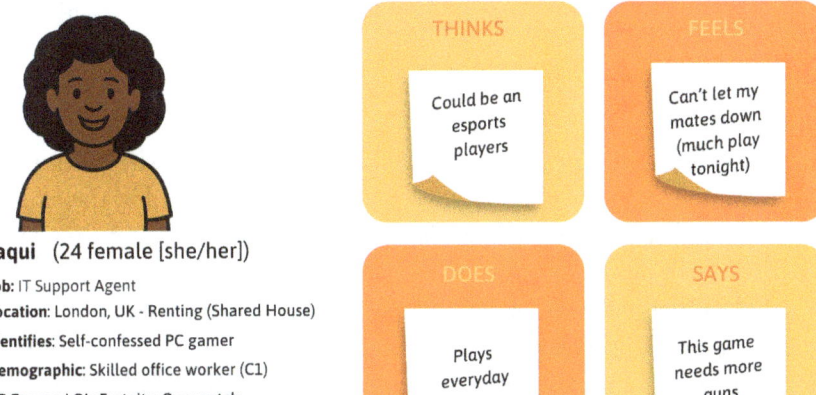

Jaqui (24 female [she/her])

Job: IT Support Agent
Location: London, UK - Renting (Shared House)
Identifies: Self-confessed PC gamer
Demographic: Skilled office worker (C1)
PC Games: LOL; Fortnite; Overwatch
Mobile: Polytopia, Raid: Shadow Legends, Balatro
Channels: PocketGamer, Reddit, Twitch

THINKS
Could be an esports players

FEELS
Can't let my mates down (much play tonight)

DOES
Plays everyday

SAYS
This game needs more guns

FIGURE 4.6   Example player persona.

PLAYER LIFECYCLE

So far, we have talked about the player's needs, but even though we are considering what they might want from a game to help with retention and to sustain their interest, we need to appreciate that players 'needs' will change throughout the player lifecycle. Part of this comes

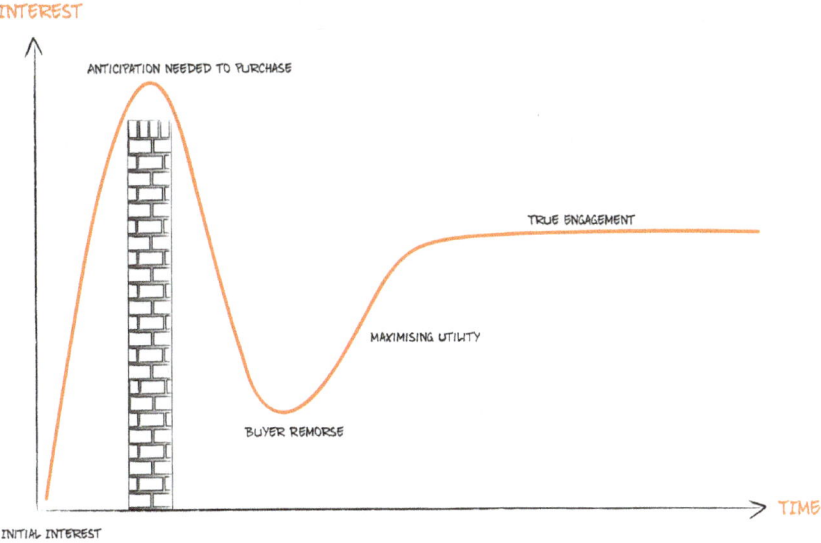

FIGURE 4.7   Player Lifecycle.

from how they are affected by playing the game itself, and other factors include what might be happening in their 'everyday lives' (which we obviously can't affect).

Players adapt and evolve through their experience and engagement with the game. They become familiar with the efforts required, the enjoyment they can extract, what they have left to look forward to by continuing to play, and especially where the game lasts years or decades, their individual lifestyle perspectives may also change. This affects what they need and want from the game.

At its simplest level, a player often will start in a simplistic state looking for some general entertainment, but as they get more engaged in the experience, what they are looking for will clarify and (if we do our job right) intensify. Indeed, there is almost a hierarchy of engagement levels (reflecting that only a smaller number of players will rise up into the different levels). This hierarchy of needs influences their willingness to engage with the commercial elements as well as the general playing behaviour – if they don't churn out.

First, let's look at a typical flow of players. In this diagram, we look at "Interest" as an arbitrary measure of player motivation over time. Whilst this is arbitrary in this image, the author has seen exactly this format when it comes to average activity since the first day of install across multiple games. It happens to match expected models around other service experiences as well as the adoption of technology products outlined by Geoffrey Moore in the classic book Crossing the Chasm.[9]

The initial promotion of the game stimulates the initial level of interest but also has to overcome whatever inherent barriers there are to adoption. If there is an upfront payment, this creates a 'Paywall' which, if the game is not sufficiently compelling, it won't generate the initial anticipation required for players to get past that point to commit to the upfront payment. However, even free-to-access content has some level of barriers related to 'Trust', practical availability of capacity to play (HDD space/device compatibility/etc.), as well as the Opportunity Cost of other games that the player might want to play. We can call this initial engagement the 'Discovery Stage' because it's the point at which the player first encounters the game.

At this point, they need very simple answers to very simple questions.

- Does it excite me as an idea?

- Why should I care?

- Will it be 'fun?'

- Can I play it now? (device/connection/controls)

If we create barriers at this stage, we lose the audience, and they will either churn or perhaps not even bother to download.

When the player first installs the game, they will experience their worst playing moments. I know that sounds odd, but at this point, they don't know how to play, they don't know the controls, and they don't know the objectives. Add to that, if they access the game for free, they also won't have any stake in the success of the game. That combination makes retaining new players extremely complicated – but you do get the chance as a designer to show them what your game is all about and give them reasons to care. It's why onboarding for free-to-play games are absolutely critical.

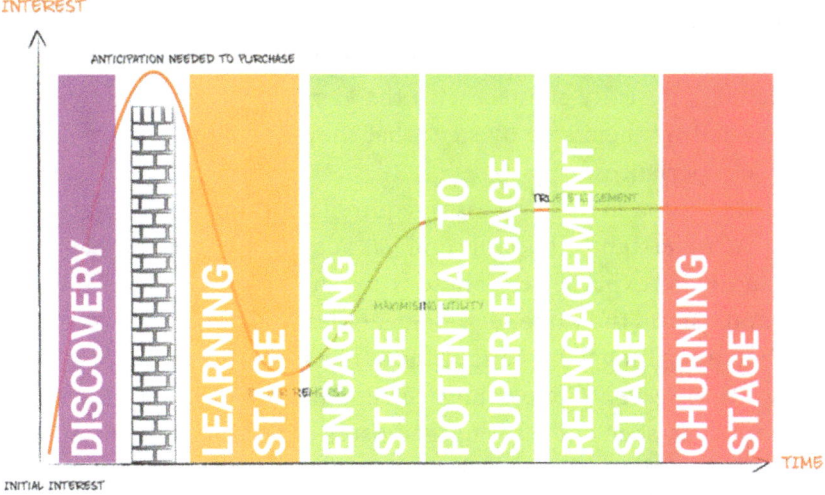

FIGURE 4.8 Player lifecycle stages.

This "Discovery" phase is also important, where the game is paid upfront; however, the bigger challenge is to get them to convert to paying before they get to fully experience the game. That requires a lot of effort and a higher level of Anticipation/FOMO and Social Capital. But on a positive side, with a Pay Upfront game players will often go above and beyond to prove they made a good decision making this purchase – making onboarding somewhat more forgiving.

Once the player has committed to the game, they enter what we call the "Learning stage" of the game, where we can build on the basic concept of what the game is about start to introduce more depth, making sure they are able to answer those questions of how to play but also setting the tone for why they should care and why they might want to continue to play.

Service games in particular which fail to foreshadow the potential longer-term excitement and goals at this point (including why the player may later spend money) will not sustain a sufficient audience to last in the longer term. If we fail to capture the players' engagement in this Learning stage that's when we will.

Building an effective onboarding process is essential – we need to consider the player journey as a First Time User Experience flow. Considering every stage in terms of how we build not just information on how to play, but reasons to care and build desire to get to the next stage, then the next. This is rarely an intuitive process and usually requires considerable iteration. Try to remember why the player wants to play, and how they need to experience Autonomy, Competence, and Relatedness to really connect with the game. Tutorials that constrain players, telling them step by step what they must do next, are usually terrible experiences.

Getting through this process is required to transform the player into one who understands the game and has adopted it as one of their go-to entertainment experiences. These truly engaged players are the ones who understand the value each element means to them and whether or not they are willing to exchange time or real money for it. In some cases, this leads to a level of 'Super-Engagement' often linked to a higher level of committed spend. These engaged users do need to be continuously reengaged, or they risk being burned out – hence the need for ongoing updates and releases that take the players with the game.

OSCAR'S HIERARCHY OF GAMES

FIGURE 4.9   Hierarchy of games needs.

Another way to consider this principle of a life cycle is to explore the evolution of player needs as a hierarchy, where our role as designers is to excite the player to ever higher levels of engagement. The base state of this hierarchy is a simple requirement for entertainment, but as the player transitions through the player experience, our aim is to excite them to build a deeper connection with the game, building on that with a sense of trust in the experience, then social validation eventually leading to a form of Game Self-Actualisation where the player takes on aspects of the game as part of their personal identity – even if temporarily. In this way, a game transitions from being a 'product we consume' to something which can even form part of our sense of self.

Social factors are too often forgotten in video game design. Because, unlike most board games, we can often play games effectively against the machine. However, at their heart, games are an intrinsically social activity where even when we don't play together, we share stories about our experiences with others. This has become even more important in the decade I wrote 'Games as a Service',[10] such that content creators have become one of the principal vectors of generating awareness and community for games.

Beyond Self-Determination, it's also important to consider the social factors at play. A key psychological model we can draw up for this is the concept of Social Identity Theory.[11] At its heart, this idea is focused on how, as humans, we readily align ourselves with the groups we feel we most align with – our Tribe. The tribes we align with may come from multiple aspects of our experience. This can be cultural, based on ethnicity, community, religion, or some other common intellectual movement. It can be based on common physical characteristics, sports, games, musical preference, movie genres, and indeed any shared experiences, e.g. Veterans, LGBTQ+, professions, and of course the development teams we support.

To reinforce our sense of self and self-esteem, we tend to positively align ourselves with some of the common characteristics and values amongst that 'Tribe' or 'In-Group' that we perceive as being shared. But that is necessarily reinforced by defining our 'Out-Group', which provides us with a distinct (usually negative) comparison. One of the best illustrations of this comes amongst sports teams where the players, managers, and even kit (arguably the equivalent of a tribal flag or costume) change regularly.

One of the fiercest of these rivalries comes from Scotland with Celtic vs Rangers. The "Old Firm" derby between Celtic and Rangers is one of the most intense rivalries in world football. It has a history rooted in sectarianism and political tensions that go back over a century. The two teams are located just a few miles apart in Glasgow, Scotland, and their rivalry represents much more than just sport. For many fans of Celtic, the club represents a symbol of Catholic identity, while for Rangers' supporters, it embodies Protestant unionist values. The conflict between these two groups has often spilled onto the football pitch, leading to violent clashes both on and off the field. Aligning yourself with one or the other of these teams has deep implications and carries enormous weight for many – influencing wider opinions, values, and political activism. But tribal membership need not be so absolute and will itself be on a

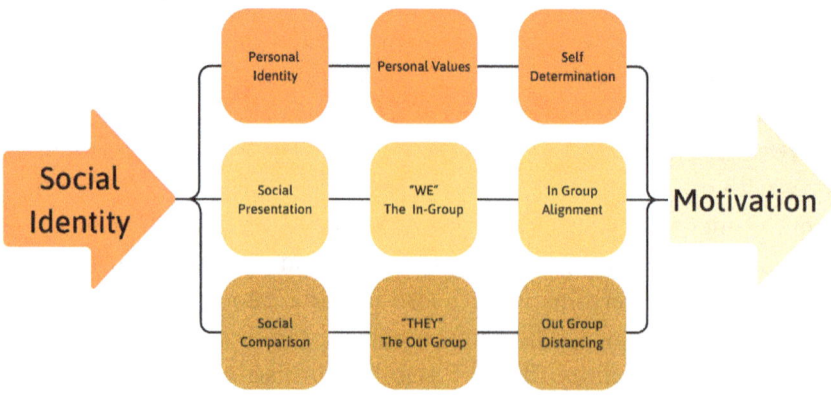

FIGURE 4.10   Social identity theory.

spectrum affected by the social context as well as the personal values of the individuals – although it is common for someone's personal values to be deeply influenced by the tribes they associate with.

How does this apply to why we play games? Well, the point is that social norms and mores (social customs) and the tribes which influence them are not something we can ignore as designers. Moreover, we can create versions of this within our playing experience which magnify the players' sense of reward and personal esteem through play. The power/impact of social elements can be represented as an inverse pyramid, where the scale increases with each higher state of social engagement.

We gain the least impact from the initial state – where I can see you play, but as I become aware that you can also see me play these increases in potential. Light competition builds this further, as does more engaged collaborative play. Personal higher-stakes competitions take this event further, but the ultimate game social experience remains when Guilds (Tribes/Clans/teams) form and compete against other Guilds, creating a realistic sense of belonging and common endeavour. Given this model of social tribalism, we can easily see why Youtubers, TikTok, and Twitch

FIGURE 4.11   Six degrees of 'Socialisation'.

content creators have had such an enormous impact on game's community and marketing over the last 10 years, and why this will inevitably increasingly transition to mobile and other personal devices where we consume gaming content as well.

In the end, understanding "Why we play" is a complex interaction between personal motivation, intrinsic and extrinsic rewards, as well as the social context in which we engage in the game. Hopefully, this section has provided some tools to consider your player and their motivations in ways we can later leverage in our game design. However, are they the same motivations that affect the reasons we purchase games… In fact, why do we pay?

Why Do We Pay?

Buyer behaviour is a thoroughly studied aspect of human behaviour. In some models, there is the assumption that a consumer making a purchase goes through a set of evaluation stages from the recognition of the 'Need' or 'Problem to solve,' an understanding of the implications, followed by the evaluation of alternatives and consequences. This in theory then leads to the buyer making a logical selection based on the fit with their "need" state. After that purchase, the buyer will find themselves doing some form of review or 'Post-Purchase' review – this is where sometimes a player can experience a desire to spend again or even find themselves in 'Buyers-Remorse'.

FIGURE 4.12   Purchase funnel.

However, this assumes a rational evaluation which ignores the impact of marketing and cultural stimuli, both of which profoundly affect how we make decisions. In his model of Consumer Behaviour, Philip Kotler showed that these decisions are not made in isolation and are influenced in part by external stimulation and personal bias, as well as the availability of information related to the 'Need State.'

In practice, the question of whether demand for a specific game is triggered by the need or rather the marketing or cultural stimuli is a moot point. However, it's important to understand that in a game there are multiple channels of influence and that all the factors from the quality of the game itself, the way that it is priced, and the channels of distribution are as important as the cultural, social, and political context in terms of influence for the buyer decision. Importantly, value can also be attributed to unexpected elements, including other factors of the game design – which, after all, is part of the stimulus we define as 'Product.' There are many games where an in-game currency intended for exchange became a measure of status in itself instead, completely changing the players' decision-making process, and in the end undermining the game economy balance.

The influence from each of these stimuli applies whether the game is being purchased upfront, or whether the player is spending money in-game for DownLoadable Content (DLC) or free-to-play content. Indeed, we would argue that even the consumption of a rewarded ad is a form of purchase transaction in itself.

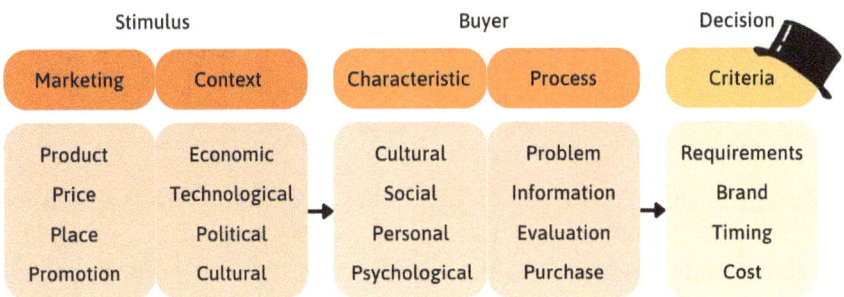

FIGURE 4.13   Consumer behaviour, Philip Kotler.

There is another perspective we can apply to understanding buyer behaviour. This was proposed by R. Bauer in 1960 and looked at "Consumer Behaviour As Risk Taking."[12] The article explores a number of elements, but for simplicity we will focus on four forces that act on our decision-making. These elements need to all be supported to some extent or we instinctively will not act to make that purchase – the default position being to not act. If we are going to be successful in making a commercial game, we need to understand how we positively fulfil each of these four elements.

Another complicating factor is that we often do not make decisions with a complete understanding of the 'good' itself (item/product/service) but instead based on our expectations of 'future delight.'

Hoseini Kiya and Mirabi (2023)[13] in "Identification and ranking of the influence of variables and behavioural indicators of lifestyles on purchase decisions and mental conflicts" stated that the following factors have respectively the greatest impact on purchasing decisions:

1. Behavioural styles of self-deception,
2. Successful people,
3. Herd or mass-like behaviour,
4. Halo effect,
5. Sophistry,
6. Behavioural gap,
7. Idealism,
8. Realism,
9. Anchoring,
10. Projection.

Their results show that the decisions made based on behavioural variables have more satisfaction and less cognitive-perceptual inconsistency, mental conflict, and psychological tension after purchase.

All of these elements apply to any kind of purchase – not just games. Think about what happens when you consider buying a new pair of jeans, a car, or indeed a game. This is the same underlying process as when we decide to purchase a game or in-game item – the only differences are contextual such as the expected 'returns', urgency and what 'opportunity costs' are relevant.

Anticipation: What is the buyer expecting from this purchase action – why is it filled with the potential for delight?

Fear of Missing Out: What is the opportunity cost of making this decision, what other content experiences are we missing out on by taking this decision, and why is it imperative that I act now rather than defer my choices to a later point? Fear of Missing Out is often stated as a 'Dark Pattern,' but it's important to realise that a motivation to "act now" is essential for any transaction. That is not the same as coercion, but care needs to be taken, or this can become counterproductive – alienating the player.

Abnegation: Why should the buyer put aside the other factors in their life outside of the context of this purchase decision? There are things that they should be doing instead of taking this action. How do they give themselves permission to take the step?

Social Capital: What is the social context of this purchase – will their 'Tribe' see this as a positive choice, will it allow them to positively show off their distinctiveness, or facilitate their identification as a member of that tribe? Or will the purchase risk opening them to ridicule or rejection?

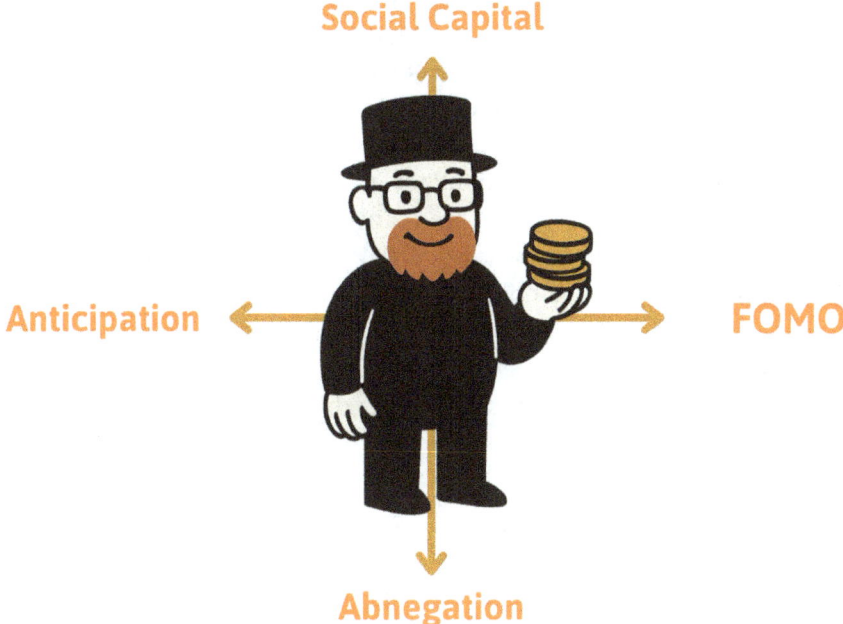

FIGURE 4.14   Buyer behaviour as risk taking.

You will note that for 'Anticipation,' 'Fear of Missing Out,' and to an extent 'Social Capital' we can directly affect those decisions through design, price, distribution, and marketing hype. However, we cannot make someone 'put aside their other needs', as that is a decision that they make within their own context. Historically, people have used the experiments by BF Skinner to try to understand this process. His concept of

"Operant Conditioning" came out of experiments including access to food/rewards/punishment for, notably pigeons and rats, in the eponymous 'Skinner Box'.

The concept outlines a learning process where voluntary behaviours are modified by associating them with consequences (rewards or punishment). There are some fascinating implications from these experiments that help us think about player behaviours in response to rewards. There is specific evidence about what happens when we add randomness of payout and how it influences compulsive behaviour in animals. Like every model, we must acknowledge not just the positive insights but also the risks of overuse.

However, it is also important to realise that the later evidence demonstrated limitations in 'Operant Conditioning' as a useful model, and that it does not apply generally. In 1959, Noam Chomsky[14] famously criticised Skinner's approach. Chomsky argued that adult behaviour cannot be adequately described in terms of sequences of behaviours or responses and, more generally, that complex social contexts may not be adequately represented by these animal models. For example, the animals were not presented with alternative options for access to that reward or avoidance of the punishment. There are many other notable scientists who contributed to the study of Behaviourism[15] including notably Pavlov and his assessment of how, as opposed to the reward of an action, a stimulus associated with that reward could itself elicit the trained behaviour. However, as critics have widely shown, humans are exposed to multiple sources for dopamine rewards (as well as other demands on their time and attention), and such experiences are nearly infinitely substitutable,

FIGURE 4.15   Skinner-box operant conditioning through food access.

reducing the risk/impact. Additionally, games are by definition an escape from the 'ordinary world' and healthy games need to deliver a sense of autonomy, competence, and relatedness that only comes from meaningful positive experiences.

Manipulation or overt pressure to ignore these needs inevitably leads to a negative experience for the purchaser. This creates a sense of 'Buyer Remorse' because of the negative consequences that they experience, leaving them feeling cheated and with a loss of trust in the brand. Something which can never be sustainable. We do have a responsibility to consider vulnerable audiences and avoid exploitative methods; not just ethically, but in the long term 'Dark Patterns' will undermine our commercial potential as they will cause audiences to recoil and damage trust in our games.

One psychological model we need to understand to help us avoid the loss of trust is known as the Hot/Cold Empathy Gap.[16] Whilst exploring attitudes amongst addicts, George F. Loewenstein showed that human understanding is "state-dependent," and in his example, addicts mistakenly categorise their addiction as an essential living drive state. This has been found to have wider applicability, for example, when one is angry, it is difficult to understand what it is like for one to be calm, and vice versa; when one is blindly in love with someone, it is difficult to understand what it is like for one not to be (or to imagine the possibility of not being blindly in love in the future). Importantly, an inability to minimise one's gap in empathy can lead to negative outcomes in medical settings (e.g. when a doctor needs to accurately diagnose the physical pain of a patient).

This model can explain some of the 'poor decisions' we end up making and what we, as developers, need to be careful to avoid when we design our game economy and purchase processes.

Essentially, the concept of the hot-cold empathy gap suggests that when we are highly emotional (hot), our current situational context and related emotional state have a strong sway over our decisions. That means that strong references to emotive topics, desire, sexuality, etc. can lead us to make decisions where we shortcut our decision-making process. Taking action without the due consideration of the consequences. When instead we are calm and collected or otherwise more detached (cold), we are free to act more rationally and plan our actions more carefully. But what further complicates this is our inability to conceive of our own attitudes and choices outside of that context.

Post Purchase Analysis is a vital stage for any buyer and one we cannot afford to ignore as it is essential for building sustainable retention. Retained users are critical to any sustained commercial model. This is even more so the case for service experiences like GaaS. Ensuring a positive outcome during this post-purchase stage is vital for positive reviews (which are vital for new user acquisition), reengagement, and repeat purchase. A returning player additionally does not have the associated cost of acquisition, and although there are costs to support/sustain that player, this is generally a fraction of the initial UA costs required.

We should note that any rationalisation will usually be in the 'Cold' or 'logical' state, and this includes all the complexity that comes from being in a different emotional state. That often leads to one of following reactions:

1. Genuine satisfaction where the experience delivered sufficiently against the expectation of delight to be considered worthwhile, even in this post-play cognitive state.

2. An attempt to justify our purchases. This can work for us as developers and is something we more commonly see in Premium (Pay Upfront Games) where players will work harder to get through the tutorial of a game that would otherwise cause them to churn. However, this justification comes with a risk of 'Player Fatigue,' which can build up if the experience repeatedly fails to live up to expectations.

Develop 'Buyer Remorse' as a form of cognitive dissonance which can sometimes go beyond the perceived opportunity cost that the buyer experienced – and can be fatal to trust.

This is why manipulation of players in terms of their purchase decision process is extremely unadvisable, not just unethical. The likelihood of backlash is considerable. We have seen this in games already, for example through the poor reaction to the implementation of Gatcha elements in games like Star Wars Battlefront 2 and the general dissatisfaction amongst Steam players around both microtransactions in AAA content and with Battle pass design – despite Battle passes, in the opinion of the author, being one of the best ways to deliver obvious value to players by focusing on them unlocking more value the more they play over the period of the offer (and especially where they are designed to support both free and paid players).

Understanding why players buy in games is no different from why people buy anything – but in the specifics, we need to understand their motivations for playing, the way that they engage socially, and the 'Tribes' we develop in our gaming community. If we respect what players value and how we deliver it authentically, we can develop amazing player experiences. But if we act disingenuously or without proper care, we risk developing what some call Dark Patterns, which can damage our game, brand, and the potential for success for the game (SEE 'Sustainability and Ethical Design').

Interview

TIME, VALUE, AND PLAYER EXPERIENCE –
AN INTERVIEW WITH JAMES PORTNOW

Game economies are often understood in terms of in-game currencies, experience points, and consumable resources. However, James Portnow[17], Game Designer and Co-founder of Extra Credits[18], proposes a unifying theory that all of these can be boiled down to one fundamental consumable resource: human time. Every game economy operates on an exchange of time for some form of commodity, whether it be gold, experience, or premium currency.

> I have a theory that I've been pursuing recently, which is that all of it can be drilled down to one fundamental consumable resource, which is human time. And that when you look at gold, when you look at XP, when you look at gems, whatever it is in your game, you can figure out as a designer how much time per unit of whatever that is and cost your game accordingly.

However, the time investment of a player is not a simple metric; it is influenced by factors such as skill, session frequency, and persistence. Two players may spend the same amount of time in a game but experience vastly different economic progressions based on their engagement styles.

> So the thing is all these things are also true even if you use a different currency. How much gold I earn depends on my skill, right? How many gems I earn, whatever XP I'm gaining, depends on my player skill, my session frequency, all these sorts of things.

Understanding what a player is actually purchasing when they spend their time or money is critical to designing a compelling game economy. We need to understand the true value of in-game commodities. The functional attributes of an item – be it a sword's attack power or a character's movement speed – are not the primary motivators for a purchase. Instead, players seek the experiences those items unlock.

> "I think of each commodity in my game as a ticket to an amusement park ride. This commodity buys you this experience. It doesn't matter if it's a sword or a ticket to a magic draft, right? What you're buying is this experience that you want, and to make that purchase satisfying, the experience that you get out of buying that thing has to match or exceed the vision you had of it when you press the buy button," says Portnow.

That doesn't mean every experience has to be a high-octane crafted thrill ride. Repeatable moments can have some level of satisfaction. This can lead to grind, an often-unavoidable part of many games. While some degree of repetition can create meaningful progression, excessive grind risks alienating players. The key distinction is whether the grind is serving as a means to an engaging experience or simply a mechanic to keep players occupied. Portnow sees this concept of a 'ticket to a ride' as a critical way to frame even grind into the design.

> Now that is the economy. Now if I beat the Jabberwocky 40 times, I'll level up enough, get the rare drop, and now I can do the next thing. So, I'm actually buying the ticket to the next ride with the grind.

However, designers must be careful not to rely on empty progression mechanics that manipulate players' compulsions rather than provide meaningful gameplay.

> We like the feeling of accomplishment, even if it is false. We like the feeling of progression, even if it is illusory. And so a lot of times what you'll see is the numbers go up, Skinner box trend, right? And that when players are grinding simply to have the empty experience of feeling like they're making progress, you will eventually hit an exit point.

Scarcity plays a significant role in shaping the perceived value of in-game items. While traditional economic models focus on supply and demand, game economies have unique levers, including temporal scarcity and difficulty-based scarcity.

> Yes, but I think that we have learned that you have to look far beyond just literal resource scarcity. Temporal scarcity is a big one, right? Every miHoYo game has this character available for the next 20 days. If you don't get it now, who knows if it'll be back, right?

Similarly, status-driven scarcity can be a powerful driver of engagement, as seen in rare raid rewards and prestigious cosmetics.

> That raid item, you see that guy walking by in raid armour and you're like, man, that guy's awesome. I wanna look like that person, right? Those items aren't scarce. There's infinite of them generated. If you could just grind them all day, you could get infinite of that. The sheer difficulty, the bar to ride, the table stakes for getting that is so high that it creates a scarcity even if there's no underlying programmatic scarcity.

A common pitfall in multiplayer game economies is the "win-more" feedback loop, where the best players accumulate more resources, making them even harder to defeat. Instead, effective game economies introduce catch-up mechanics, such as Mario Kart's blue shell, to maintain engagement for a broad spectrum of players.

> "You want to have that closeness and so finding ways to make sure that you're rewarding the player without having mechanics that get them so far ahead is a tightrope to walk but one that is worth the walking," Says Portnow.

Every persistent game economy must have mechanisms to remove currency and items from the system. Without effective sinks/drains, in-game currency devalues over time, leading to inflation, and loss of meaning for rewards.

> Every time a new monster spawns, it's literally printing currency, right? Every time I defeat a monster, it's a loot box, it's a treasure chest, it's a pack of cards, right? You open it up and boom, there's something that wasn't in the world before that is usually convertible into some form of currency.

Beyond basic consumable purchases like health potions or weapon repairs, effective sinks should feel rewarding rather than punitive.

"The biggest thing about sinks is actually player perception more than anything else, because you need those sinks. But those sinks should also feel good. Buying a group of potions and powering up certainly feels better than simply having gear degrade over time," says Portnow.

Rather than targeting a small percentage of ultra-high spenders, a well-designed free-to-play economy should encourage sustainable spending habits across a broad player base.

If you can get the average revenue per user to be $5, but actually have it be the mean revenue as well, rather than having 20 users who spend $10,000 and everybody else spending nothing, your game is much better and much more stable and much more long-term sustainable.

CONCLUSION: CREATING MEANINGFUL AND LASTING EXPERIENCES

At its core, a well-designed game economy is about more than just numbers and balance – it's about creating memorable experiences for players that keep them engaged and invested. Whether through time-based currency balancing, compelling progression, or effective sinks, game designers must always keep the players' journey in mind.

"Games are in themselves fundamentally an illusion. And so a lot of the time when I'm looking at my sinks and things, one of the things I very often do is look at presentation. Does it feel good? Does it feel like you're getting something rather than losing something for putting money into this sink?" says Portnow.

By carefully designing economies that reward effort, encourage engagement, and provide meaningful choices, developers can create systems that feel fair, enjoyable, and ultimately sustainable.

NOTES

1 https://mud.co.uk/richard/hcds.htm
2 https://amyjokim.com/
3 https://quanticfoundry.com/
4 https://newzoo.com/resources/blog/overview-newzoos-gamer-segmentation-and-gamer-personas

5 https://www.gamerefinery.com/gamerefinery-player-motivations-archetypes/

6 https://en.wikipedia.org/wiki/Self-determination_theory

7 https://psychologyfanatic.com/intention-behavior-gap/

8 https://www.inverse.com/article/53414-this-person-does-not-exist-creator-interview

9 https://www.mrs.org.uk/resources/approximated-social-grade-on-the-2021-census

10 https://www.taylorfrancis.com/books/mono/10.4324/9781315849102/games-service-oscar-clark

11 https://www.simplypsychology.org/social-identity-theory.html

12 https://www.jstor.org/stable/1250198

13 https://www.jvcbm.ir/article_182759.html?lang=en

14 https://pmc.ncbi.nlm.nih.gov/articles/PMC2223153

15 https://en.wikipedia.org/wiki/Behaviorism

16 https://en.wikipedia.org/wiki/Hot-cold_empathy_gap

17 https://www.linkedin.com/in/james-portnow-1506365

18 https://www.youtube.com/extracredits/videos

CHAPTER 5

What Is a Game Anyway?

DOI: 10.1201/9781003592471-5

WHAT IS THE ANATOMY OF A GAME?

Before we can dive into economic structures, we need to agree on a common starting point for how we define what a game is and how it operates as a collection of systems. This is a topic of endless debate and disagreement, as there is simply no such thing as one approach to games. However, there are some common principles.

First, we can establish some basics.

The word 'game' has around 30 definitions in the Collins dictionary, including:

- an amusement or pastime; diversion

- a contest with rules, the result being determined by skill, strength, or chance

- an event consisting of various sporting contests, especially in athletics

None of these adequately capture what we mean by games in the context of the video games industry. Raph Koster's excellent 'Theory of Fun' focuses on games as a framework for triggering the brain's reward system through pattern matching. In his 2013 GDC Next talk, he further stated that "Play is the wiggle room. It is space. It is explorable areas."

In his critique of Homo Ludens, "Les jeux et les hommes,"[1] 1958, Robert Cailllois outlined six core characteristics of a game:

- It is free, or not obligatory.

- It is separate, (from the routine of life), occupying its own time and space.

- It is uncertain, so that the results of play cannot be predetermined and so that the player's initiative is involved.

- It is unproductive, in that it creates no wealth and ends as it begins.

- It is governed by rules that suspend ordinary laws and behaviours, and that must be followed by players.

- It involves make-believe that confirms for players the existence of imagined realities, that may be set against 'real life.'

But does that help us get to the core bones of what makes up a game?

I think we need to go deeper – and fair warning, this section will very much be about logically 'splitting hairs' of definitions. Let's take Monument Valley, one of the greatest mobile playing experiences ever made, but is it a game? Given that the results of play cannot be predetermined. There is only one solution, but the discovery of that solution is not guaranteed, and in the act of that discovery, we find the challenge.

In our interview with Jennifer Estaris, we defined three kinds of structure which impact the purpose of play and that greatly impact how we manage, particularly, player progression.

- Linear puzzles are unidirectional and rely on solving the puzzle to unlock the next stage, to deliver progression.

- Branching narratives offer some level of autonomy – even if only really at a perceived level, such as with the classic The Walking Dead: Telltale Series[2] but which does have some level of meaningful choice.

- Emergent gameplay consists of games which are based on replayable systems, and often more ambiguous goals, and often where the player can engage in unexpected ways.

Within a linear puzzle experience, we are expected to solve the specific problem set at the specific point in the experience. Puzzles are generally the core method we use to drive the game forward, unlocking new levels and narrative elements. Rewards, which further unlock other forms of interaction in the puzzle, risk directly undermining the puzzle solution design or, in the best-case, making the core puzzle design ever more complicated. Adding progression other than in terms of unlocking the next level (and narrative) risks derailing the player from the core objective.

Branching narratives have basically the same restrictions, but here the options you choose inherently affect the outcomes, making replayability for the game possible.

Why does this matter? Surely puzzles are a completely valid form of play? Yes, of course they are. Does that mean they aren't fun? Of course not. Some of the most meaningful forms of playing entertainment we experience, like Monument Valley, take this form. However, for this book and for us to explore design to the full, the distinction matters. This is because only in what we have described as 'emergent games' do we find the

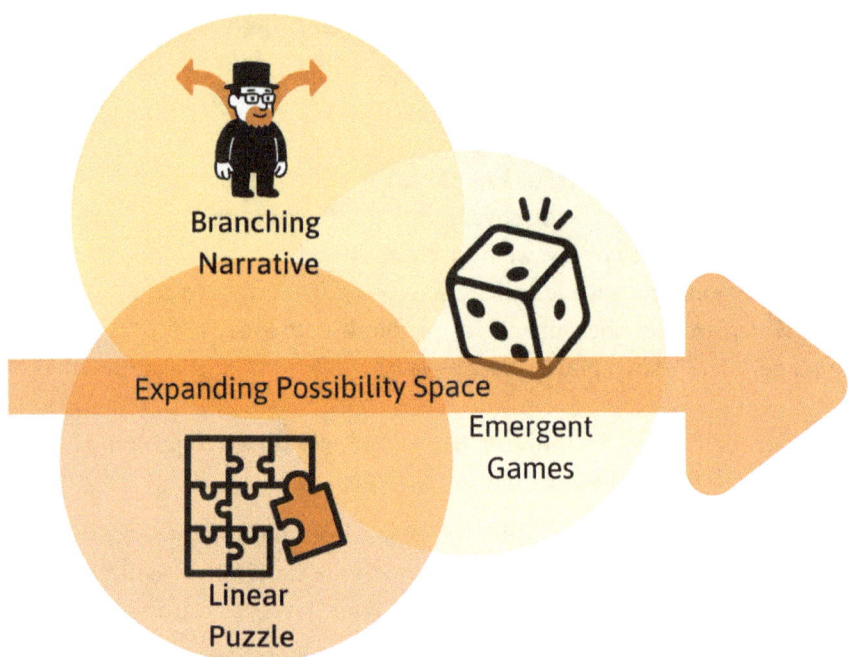

FIGURE 5.1   Possibility space expands with different design paradigms.

full scope for replayability. Games where there is space for the application of speed, skill, strategy, even 'grind,' to affect the outcome. The full arsenal of economy design works best where there is a 'possibility space' on which a functional economy can be developed.

That doesn't mean we can't use the economy design principles outlined in these other game structures. It just means we need to be aware of the constraints on the scope of 'possibility space' we can leverage and the impact these structures have on player purpose and progression. For example, applying progression elements in layers, e.g. the use of narrative and the restoration of your inherited house in Merge Mansion from Metacore or the Homescapes from Playrix.

PLAYING PIECES

Now that we have established the kind of playing experience we have defined as 'games' for the purpose of economy design, we have a clearer focus to allow us to start providing some definitions of the functional components of the game. This starts with the things that we actually do in play. There are so many variations of how we can look at games, so what we're establishing here is a framework to look at games for the purpose of offering a common language for the components within game mechanics. Of course, no framework can include every edge case, but the following is an attempt to break games down into six manageable aspects, each of which has six variant characteristics, useful to understand the differences in the playing experience. This framework can be helpful during the game design process.

1. **Objectives**: The essential 'Why' of the game – for the overall game, or for any specific moment of play. What are we expected to achieve as players – whether directly communicated or not? Objectives range from personal to social interactions, including:

   - **Curiosity**: Stimulating exploration, creativity and discovery through the context of the game experience.

   - **Ownership**: Focus on the acquisition and control of resources.

   - **Identity**: Creative personal expression for the player through the actions of play, through creativity or choice of action, includes a sense of belonging via some form of self-identification with an 'in-group'.

   - **Escape**: Actions to evade the game setting conditions (as well as more widely to escape/distract from pressures of the real world).

   - **Mastery**: The expression of skill, whether physical dexterity or the application of mental acuity through tactical, strategic, or economic decisions.

   - **Collaboration**: The shared resolution of a common endeavour along with others in my group, and potentially against other players and player groups.

2. **Challenges**: The obstacles which get between us and the set objectives, which provide a sense of meaning to the experience. These can include a range of vectors including:

   - **Tasks**: The completion of a specifically defined activity or series of activities which sometimes needs to happen in a specific order. 'Go Fetch' missions are typical examples used in MMO or Sandbox side quests where the player is asked by an NPC or equivalent to gather something which can only be obtained after resolving a number of steps such as defeating an enemy, resolving a puzzle, and then gathering the item. Even a series of narrative checkpoints could be considered a set of defined tasks.

- **Puzzles**: The resolution of a logic or physics-based problem using a defined set of tools or interactions that test the players' ingenuity or knowledge. There is usually one solution which has to be derived, but in each iteration there usually will be some form of progressive 'twist' that complicates prior learned patterns.

- **Contest**: The direct function of the player against other players is, to demonstrate raw playing skill. This can take the form of direct combat, resource management, or domination of territory.

- **Collect**: Locate and gather an array of unique items or tokens through a set of activities. This can be similar to a 'task' and may involve 'puzzles' or enemy drops and tends to be a longer-term set of actions. Alternatively, rather than unique items, this can be used to unlock sets of 'hidden information' that update and amend the players' future activity.

- **Survival**: The ability of the player to locate, secure, and apply a series of resources and systems which require maintaining in a dynamic equilibrium. This means that more complex systems have respectively higher costs to sustain in context with the benefits they convey.

- **Creation**: The use of the game's tools to create new elements in the game world. This usually, although not necessarily, includes a sense of expression and potentially some selection dilemma either by having to choose specific variations (such as in Gardenscapes). In some games (such as Tiny Glade), the whole point of the game is the expression itself.

3. **Interactions**: What the players actually do in the game to trigger the interactions and pattern matching is key to the physiological sensation of play. This combination of physical, logical, and emotional responses creates a visceral level of immersion in play. These can include:

- **Tap**: When using mouse, controller, or touch screen, the simplest interaction is a tap – this triggers a range of effects at the specific position on the screen, from collect, open, interact, shoot, stab, etc. In games with 3D environments, we have to interpret those interactions on objects with the context of facing and distance from the player's avatar/cursor/etc. On touch screens, this can be even more visceral through the use of swipes, but this also can add to the complexity of the feedback process.

- **Hold**: Requiring the player to specifically maintain the tap and hold it for a period of time, sometimes whilst doing other activities to intensify the experience. This allows us to make the moment of release vital to the outcome. Classically, a power bar might fluctuate from low to high, whilst the player attempts to time the release perfectly to obtain the desired 'power' for their action, e.g. kicking a ball, releasing an arrow.

- **Drag**: A further adaptation of Hold, where the user is required to move an item within the game world to a new location in virtual space. This methodology can also be used to change the shape and size of in-game objects, or even to scale camera perspectives.

- **Move**: The player uses the control system to traverse through the virtual environment in either 2D or 3D. Movement can relate to the position and facing of the character and/or camera view and needs to consider rapid changes such as acceleration, braking, or falling in ways that mimic the expectations of the type of character or vehicle being represented. Think about how we expect Mario to jump in a Nintendo game[3]? Critical to this is how the camera and characters fit into the space do the tires on the car feel like they are gripping the ground? What happens when the camera 'clips' through walls or tries to move through other objects or characters? Reaching new locations can trigger other interaction types. For example, moving the camera to face items in the game world that can be tapped, held, or dragged even if the player's character does not change their virtual location.

- **Choice**: The player is presented with a set of options which they directly choose. This can be overt, such as the selection of a conversation choice, or indirect, such as the placement of objects in specific locations or the completion of tasks in a specific order.

- **Activate**: The selection of an asset or activity type to be played, often from some form of inventory. This can be the use of a player ability or item, the selection of a button, or something else which the player has immediate access, rather than requiring the element to be in-world.

4. **Resolution**: The conditional parameters which allow us to understand what success looks like for the game. This can be a measure or a flag of some form denoting completion.

- **Score**: A performance metric which provides a level of ranking or required threshold of performance. Scores can be based on diverse factors from 'Hits' or 'Kills,' to goals, distance attained, getting yourself or an item to a predefined location, etc. Typically, the scope of a score has no inherent cap other than that possible practically in the available duration.

- **Time**: The duration that elapsed before the player attained a specific checkpoint in terms of location, decision, score, or other defined outcome. Different games will identify a low or high time as good in any given game – and indeed time is often converted into a score metric in many games.

- **Boolean**: Player action setting some condition to either True or False. This can be the player achieving a simple 'Pass' condition, such as reaching a specific location marker, or selecting a specific narrative option.

- **Deadline**: A preset factor which limits the player interactions, such as time, or a number of moves, health, fuel and other factors, which when they expire, form the end of that player session. There are usually some secondary resolution factors which are tracked alongside hard ending factors including time, score, and distance.

- **Checklist**: A set of actions or resources which have to be collected/completed before success can be defined in the session.

- **Levelling**: A transition point in play where sufficient score/resources/currency checklist completion has occurred to trigger a threshold of activity which changes some status of the player or the environment.

5. **Perspective**: This is about how the game is presented to the player and incorporates visual and narrative storytelling elements. Games often use combinations of camera and storytelling techniques which may not work in other media. The kinds of perspectives seen in games can include:

   - **1st Person**: In terms of camera, this is where the screen shows what the player sees, and where the narrative is told directly from the point of view of the player as protagonist. Note, the second person perspective is very rarely used as it's generally too confusing – e.g. the view of the player character from the perspective of their enemy.

   - **3rd Person**: This is a very common camera perspective used in games, and has the advantage over 1st person in that the player gets a sense of things that are around them, rather than just the field of view presented by the screen. However, it does lose a little in terms of immersion and the sense that these are your own actions. In narrative terms, the story is being told outside of the player perspective and can be 'Omniscient' or all-knowing, including the inner thoughts of a character, 'Restricted' where the player hears the inner perspectives only of the character currently narrating, and even 'Unreliable' where the information from the narrator cannot be taken at face value.

   - **Observer**: This is less commonly about camera perspective and more about the role of the player in narration. The player is observing the action and decisions of the narrative protagonists and is in practice little more than the 'sidekick' or cannon fodder in the game. This is particularly the case in games like 'Gears of War' where the player completes combat missions between sets of cutscenes with story exposition.

   - **Branching**: A narrative technique at which games excel is the ability to introduce alternative perspectives through options selected by the player. This can include character swaps, branching narrative choices, or the selection of one or the other option in a dilemma-based problem. The act of choice opens up new perspectives and choices and can even change the ways we present information and UX elements in the game. Branching doesn't need to become overly complicated, as demonstrated in games like The Witcher, where most choices are simply opportunities to access additional narrative information.

- **Twist**: A present condition in the game which, once triggered, affects the narrative flow of the game. This could be a reveal or jump-shock moment, but generally triggers a change in tone in terms of narrative or visual style. Twists can also be relevant to puzzle resolution, where some constraint prevents the application of one of the established tools or solutions but something in the environment or in combination with another tool the player can still resolve the problem logically. E.g. I need to position a mirror to be able to deflect a laser, which is required to open a gate.

- **Catalyst**: A narrative component which can either build over time, or change instantly at a specific checkpoint or threshold, triggered by a specific form of player action. For example, in an extraction shooter, this could be a change in enemy behaviour, triggered when the player prepares to depart, or once an item or switch is activated e.g. once a player triggers the bomb, the objective instantly switches to finding cover.

6. **Rewards**: The pay-offs in games come in many different forms and these will be some of the principal vectors we will explore later in the economy design. For this section, here are some high-level categories:

   - **Currencies**: The basic form of reward, typically 'Gold,' which is the basic in-game form of exchange required for any in-game transaction. Currency can be 'Soft' (acquired readily in-game) or 'Hard' (largely purchased with real money).

   - **Resources**: At a basic level, these can be considered 'flavoured' currencies used to convert to specific kinds of in-game functions and inventory items; often used in the crafting of various kinds.

- **Anchors**: These are forms of exchange (often currencies) which can only be obtained through play, but which form a baseline for exchange that necessitates progression in the game. Experience or XP are typical examples.

- **Ratchets**: These are limits based on progression, and the sink of Anchors required before the player can access specific upgrades, abilities, or other forms of playing options – potentially including cosmetic items.

- **Consumables**: Items which the player can acquire and that are consumed when used. These can include power-ups, fuel, health potions, and any other form of player utility (what a player wants/ needs). They often have some capacity limitations restricting how many can be owned or held at any time.

- **Durables**: These are more permanent inventory items that players unlock and get to keep – they are not consumed upon use – although they may in some games partially or fully deteriorate over time. These can include functional items as well as items which are purely cosmetic.

This is not an exhaustive list, but hopefully provides a set of tools or lenses from which we can start to understand what is going on in any game. However, this is just the building blocks. Games, as we have stated, are systems, and as such it is as much about how these elements work together to create the player experience, as each individual part.

To understand games as systems we need to break them down into loops. For the purposes of this framework, we will define three layers of loops. The Core Mechanic, the Context Loop, and the Cultural Loop.

UNDERSTANDING LOOPS

The fundamental aspect of play that is often the focus for game designers is the Core Loop. This is the basic level of system design we consider and helps us understand the transitional states of what play delivers for players. In a typical game, this loop cycle begins with a **Start Condition**, where the player is introduced to the playing setup. This is followed by the communication of a **Challenge**, which frames the activities or difficulty that the player must overcome. The player then uses the systems of the game to create a **Resolution** and when successful (or unsuccessful) in completing the

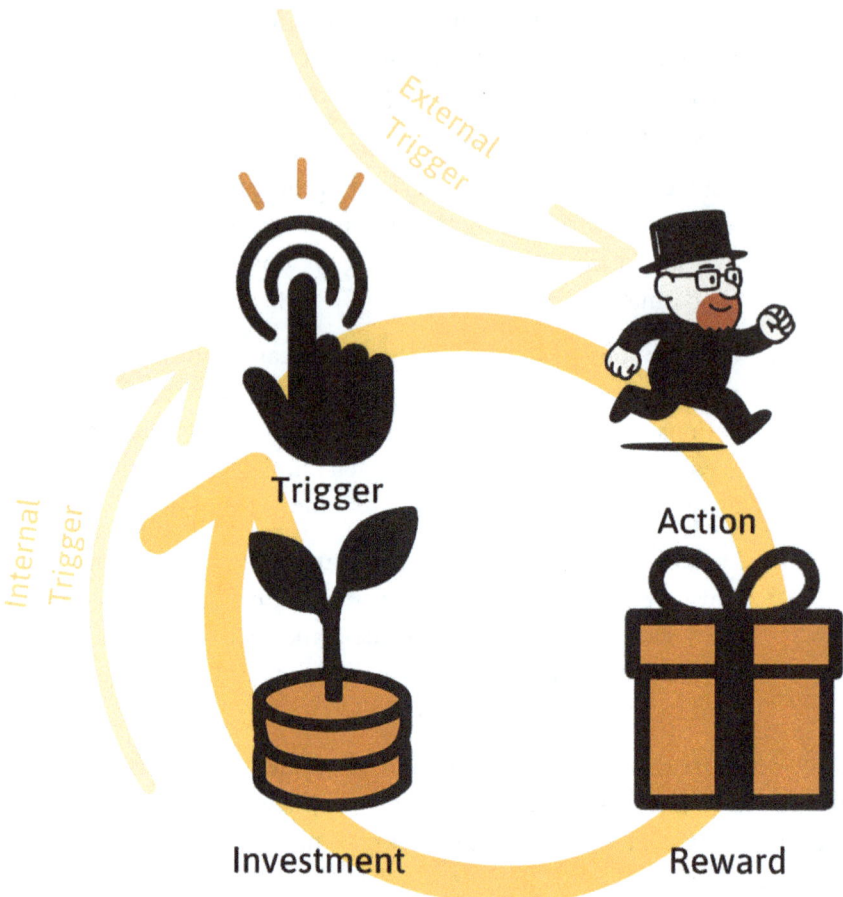

FIGURE 5.2   The hooked model by Nir Eyal.

Challenge, a **Reward** provides feedback and stakes that incentivises the player to continue to further invest their time into the loop cycle.

This concept of looped behaviour has been explored further and wider than just for games. In Hooked: How to build Habit-Forming products[4] Nir Eyal explored this in his 'Hooked' model, showing the flow from a trigger motivation, to action, reward, and a level of investment by the consumer (or in our case player).

This model reminds us to consider that there will be intrinsic and extrinsic motivations bringing consumers to the experience; including the range of external stimuli we have explored in the previous chapter. Those motivational triggers therefore have to be aligned and communicate the action we want these consumers to take – such as play the game. In return for that, we need to offer those consumers some level of reward in a form that stimulates further engagement. In Eyal's model, he also shows that some level of personal investment in the experience is necessary to impact the level of retention those consumers will have with the experience, and hence their likelihood of continuing to play (and where relevant, pay).

However, we need to make some important caveats. Key to this model is that we have a deep understanding of the intrinsic, not just extrinsic, motivations of our audience – and offer an experience which sufficiently delivers on that expectation, not just in the Rewards, but in the way that the actions deliver a profound sense of investment in the experience as well.

Using external stimuli to affect individual actions has a complicated history and is one of the recent forms of this 'Nudge Theory'. Nudges aim to influence people to make better decisions. For example, authorities may set a "better" choice, such as donating your organs, as a default. Or they could make a healthy food option more attractive through labelling. Research seemed to show highly exciting outcomes. However, although this area of study is still interesting, more recent meta-analysis has not shown the expected results, despite huge levels of investment in many countries. Indeed, there are some who question whether it has any effect at all.[5] This should serve as a reminder that whilst we attempt to use evidence-based approaches to game design, a lot of the results are affected by the reality that we do not (nor should we try to) control the subjective perspective of players.

Instead, we can think of gameplay in terms of the Loop as a model to help understand the player experience, set up expectations, and respond to the intrinsic motivations to play. Further, we can use it to understand the emotional flow of players within our experience and how we can create a dynamic equilibrium that allows the players to stay in that state during play, as well as to then be able to leave and return time and time again.

We will explore the Three loops (Core, Context, and Culture) later, but first we will explore the dynamic nature of two emotional vectors during play. The first explores motivational emotions from Anticipation to Fear of Missing Out (FOMO), the second, Absorption, looks at how immersed or absorbed in the experience we are at that point as we move between Relief and Tension.

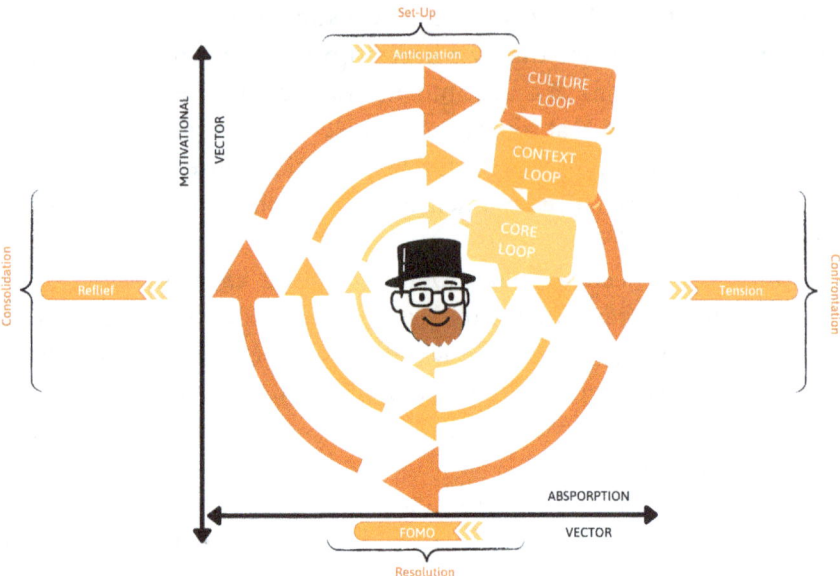

FIGURE 5.3 Motivation and absorption vectors across loops.

Motivational Vector: Anticipation vs. Fear of Missing Out

FOMO as a concept is an aspect of Self Determination Theory and refers to a sense of anxiety related to being left out of activities being enjoyed by others, especially those in your in-group (or "tribe" in 'social identity theory'). This term can often be portrayed as a purely detrimental or exploitable factor, not entirely unreasonably as excessive FOMO can lead to stress and unhealthy comparisons. However, it is also important to appreciate the positive role FOMO can play as an important psychological factor necessary to motivate action, especially beyond our 'typical' routine expected behaviour. FOMO can be key to encouraging us to both try new things and stick with actions that require extra effort to sustain.[6] FOMO provides us with a reason to act now, without which we will, all other things being equal, not act. Similarly, this reaction, when overemployed, can become significantly detrimental and we need only look at the epidemic rise in mental health issues attributed to social media and general online social engagement.[7] As game designers, we need to leverage the human reactions to the risk that the player may fail, or miss out on some in-game experience, without creating such a reaction whereby players feel that the burden of these demands becomes detrimental or even anxiety inducing.

The opposite end of this emotional spectrum we will explore is Anticipation. This is the positive delight derived from the expectation of a future reward, and just as FOMO is a vital aspect of motivation, so is a predictive expectation of the rewards of that action. Designing for this seems, on the surface, to be a purely positive factor, but just as FOMO has to be managed carefully to avoid detrimental impact on the player, so does Anticipation. Think about the impact of 'Hype' and how the prior idealisation of a film, game, or technology leads to an overinflation of expectation that is profoundly misaligned to reality; causing equally overinflated negative reactions when the real experience is revealed. The damage to that film/game/technology can be profound and potentially irreversible. The quintessential example of this in games was Hello Games' 'No Man's Sky'.[8] The founder, Sean Murray, understandably wanted to share his vision of the game, but in sharing it, the hype that built up went far beyond what the team could deliver at launch, given the conflicting pressures of time, technology, quality, and presumably pressures from publishing. The disappointment from the players was palpable – it was deemed a failure at the time – despite delivering an incredible, engaging, unparalleled space exploration experience. Unlike the vast majority of projects which fall victim to hype, Hello Games went on to perform a miracle and continued to deliver on the game, turning around the critics but at considerable cost, time, and effort.

However, this is another risk when it comes to anticipation – satisfying that expectation. That may sound odd, of course, if we present someone with goals, we need to provide a point where those promised rewards are delivered, don't we? This is where we have to remember Victor Frankl's emphasis on the human pursuit of meaning over 'happiness' per se. Providing anticipation is more than just presenting the promise of something valued by the player, we need to understand that value is inherently measured against the intrinsic characteristics, effort to unlock and context. This is further complicated in that anticipation is subjective, and the value we attribute to promised rewards is affected by our sense of how obtainable that result is for us. If it's too easy, the value will be seen as low, if it's too hard or requires too great an opportunity cost in terms of effort/ time or real money, it will be seen as unobtainable and ironically lose its effective value, even if it retains aspiration.

Neither Anticipation nor FOMO is a static variable, they form a dynamic equilibrium. In our game, we need to ensure that we balance these elements and create a journey where we take players through layers of Anticipation,

FOMO, and pay-off, which if done well leads to additional future Anticipation, FOMO, and pay-off. These are also both anticipatory emotional reactions to the perception of goals. For that to function, we need to ensure that they are effectively communicated, but an essential aspect is to deliver this with a degree of ambiguity – Predictable Surprise! The impact of an outcome which captures attention being based on the observers' expectations. We assume, often erroneously, that outcomes will match some statistical model based on our prior experience. As designers we can play with those assumptions to reinforce those perceived expectations, which helps to reinforce behaviours and excitement derived from play. Of course, remember the caveats we have already stated re: behavioural conditioning and the arguments against 'Skinner Box' methods and the manifold reasons to act responsibly as designers. From a design theory perspective, what is interesting is that there is a direct connection between the expectation of such surprise and the attention of the player which has been backed up in a paper on "Bayesian Surprise and Human Attention",[9] which states that "Surprise represents an inexpensive, easily computable approximation to human attentional allocation." However, we should be careful not to read too much into this study as it only included a very small sample size.

It should also be noted that in real-world scenarios we tend to be more averse to 'Ambiguity' than 'Risk' and this can act to inhibit action.[10] The difference being whether we have the information to act rather than the likelihood of success. As studies into this area note, neural responses to risky and ambiguous situations also depend on individual attitudes. Given that games, by definition, are about an escape from the real world, they provide a safe environment for the player to practice their predictive methods, taking on riskier or more ambiguous activities than we might consider given the permanence of real-world consequences. As a result, we can gain significant pleasure from the resolution of such predictable uncertainty, where the game includes a suitable level of restricted information and discovery, much more so than where the issues/risks, and rewards are directly communicated.

We feel a greater level of attention in an experience and from the rewards we receive when there is sufficient ambiguity, effort, risk, and delayed pay-off.

Absorption Vector: Relief vs. Tension

Flow[11] as a concept was developed by psychologist Mihály Csíkszentmihályi and is considered a vital component in understanding game design.

This is a state of being fully immersed in an experience with a feeling of energised focus, full involvement, and enjoyment in that activity. It's that experience where we are so engaged in a game, that we look up and suddenly realise, without regret, that hours have passed. Achieving this state requires a number of things to be the case. We need to feel that the experience has outcomes which feel attainable, whilst at the same time having a visceral sense of meaningful challenge. There needs to be a sense of the activity being effortless or at least where the interactions can become instinctive. And at its heart, the experience needs to be deeply immersive, intrusive activities such as ad breaks, or forced tutorial actions that can potentially catastrophically disrupt that immersion.

FIGURE 5.4 'Flow'.

Understanding the interaction between Skill and Challenge is vital to creating the conditions where players can enter the 'Flow' state, which occurs where the Challenge is high (but not perceived as impossible) and matches the players' Skill.

Challenge and Skill are relatively subjective concepts and highly context dependent. They are also factors which change over time based on familiarity and practiced behaviour. It's essential to realise that we cannot sustain a low state forever and that it is inherently dynamic. The more practiced we are the more our skill grows requiring more challenge in order to sustain the level of engagement which delivers this idea of an optimal 'Flow State.'

As designers, we can also be playful with this principle. Adjusting the challenge dynamically can introduce the sensation of Tension or Relief building emotional texture in the player experience as a direct result of what we do in play. Something we can reinforce through rewards, narrative and even consequences. However, we have to be careful as one of the challenges of play, especially on mobile, because our device is so easy to access, is to ensure the player can break out of the experience. This is important for two reasons. The first is that we need to be responsible as designers. We should help minimise the potential impact on vulnerable players who perhaps due to external issues may be at risk of becoming overly dependent on the game. The second applies to any player and has a direct impact on engagement across all players. We need to avoid the risk of 'Player Burnout'. This form of burnout in the context of an individual game, can be deceptively simple and present in a player as a feeling that the expected effort and commitment to play another session exceeds what they feel they can commit to right now, prior to starting again. This is situational, but we have observed players avoiding games they reportedly love to play on mobile because the game has too long a window between moments that experience can naturally be interrupted. Indeed, we probably have all experienced this to an extent, think about the frustration one feels when a family member needs to talk, and you can't readily stop and listen without getting your character killed. We know that they aren't being unreasonable, but the timing sucks.

The observation we have made indicates that in general, mobile games need an opportunity to break away in no more than 90 s chunks of playing loops; and the player should have the option to break out and respond to an interruption, before diving back in. That doesn't mean that the player won't continue to play for extended periods, e.g. 20–60 minutes on their device (battery permitting). It simply means that the potential for a break in immersion, or at least texture in the emotional flow, allows the player to avoid burnout, and avoid the game unduly impacting their 'ordinary' lifestyle. Similar issues affect PC and console experiences, but usually at different levels of periodicity, for example, building an unending sequence of required daily challenges, which puts the player at a significant disadvantage to others, can become gruelling very quickly. This principle of having natural breaks is also a vital aspect to avoid the player from getting into unhealthy habits that are associated with behavioural addiction, particularly an issue for vulnerable players.

To support a positive engagement with the Flow state, we need to look at the way we engage and absorb the attention of the player through the transitional states of Relief and Tension as we mentioned. As we take the player through the journey of the Core Loop, an important aspect of building immersion and engagement is the way the mechanics help us transition the player through states of calm (Relief) and intensity (Tension). We want the player to feel that they can dive into an absorbed state and also turn down the intensity so they have an opportunity for rest without shocking them out of immersion. This is a dynamic equilibrium, not just because of the continuous learning process but also because if we instil the 'Relief' state too completely, the player will become bored and no longer be absorbed in the game. Similarly, if the game is too intense or difficult, the frustration becomes the cause of churn and we see the classic 'Rage Quit,' from which there is rarely a return.

The experience of such frustration, and the intensity of reaction, happens to also be a key component of what players love about games, and for many there is a point where we get so close to giving up, or to throwing the controller through the TV screen. A point where we can feel almost an intense hate for the game, yet we play again, and where subsequently we win, we most love the game. This very tension is how we best experience the game. We will explore this further when we talk about Difficulty and Drop rates. The thinking on this phenomenon has been profoundly influenced by Florian Steinhoff's GDC 2014 talk on the Wooga game, Jelly Splash.[12]

We will argue that the purpose of the Core Loop is not just to act as a map for the player experience, but additionally as a tool to direct and manage the elements required to sustain the dynamic equilibrium along both vectors, to deliver Motivation and Absorption in play.

Interview

PURPOSE IN GAMES AND BEYOND PLAY – AN INTERVIEW WITH JENNIFER ESTARIS

Jennifer Estaris[13] is a Filipino-American designer based in South London, best known for directing *Monument Valley 3*, a meditative puzzle game exploring disaster recovery and rebuilding a nature-resilient community. She previously worked on high-profile titles like *Subway Surfers*, which reached "four billion downloads."

Games are a unique medium where players act and get feedback on their actions, and as a result present opportunities not just to entertain, but to potentially also explore something more. In our conversation Estaris described her guiding motivation as "the ability for games and for interactivity in general to help make the world a better place."

This is a sentiment shared by a lot of game developers, often indie, but that speaks to a deeper ambition than just the obvious commercial necessities of the industry.

We started our conversation exploring the question of the structures of a game that drive the nature of the purpose of play in a game, and we broke this down into three broad types:

- **Linear Games**: Games that tend to be unidirectional, including handcrafted puzzle games like Monument Valley versus stories that have branching narratives. These experiences tend to be "designer heavy," where players aim to decipher what the game's design is about and how to exploit the world's logic.

- **Branching Narratives**: Games which generally offer some level of perceived "autonomy" and have the benefit of more scope for replay where the player wants to explore different approaches and tactics to unlock different story perspectives.

- **Emergent Gameplay**: Games which tend to be more open in terms of replayable systems, potentially including more ambiguous goals. In these, the player interacts with that design and comes up with different surprises and gets to put them together in unexpected ways.

Thinking about games in these ways allowed us to explore different mindsets and design strategies, which frame the kind of experience we are making (and commercial model). This also has a specific impact on how we understand what 'Balance' means and the role of an economy for that game.

For example, in more linear games like *Monument Valley*, purpose is led from the flow of the experience, moving the player from one moment of play to another within the range of the experience.

> "For me, the balance in a more linear game is about balancing the content against each other. So, balancing that journey that the player is taking. Because you're only balancing for the most part one journey, then you really get the chance to curate that experience. Like a film director, you really get a chance to bleed into the different aesthetics and make sure they layer well. make sure they contrast, make sure they help deliver that emotional journey. And you can do that in systems games. It's just less curated and it will be more about what the player, what you and the player make it together. The linear journey is more about what the director and what the rest of the development team creates," explains Estaris.

Estaris further explained that for *Monument Valley 3*, design decisions began with the emotional arc:

> "We wanted to provide contrast between this really sad, painful moment to something with a little bit more hope." Chapters were arranged to deliver "synesthetic pleasure" and the story was used to "weave everything together holistically."

She emphasised that in this process, "the moment-to-moment feel" must be in harmony with the holistic themes. They used a lot of playtesting across various player types to ensure not just that this worked but also that both new and returning players could navigate and enjoy the game. Given the puzzle nature of such games, you need to build up a set of consistent methods of interaction, with rules and ways those rules can be logically subverted. Estaris compared this with writing jokes.

"I also like thinking about it, like the structure of a joke where you set up the setting and then you lead up to an ending, but then you surprise them with a twist. And that's exciting to think about how you would do this in a systems game or an emergent game because it's hard to plan for," said Estaris. Describing it as "Whatever the equivalent of comedic timing is for a linear puzzle game."

Building on the idea of "moment to moment feel," Estaris further highlighted the soothing effect that routine actions can in games:

"I was thinking about Sky: Children of the Light, [which has] this kind of brain smooth experience where I'm just collecting light today because I know I'll do a battle tomorrow. I'll do the big event tomorrow. there's something beautiful about [that]," she said.

This ability to frame different forms of purpose when we design playing activity is transformational. We can choose to develop relaxing, repetitive, even sedentary experiences that can feel almost therapeutic and those can be just as satisfying as highly energetic, tense action moments.

However, developing games without traditional currencies, Estaris pointed out, means that you are left with a narrative arc and "customisables" to communicate what she described as soft progression:

"That is your way of showing how you are depicted in a game," she said.

The issue that raises is that customisation without a 'Vanity' loop severely curtails the potential impact of such methods, but Estaris defended the power of personal expression even in single-player games, saying:

I also play a lot of single player games where I just spend so much time doing character creation and character dress up. Sims, for example, where that is the main play and you're showing off to yourself.

Progression in emergent games is a different beast and often led by numeric pathways, but even these can be exploited by smart players applying the mechanics in unintended ways.

I played a lot of World of Warcraft, and in the battlegrounds, you could cap out for each level band. So level 10 to 19 [players] would battle against each other. One of the favourite activities I did with a few others was to make level 10 maxed-out characters that would easily defeat the level 19s. And that was a progression in a sense, right? It was understanding how to find the loops that would help you max out a level 10 character. I formed my own progression path along with a few others.

The idea that even the intended purpose and progression in a game can be entirely subverted by players is something that designers need to embrace; rather than just assuming that the game will be played entirely as we envisioned it originally.

We continued our discussion by exploring how we bring purpose to the first-time user experiences. In particular, when you have different skill levels of players.

> One of the greatest challenges is how to do onboarding without people recognizing that they're doing onboarding. And we had the added challenge as we had with the third Monument Valley. Some players had played the first two, which is essentially the onboarding for the third game, whereas others haven't. And so how do you accommodate all the different player types? But we do lean into a lot of these subtle hints, like textures that appear on the geo or little glows that appear to help remind you of things that are happening, but they're quite subtle and you don't recognize it unless you've been playing.

The issues for new users are commonly discussed but with a game, like Monument Valley, which will inevitably attract a large share of returning players; who perhaps have not played the game in years this presents different challenges. Challenges which have parallels in Emergent games (usually with long-term LiveOps), which have players coming back months or years later. We asked Estaris about how they approached the 'Lapsed' players.

> "We do a lot of playtesting with all types of players and we have the fortune of having a game that's been out for 10 years so we are able to – we made sure to identify which players were new to the genre or new to the series," Estaris outlined.

The team identified three kinds of players. Those who had recently played Monument Valley, those who had never played and those who had not played for a long time (e.g. 10 years ago).

> "[We] tried to make sure it accommodated all of them." She stated.

This theme of purpose led us to go back to the beginning of Estari's time with Ustow and when the original approach for the 3rd sequel to such a beloved series was first discussed. Estaris revealed that the team were open to finding new ways of working and even business models.

> "One of the original reasons why I was brought on was to explore whether or not a free to play Monument Valley was possible. We went with a different direction, but still think there's a kernel of excitement in that. If we were to have Monument Valley as free to play, would it change the nature of the game? Sometimes change is good. And it might be for the best. But it's a bit risky as well," Estaris said.

This demonstrates how important it is to always consider what the right model will be for your game openly, but also that in the end the decision has to be right for the game, the players, and the team, and be balanced with the risk.

As we have stated elsewhere in this book, games are now the single largest form of entertainment on the planet, with billions of players enjoying video game content on a regular, often daily, basis across all the platforms. This scale of connection with an audience creates an unprecedented opportunity for designers who have a shared sense of purpose to communicate meaningful ideas as well as delightful experiences.

One such initiative is *Playing for the Planet,* an initiative in the games industry supported by the United Nations Environment Programme. This alliance aims to address some of the world's biggest environmental challenges through creativity and technology. The aim is to connect players with the genuine issues and programmes affecting real-world change directly within the games and something which has tremendous reach. The author was lucky enough to be invited to the initial launch, which had less than 30 people attending, but despite this, the games of teams represented there added up to around 250 million daily active users.

This is just one example of how games have (and continue to) aspired to go beyond the simple act of play.

Estaris' commitment to this project stems from a belief in the medium's power to support "our sustainable futures."

> "I firmly believe in free to play because of the reach, because it can reach people who don't have the means or the socioeconomic

means at their disposal to buy a game upfront. So I'm excited about this. People who only have a mobile device or people who live in countries where you can only play offline. There's just a lot of opportunities to democratize the play experience and I want that," Estaris concluded.

NOTES

1 https://en.wikipedia.org/wiki/Man,_Play_and_Games
2 https://walkingdead.fandom.com/wiki/The_Walking_Dead:_The_Telltale_Series
3 https://www.youtube.com/watch?v=7daTGyVZ60I
4 https://enosta.com/insights/hooked-model
5 https://www.bbc.co.uk/future/article/20220804-does-nudge-theory-work-after-all
6 https://medium.com/@GigaStar.Official/embracing-the-positive-side-of-fomo-how-fear-of-missing-out-can-propel-growth-5ac4a157e20f
7 https://pmc.ncbi.nlm.nih.gov/articles/PMC7504117/
8 https://en.wikipedia.org/wiki/No_Man
9 https://www.academia.edu/9371825/Bayesian_Surprise_Attracts_Human_Attention
10 https://www.jneurosci.org/content/29/6/1648.short
11 https://en.wikipedia.org/wiki/Flow_(psychology)
12 https://www.pocketgamer.com/news/gdc-2014-wooga-on-using-the-fuuu-factor-to-hit-the-top-of-the-app-store/
13 https://www.linkedin.com/in/jenniferestaris/

CHAPTER 6

The Three Loops

DOI: 10.1201/9781003592471-6

THREE DISTINCT LOOPS

As mentioned in the previous chapter, games can be broken down into three discrete layers based on the things that we do in play, what keeps us playing, and the elements that affect our engagement with the game which are not specifically focused on the game itself (the literal definition of a metagame).

These layers allow us to dissect the game into systems directly tied to the principle motivations outlined in Self Determination Theory:

1. The Core Mechanic Loop or "**How** We Play" is directly related to the player's sense of competence based on their ability to assess the requirements of the situation and use available tools effectively to maximise their reward.

2. The Context Loop or "**What** We Play" supports the player's sense of purpose, progression, and autonomy, which relates directly to their sense of autonomy. This allows them to not only explore the game's narrative, but to weave their own narrative into the story.

3. The Cultural Loop or "**Why** We Play" explores relatedness by looking at the extraneous elements of the game (arguably the true definition of meta!). This covers the lifestyle fit of playing that game, the cooperative and competitive social factors, and the wider social impact of the game, including why someone would watch someone else playing this game. All these factors have become increasingly important to the development and promotion of service- and community-based experiences.

Within this chapter, we will show how these three loops can be defined through the lens of the motivational and attention vectors we covered in the previous chapter, and through which we can build an effective, dynamic equilibrium of play.

THE CORE LOOP

The concept of a game as a verb really comes to life with the base level of the core loop and how it describes the 'How' of a game. Here we define the basic elements of play, the things that we actually do. The player needs to understand the game environment and the means available to them to interact in that world with the relevant elements, in terms of the explicit or

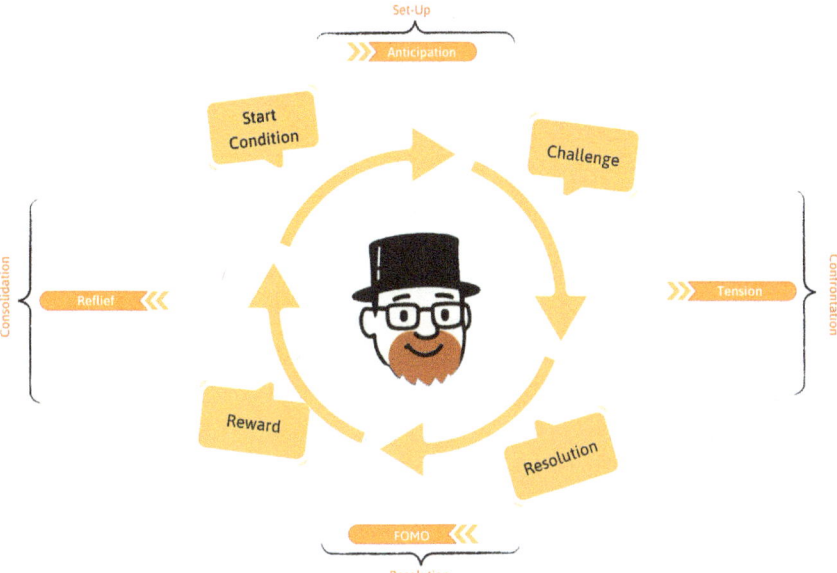

FIGURE 6.1   The core loop.

implicit challenges. The game then needs to provide feedback to the player for those interactions, often through some form of animation or narrative component. This can often be associated with virtual items that further the player's engagement in some form.

In a first-person shooter, there is movement, weapons, targets, and a trigger controller which unloads our virtual firepower at the target our camera is pointing at. For a cosy farming game, there is typically an environment and tools which allow the player to prepare the ground and plant a future harvest. There may be actions necessary to support that growth over time, such as watering or weeding, and then the player eventually gathers produce from their efforts.

Building on the ideas presented in the 'Hooked' model we explored earlier in this chapter, we can break down the core of play in any game into four steps:

Start Condition

The first aspect of any game is to establish the opening experience of the session, setting the scene for the player to understand what to expect. The most vital variation of this is the first-time user experience, where the game needs to rapidly establish a deep connection with the game player, help the player learn the playing methods and interactions, and how the game will fit into their routine in the longer term. However, putting those considerations aside for now, let's establish some more basic principles.

Players need to be able to enter the Start Condition in a relaxed or 'Relief' state. Players are seeking entertainment or escape from their daily routine and have chosen your game to do that with. This means the Start Condition usually needs to offer a moment of calm before the intensity of the playing experience to come. This moment needs to reinforce any intrinsic anticipation that the player brings with them and frame the rationale and challenges for the upcoming interactions. This is a moment for the player to start the immersion process, suspending disbelief and preparing to focus on the future playing tasks and mysteries ahead. The Start Condition also applies to players who have just completed a wave or loop of the experience and are wanting to go straight back in. In this instance, the relaxed or 'Relief' state becomes ever more important as it provides an opportunity for players to gather their thoughts, rethink their prior success or failure, and prepare mentally for the next round. As has been also mentioned previously, it gives players the opportunity to decide to break out and come back later if they have other constraints – and helps mitigate the risk of burnout or negative addictive behaviour.

In the Start Condition, the design needs to provide a base grounding state for the player, allowing the environment, audio, and narrative context to provide a solid basis from which to take on the Objectives (as we outlined in the previous chapter). This means that once the challenge is communicated, the player immediately understands and cares about the stakes and consequences. Additionally, this is usually where the game establishes the 'perspectives' (again, as outlined in the previous chapter) of visual and narrative devices the game will be using in play. The game provides visual clues from the camera as well as elements from the environment, whether 2D or 3D, to help communicate directional momentum, openness, constraint, and even build an emotional connection.

Mike Bithell's Bauhaus-influenced[1] use of solid colour, shapes, and sharp angles in the originally planned opening of Thomas Was Alone provided a subconscious emphasis of purpose. Combined with the audio narration by Danny Wallace, this made the experience "feel important" and something that emotionally connected the player with what was otherwise just a pixel block.

In Slay the Spire, the player selects their character and is sent off on their mission to climb the spire with a deck of cards, a relic, and some other constraints. The player selects a node on the available path and is presented with their first opponents (or mystery encounter).

In Skyrim, as part of the first-time user experience the player finds themselves on a cart being taken for execution, a fate averted but leaving them with a start condition where they need to make choices to survive, locate equipment, and decide on an initial faction to align with.

The Start Condition is not a passive concept; it requires careful thought and preparation to provide an opening step that delivers rapid immersion and acceptance of the 'rules of play' as well as a call to action for the player to play again. This is the moment where the game establishes 'Need States,' scarcity, and narrative foreshadowing. It is the framing structure to help translate the intention of the game's design and narrative into engaging, playable elements.

Challenge

The Challenge is the presentation of the obstacles and options immediately facing the player that need to be overcome through play. This can be as simple as fighting an opponent, moving a box to clear a path, a shape to move on a puzzle, or it can require a complex series of interactions and choices, including the types outlined in the previous chapter. Delivering a sense of competence is key to the role of the Core Loop, and this is measured against the obstacles the player faces in the game.

What is important is that the Challenge introduces tension into the experience, as well as setting up enough information to signpost the player into performing the necessary decisions and actions to progress the experience.

The information on what has to be done needs to be clear and effectively communicated, but that doesn't mean it has to be complete or even that it can't be deceptive. The purpose is to illuminate the stakes at hand and the necessity of action. How we communicate the challenge will also frame the players' expectations about the method of interaction and range of choices. The game can offer alternative paths, different interactions, and even cheat the player to an extent as part of establishing the wider play experience. Take the example of The Stanley Parable,[2] where early on the narrator tells us that "When Stanley came to a set of two open doors, he entered the one on his left." Yet, we do not actually have to accept that choice. The narrative pay-off establishes the many future choices the player may get to make. Puzzle elements may similarly present as a method we have previously resolved but usually will constrain some twist or constraint, which prevents us from employing a known solution, requiring the player to devise a new approach that previously they had not needed to consider.

Additionally, for the purposes of this approach, we are not considering alternative mechanical elements as separate loops – although that can be valid in terms of practical design, instead we see those as alternative methods to resolve the Challenge and potentially gain different rewards. In Deus Ex, most game problems could be resolved ultimately via a stealth action, a hacking action, or combat – the choice has some implications, but the experience could still be completed whichever you chose.

The Challenge is about signposting the stakes and potential rewards in such a way that reinforces the anticipation for play, but where the player can now feel sufficient tension that ensures that taking the step into the resolution is meaningful. This is even the case for a Cosy game, but the implications and consequences for failure will generally be less dramatic, whilst the pay-offs will tend to reinforce more emotional values than other more 'hardcore' games.

Resolution

This is the point where the player actively uses the interaction tools in a game, understands the initial stakes (and indeed these may well ramp up as the game reveals more information), and it is up to the player to overcome the reality of the challenge that was set. This is the stage where the player uses the interaction methods (as described in the previous chapter) to resolve the challenge. It is essential that the actions in the resolution are meaningful, and the application of skill, persistence, and logic in the use of those interaction methods needs to be reinforced by the emotional stakes.

Balance is critical at this stage as the game needs to deliver a sense of 'Fear of Missing Out' and 'Tension' that sustains both the motivational and attention aspects of play. That means understanding the balance of difficulty and perceived reward. Players need to feel that any failure is theirs, because if they feel that it's the game that's being unfair, they will churn. This means that the player needs to feel that the challenge is real, but not so difficult that it is beyond them. Failure should always be an option in some form, but this doesn't have to be punishing in all cases, and a common mistake in games is that players who fail lose all of what they have earned so far. That level of punishment suits some extreme games but can be highly polarising. For example, if you let the player earn XP or Gold or some other form of exchange related to progression (even if they lose other rewards), and this gives them the chance to improve their characteristics and chances of success, you can offset the risk of making players feel that continuing the game is pointless.

The resolution usually needs to be intrinsically compelling, but there are some simple examples where it can be reduced to just a click on a screen. Games like Adventure Capitalist[3] from Hyper Hippo are essentially this, but despite this, the timing, choice selection, and inherent humour integrated into the experience transform that into something magical. Indeed, you could argue a rhythm-action dance game is nothing more than a button-clicking exercise, yet the necessity of accurate timing and an engagement with the beat provides something deeper and more emotionally connecting. There is something deeply human that happens when connected perfectly with the beat in a music experience.

The building and sustaining of tension, with the risks that allow the player to get a positive sense of FOMO through play (e.g. what if I miss the next beat and lose my streak!) create an enormously engaging sensation. However, it takes energy, and there is only so much tension a player can take before it becomes overwhelming. As designers, we have to balance this aspect just as closely as we do the underlying difficulty. We need the player to feel that success and completion are just after the next action.

Reward

Instant feedback is the superpower that games have over other forms of media. It's important to understand that games are verbs, i.e., we do. The functional benefit of this comes from understanding the importance of the feedback and associated rewards. In essence, a reward is the delivery of an expected return for effort and/or recognition of success achieved through action. But what exactly does this mean in practice?

Rewards come in many forms, as discussed in the previous chapter, and serve multiple functions for the player:

- **Exchange**: The purpose of the reward is its ability to act as a form of exchange within the game economy. This can be a generic currency or a 'flavoured' resource used in a specific type of exchange. In essence, these tend to break down to a simple equation of time vs. unit value subject to scarcity and scope of utility. What we use the currency or resources to exchange for will vary between games, but in essence, it will be for something related to our rationale for playing. Items which support our 'Competence,' 'Completion,' sense of 'Control,' or 'Social Capital' within the game – although Social Capital can extend beyond the game itself and into the wider community. We will explore forms of Utility in later chapters.

- **Status**: These are rewards that specifically act as a marker of achievement for the purpose of comparison, of your own actions as well as in comparison with your peers. Score is the classic marker and generally provides an absolute level of rank. However, this can quickly become meaningless when compared to too large a peer group. There is next to zero sense of personal achievement to go from rank 119,345th to 119,344th in a leaderboard. Achievements, trophies, badges, or similar mechanisms are usually more overt markers of specific activities, performance, or progression. These can provide a personal marker to demonstrate 'Competence' by marking the overcoming of difficult challenges or passing some skill-based measurement. They can allow the player to map their journey through the game, showing their progression through 'Collection' (and acting as further incentive to continue), and obviously, this has the potential for inherent 'social capital' value as well.

- **Gateways**: These rewards are generally the recognition of the player reaching some stage in the game and can unlock access to new elements of play – sometimes even new game modes. They may well be associated with Status rewards or even specialist Exchanges (such as building a required item to move into a new region of the game), but in essence, they mark a transitional point in play. These rewards may not even be presented in the same way as other rewards, they may be as simple as unlocking a door that previously could not be accessed or the introduction of a new monster that occurs only when the player has reached a specific point in their character progression.

Gateways also serve the purpose of limiting access to game elements that may be overwhelming to new players, or simply provide a way to ration access to content, providing a consistent delivery of novelty for the player and allowing us to sustain their engagement over time.

- **Advantage**: Rewards which provide direct utility in play augmenting the effectiveness of players' actions in the context of the game. These may be consumable or durable items which the players can use in future playing experiences. These are critical components of a game economy and are either earned directly or through an exchange via some form of currency. For our purposes, we make no distinction between advantage rewards which take the form of items our character uses and direct improvements made to our character, e.g. through level progression. There are different design advantages from using equipable items as opposed to innate character abilities in games, but at a basic level, they serve the same fundamental purpose of giving the player some advantage over their base performance.

The way we communicate rewards is key to building the player experience, and for that, we need to understand the impact of different approaches. In its simplest form, the expectation of future rewards is a core aspect of motivation. However, there is more to incentives than this basic approach. As such, we should also look at the implications of other ways to leverage reward systems.

Random Factors: Predictable surprise can be a powerful motivational factor, especially to support the player's attention. However, there is a risk that it undermines some of the core motivations of play – especially where this breaks the connection between competence and success. Indeed, too great a reliance on random payout creates an experience that more closely resembles gambling systems like slot machines which undermines the meaning of player action and can lead to player churn or burnout.

Risk Factors: Players having a sense of a stake in the game, such as putting their potential rewards at risk, with the promise of an increased payout but at the price that they could lose what they have earned so far, can magnify the motivation and attention vectors in a game. However, these systems need to be considered very carefully as the impact of failure can be dramatic, creating a serious risk of player churn. This should not just be seen in terms of a gambling-style experience, for example, in Dark Souls, we face extreme risks with each new opponent, with (almost inevitable) failure resulting in us being sent back to the start. The same issue applies to Rogue-like titles like Balatro[4] and Don't Starve,[5] are all about surviving as long as possible, with a complete restart as the consequence of failure. At a more general level, we should consider the principle of Deferred Gratification within games. This means considering the risk levels adopted by players to allow them to adopt the cognitive strategies to hold off from instant feedback in return for an increase in reward that will result from such delay. An example of the complexity behind this comes with the infamous Stanford Marshmallow experiment[6] by psychologist Walter Mischel, where children were offered a choice between one small but immediate reward or two small rewards if they waited for a period of time. The initial study suggested that this was delineated by the development stage of the individuals (essentially age related), however, subsequent research has suggested that economic status and other issues may affect the results.

Diminishing Returns: Rewards provide extrinsic motivation for activity, which becomes less engaging as the novelty dissipates, but rewards themselves diminish in effectiveness as a result of a number of factors, including:

- **Diminishing Marginal Utility**: The increase in reward items negatively impacts the proportionate perceived benefit of additional items; in other words, each successive unit of a commodity adds a smaller increment in perceived value. This directly relates to the gap between necessity and surplus of the assets, but also to psychological factors such as the way humans judge numbers.

  The closer the player is to satisfaction in terms of the target expectations (need) for a specific reward, the less we perceive the value of that effort. In a game, this is further magnified by the ways in which our skill in an activity is slow to start but quickly peaks. The relationship between Power/Skill vs. Cost/Effort can take time initially, rapidly peak, and the perceived value then will plateau.

- **Matching**: The alignment or pairing of resources, tasks, or efforts with the right opportunities or needs is referred to as matching.[7] It is usually used to align labour markets to assess the connection at a macroeconomic level between work and workers. In-game rewards, to an extent, could be described as fulfilling a similar need, and as such, the rewards we offer need to relate to the available audience for this experience. In his 2017 paper, Jan Kubanek[8] demonstrated a connection between optimal decision-making and matching through diminishing returns. Applying this thinking for game design means we need to not only think about how diminishing returns affect players in-game from typing to maximise their rewards but also the impact that has on players choosing our game at all.

- **Diminishing Novelty**: The pleasure we derive from the receipt of rewards has a deep neurological connection with the brain's reward and mood mechanisms, in particular in reference to dopamine and serotonin.[9] The fresh excitement from the introduction of new activities and rewards provides a peak level of return, but this impact diminishes over time as the novelty diminishes. The Skinner Box experiments showed that random responses could maintain engagement for longer periods, but in practice, excessive reward giving itself has a diminishing return, with players becoming desensitised to the dopamine release.[10] This usually leads to the player churning, unlike with gambling behaviour where it is easy to escalate the excitement with larger and more risky bets. But that doesn't mean games can ignore the potential impact on vulnerable people, especially those with mental health issues.

- **Inflation and Value Escalation**: One real-world consequence of too great a supply of currency in a market is inflation, and games are not immune from these phenomena.[11] To a certain degree, this is an inevitable consequence given that currency is given for most actions, and over time players can focus on maximisation of such currency. We will explore the role of 'Sinks and Sources' in a later chapter, but a common response will be to either offer bigger-value commodities or rewards instead. This can be effective in the short term (provided you can communicate the value and that this matches the 'Need States' of the player). However, once you start down this path, you can't go backwards, you need to continue to offer greater perceived-value rewards that both serve to undermine lower value items and risk becoming game breaking in themselves.

- **Satisfaction and Unfinished Business**: Oddly, attaining satisfaction is not in reality beneficial to either the game or the players, and in order to understand rewards we also need to understand the future actions that our rewards will deliver. Of course, a reward should be intrinsically satisfying, it should resolve some form of short-term need. However, we also need to consider the longer-term implications within the context of the game and the emotional connection that has to deepen the engagement of the player. The development of a sense of 'Unfinished Business' has considerable impact on providing reasons for the player to play giant. This is magnified the closer the player perceives that they are to success. The sensation of 'just missing' a target number of rewards required to complete a future action is a considerable motivation – however, this has to feel natural, not contrived. If it feels manipulative, this will breach trust and be a reason to churn. However, done well we can integrate levels of reward pay-offs to player optimisation, allowing any 'near miss' to be based on player choice, skill, and performance, instead of unfair game mechanics which reinforce a sense of autonomy, rather than undermining it.

THE CONTEXT LOOP

The term 'Meta' (short for Metagame) has, in the last decade, come to be applied to aspects of game design for longer-term play but, again to split hairs, the term really refers to interactions between players and elements not directly part of the game. The elements which directly deliver reinforcement for longer-term play are actually gameplay and intrinsic to the experience – not external. Hence, instead, in this book, we will use the term Context Loop to better understand the functional delivery of this experience. This layer of the game is all about the 'What' of play or, in other words, what the mechanics allow us to do in the pursuit of the wider game experience. This encompasses the reasons to act and their consequences and returns. All within the playing experience.

Looking at Context as a system we can mirror the approach taken when looking at the Core Loop – indeed in itself this has a Start Condition, a Challenge, Resolution, and Reward stage. However, to appreciate the 'What' of a game, we apply a different lens to this layer, one related to understanding the player journey through the game experience.

FIGURE 6.2 The context loop.

Purpose

At the start of the experience, it's essential for the player to understand the purpose intended for them at this point. It is more important that there is a sense of purpose than whether the player accurately understands the implications or factual basis – indeed, the nature of purpose can and does often change over time, and in response to the evolving nature of the specific game.

As we have said, the 'Start Condition' is all about setting the scene for the player to understand what they are to expect. When considering this through the lens of the Context Loop, we need to establish a rationale for what the player does beyond the specific turn, and how this will connect the rationale to repeat that Core Loop again and again. And just as with the start condition, the player generally needs to be able to enter the experience in a state of relaxation and 'Anticipation'.

Defining this purpose is deeply connected to the core unique idea (Game Vision) underlying your game. It's about understanding the relationship between Player and Character Motivation, which includes:

Internal Motivations: As we have discussed, players have specific reasons for playing related to seeking a way to show competence or escape along with desires for completion and social connection. But in terms of playing specifics, they may be motivated by unlocking stories, pattern matching, and hand-eye coordination responses, but these need to be connected in some way to some form of attainable goal expressed within the game.

Contextual Framing: Players need clarity on what they are expecting to discover within the game. This often includes some clarity of the playing methods and game modes, although many games will later in the experience deliberately subvert those expectations. Part of this clarity is to understand the overt intention of the experience. This means some basic principles of what the game is likely to unlock for the player. This kind of framing story provides a basic shape for the player to make sense of the experience and what role their actions and their character play. It also impacts the reward structure associated with progression, but we will come to that later.

Possibility Space: Purpose doesn't just come from concrete information and statements of narrative. Ambiguity and emergent potential are vital components to help the player understand where their actions can provide meaning. Whether the game follows a linear structure or supports emergent choices, the sense that the player has autonomy and can deliver a meaningful contribution to the experience in some form is vital for sustained playing experiences.

Progression

Once we have defined Purpose, we need a method to measure our Progression, or steps towards completion. Most frameworks consider the Progression just in terms of how players use the rewards they obtain, such as XP, Gold, or Crafting materials – to move their character or the story forward. For our purposes in the Context Loop, we look at progression in the same way we define the 'Challenge' in the Core Loop such that we look at its role in communicating the arc of the playing experience, allowing the player to understand what is required from them over multiple sessions rather than just specific actions required to resolve the moment. This allows us to communicate longer-term development in terms of power, status, and narrative arc that players unlock through multiple playing sessions. It allows us to create a framing structure that delivers sustainable longer-term motivation and attention. Progression can be shown as our position on a Candy Crush style "Saga" map, RPG style levelling or unlocked game tools and modes we can access. The actual resolution of progression will be unlocked through play of the Core Loop but can help the player make choices about their short-term objectives and even which game modes they activate in each session. For example, if I want to unlock a given resource, I may use an aspect of the game that is focused on gathering, rather than, e.g. fighting. Success and progress may be driven by some currency factor like XP which I can exchange for advancement or through completing some milestone, e.g. completing a specific level or passing some checkpoint.

Progression shows us how far we have come and at the same time provides signposting to foreshadow to the player what may be ahead. This information need not be complete and can simply imply that something is ahead and that it needs to be discovered. Just as with Challenges, ambiguity plays an important role in how players' attention and motivation. Successful actions can unlock new information or even upend our prior expectations within the context of the game's premise, provided that we don't stray too far from relevance or ever undermine the player's sense of autonomy. The whole purpose of the Context loop is based on satisfying the basic human need for a sense of personal control. In the end, we need to consider how the communication of progression helps move the player from a relaxed state with Anticipation to one where we raise the tension to sustain the attention of the player.

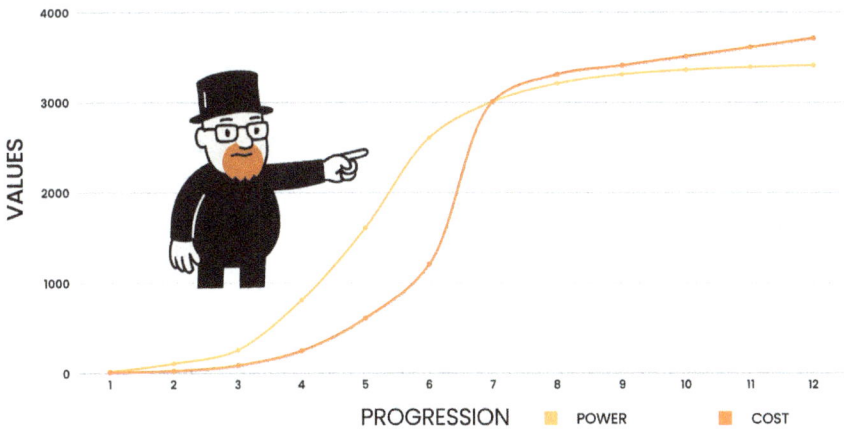

FIGURE 6.3   Learning curve vs powercurve.

There are a number of factors which underline how we can deliver an effective sense of purpose and how these frame expectations of rewards, unlocking information, and reaching attainable goals. These include:

- **Power**: The basic expectation of a progression system comes from signposting the acquisition of power or capacity to execute your choices in a game; as you proceed in the game you want to feel the benefits and your power increase. There is a natural aspect of power which comes through familiarity and practice with the game, systems, but how that changes as the challenge level increases in play, needs to be offset against a sensation of an increase in my capacity and my stakes in the experience. Unlocking powerful upgrades feels extremely rewarding, but only where we experience a corresponding increase in challenge. The irony about power is that in essence the upgrades we value as a player, undermine what makes the game meaningfully enjoyable. Consider the prototypical 'Rat' that is a very common opening level monster in Massively Multiplayer Online (MMO) games that presents the base-level of challenge, against more challenging monsters such as another typical example of a 'Giant Spider'. However, when the player has acquired the skills, equipment, and power-ups available, this will have reduced the difficulty of the Spider. Comparatively, the challenge will have dropped for this encounter, so it becomes as trivial as the original Rat was before. Power is a relative phenomenon which is more about communication than reality for most games.

- **Checkpoints**: Rather than just raw power, another aspect of Progression is the milestones or checkpoints we need to reach in order to unlock new capabilities. This can be related to specific levels of content, the gathering of 'Anchor' currencies such as XP, or the creation of some item that requires a combination of tasks to complete. Such checkpoints demonstrate a level of commitment to play, effort in terms of grind, but also provide a clear communication of the passage through the experience. Whether a map marker, status token, or numerical signifier, they establish a common comparable status which players acknowledge in relation to the percentage of completion of their current expectations of the game, as well as a way to communicate that with others. Not all games will have linear checkpoints, and many games will have discoverable actions which can communicate progression through side quests or even sandbox exploration elements.

- **Collection**: Often a secondary set of progression markers, but games will often have unique elements which show the players their progression in the game or reveal what new elements remain to be discovered. This form of progression is exemplified in the Pokemon tagline "Gotta catch them all!". This common human characteristic is prevalent whether collecting stamps, baseball cards, comic books, commemorative plates, or original Star Wars action figures. The emotional satisfaction that comes each time we add a unique variation to our collection is a manifest experience, but the remaining gaps, especially driven by their rarity and difficulty to track down, can be extremely motivating. As a factor in defining the progression system in the game, we benefit from collection systems which give some indication of what we may be out there and how we may be able to access it. However, it's important to remember the value of ambiguity to motivate players through discovery and to create a perceived unattainability. An element of intrigue can help players feel a greater sense of value versus the effort required.

- **Attainable Goals**: For players to be motivated by the requirements set out through the progression system, the steps needed to be completed must be seen as achievable – eventually at least. Meaning is connected to a delicate balance between sustained effort and the associated pay-off, but importantly we need to be able to visualise ourselves as reaching the conditions required. However, whilst games which have a clearly defined start, middle and end can be extremely satisfying, they don't support longer-term experiences. However, we can extend the experience by revealing new attainable goals when we reach (or near) our original goal. Techniques like this are used all the time in TV shows, even some movies, where the audience is presented with a cliffhanger or unresolved element which leaves room for the sequel. Arguably we tend as an industry to focus on this style of storytelling in games, and perhaps a better model of storytelling could be derived from looking at TV series structures which often have an A and B plot structure, one of which is resolved in the session, the other resolved over multiple episodes.

Even more sophisticated approaches could be attained if we think of our game in the way soap operas are written through overlapping personal narratives between individuals that play out over time and evolve as those characters evolve – each new story opening the potential of new options to explore. However, progression is not the story itself, it is the communication of the players' progress through the experience, allowing them to understand how far they have come and the direction of travel.

- **Ambiguity**: Creating compelling attention and motivation benefits greatly where there is space for the player to be able to exert their intellect and judgement on the experience. It is vital that we create a 'possibility space' not just in terms of the players' application of the tools of play through their skill and persistence, but also in terms of their ability to predict the potential outcomes and rewards from those actions, especially over time. Absolute charts of progress and power improvement over time in terms of rewards against effort aren't as effective as progression systems which leave the player room to interpret and apply the results creatively. This will become an essential factor next when we talk about the Optimisation stage of the Context Loop.

- **Gatekeeping**: Progression systems serve an additional purpose which players might not appreciate immediately, they allow us to delay access to resources, features, and game modes. With a player mindset we might reasonably think that we want access to the 'cool' bits of the game immediately; indeed, we might be annoyed that the design does not make it possible to do everything immediately. However, there are multiple reasons why this would be a bad experience. Firstly, we don't have the capacity to learn everything at once, and too much information too quickly can kill our interest in a game immediately. Secondly, if we don't have to work to access some game mode or ability, we won't appreciate how it functions or its actual purpose. In the game Infinity Nicky,[12] during the onboarding, the game introduces that the character changes 'dresses' to perform specific actions, but this is done so abruptly and without context that they miss an opportunity for the player to feel empowered – instead they are left confused. Thirdly, if there is a memorable point in the progression that requires specific actions/successes to unlock, we remember that process and add it to our personal narrative of playing that game. Finally, linking access to resources, features, and game modes to progression allows the player to sustain their experience in the game for longer, maximising their delight and value derived from each of the systems in the game.

Optimisation

In the context loop, there is also an equivalent to the resolution stage, in the form of Optimisation. At the core, this is where players most readily get to exercise their sense of autonomy in a game and a key differentiator between the structures we defined earlier in terms of linear puzzle and emergent games. Player actions go beyond simple functional actions and instead are elevated into a mental space where we can form strategies and challenge the obvious applications of choice in play. This doesn't have to be a huge mental overhead; it can be a simple act of predicting against uncertain consequences to deep mental exercise. On the other extreme, we once hired Garry Kasparov, the world chess champion at the time, to launch a chess service. Watching his face change when one of the extremely bright kids playing him (there were four simultaneous tables) made a very bold move was extraordinary. It provided a small glimpse of the depths of strategies that Kasparov was capable of. Optimisation arguably even extends beyond the constraints of the game itself, in terms of the allocation of a player's disposable time and finances and their application in a game. At its heart, the gap Optimisation is a factor that arises in the "possibility space" that arises where there is genuine impact from player performance to the results in a game. This arises where there is a gap between the perception of the "perfect" reward and the actual reward obtained by the player and in particular where in service of longer-term objectives such as the next level, new game mode, or even to acquire powerful or symbolic assets. There are a number of factors underlying this, including:

- **Variable Rewards**: We have already mentioned that player attention is enhanced where there is some variability or predictable surprise in a game. More specifically for optimisation, we note that this feels more meaningful and satisfying where that variability is connected to the player's performance in the session. A number of factors can affect that performance, from a slip on the controls, a mistake in understanding a decision, a dilemma where we have to choose between conflicting options, and at the end of the day, our skill in solving the technical, physical, or logical problem we face during the 'Resolution' stage of the core loop. The Optimisation stage of the Context loop reflects the decisions we then make as players about our intention to maximise that pay-off during the next level or session of play. Even where the player's actual ability to impact the outcome may be limited, the perception of autonomy is central to their motivational purpose and the allocation of time and effort.

- **Ambiguous Information**: The level of information available to the player between sessions can directly impact their motivation and decisions to act. Humans generally hate ambiguity, and unlike risk, where there is a chance of failure, ambiguity forces us to confront a lot of unknowns and massively inhibits our ability to make effective choices. The 'Unknown Unknowns' in game development can be massive hurdles for both players and indeed game development itself.[13] However, a level of ambiguity is usually necessary to create compelling tactical and strategic choices in games. Magic: The Gathering does this in the gap between the application of rules from each new card. The layered interactions of cards in the players deck against the opponent's deck is an inherently complex system. Understanding all the specific possibilities requires a huge depth of knowledge, and yet most players can still engage with the game because the discovery of those moments delivers information and helps the player plan future use of those cards. The randomness of the card draw process reinforces this ambiguity, and players are motivated to make the best outcome based on the constraints of their current hand. What is ironic in a game like Magic: The Gathering is that the more ambiguity there is the more some players will be convinced that they have worked out the optimal strategy! Ambiguity need not be as overt as with Magic: The Gathering, it can simply relate to mismatches between pay-offs of different variables. If the player needs ten Wood, but each action generates three, should they continue to collect 30 before switching to the next asset? What is the optimised strategy in their circumstances? What happens if they only have 25 units of storage capacity for that wood? Each of these questions raises different levels of ambiguity in the decision-making process in the game.

The pay-off in terms of Optimisation for games which rely on ambiguity comes from the unlocking of information and the application of that understanding in the next session. We need to reward them for that earning process to retain their attention and motivation, but we can, as the game evolves, also continue to positively frustrate the players' expectations by updating the context; modifying the rules through additional constraints – but we should never undermine the core lessons learned so far.

- **Shortcuts**: Games which require a one-to-one connection between action and result are very hard to balance. Very quickly, the direct application of skill dominates the experience and provides very little space for long-term engagement, except perhaps for the most skilled players. This can make it more difficult for the game to scale as it excludes less skilled players from engaging. Having the ability to apply some form of modifier effect, such as a numerical variable, to influence the result can transition the experience. This unlocks innovative ways we can flavour different kinds of actions and build the range of choice of action and strategy. The granddaddy of table-top roleplaying games, *Dungeons & Dragons*, was built on the principle that the player's character has statistics to represent their abilities. For example, Strength modifies our ability to use melee attacks and physical actions, whereas Wisdom allows us to hold off against some magical attacks but also affects our ability to spot hidden things. When we think of this under the banner 'Shortcuts,' we can include any element that helps the player with the resolution step as well as those which help optimise our longer-term progression. How players experience these benefits can also take a variety of forms, such as equipped items or tools, even vehicles or pets that the player takes with them into the adventure. This includes progression choices we make that enhance our abilities or potions which grant us short-term improvements. They can be accessed directly as rewards or via some levelling system in the game. Levelling isn't just relevant to characters; the evolution of your base in Clash of Clans presents progression and the unlocking of capabilities and resources inside the actual playing experience. As designers, we can maximise the impact of these optimisations by offering choice as well as constraints such as a capacity of items we can carry or deploy in the game in each session. The use of linear values for shortcuts is common and can be effective, but it's important to note that such items are immediately undermined when the player can access items of a higher level. When a +2 sword arrives, what is the point of ever using the +1 sword you previously had again? This can be intentional as a form of 'sink' or a way to remove items from the economy. Alternatively, we can find ways to continue to use lower-level items; such as tournaments that have a cap on higher-level items; or adding additional dimensions to the scope of the item. For example, if I have a +1 Fire Sword and I'm facing 'Earth' elemental enemies, I might choose to accept the reduced numerical advantage because the vulnerabilities of such enemies to Fire damage mean the increased damage makes that worthwhile.

- **Strategies**: Alternative approaches to play arise inherently in different games, often in ways we as designers never intended. This can be as simple as the order in which we decide to resolve a level, such as deciding if we take on the high-value targets first or focus on taking out weaker options in the hopes we collect useful resources to make it easier to take on the higher-value challenges. Between sessions, it's normal for players to review their choices in play and try alternative approaches to resolve each session. As designers, we can reinforce this decision process by presenting additional information, offering shortcuts which bias such decisions, or even by setting challenges with additional rewards. There is another option available, which is to directly offer alternative solutions. These can be as simple as, say, introducing new weapons, e.g. the Shotgun does huge amounts of damage in one go, but takes considerable time to reload, aim, and fire between shots. However, the machine gun has a larger volume of ammunition and does a smaller amount of damage as long as the enemy is focused in the player's crosshair. Both weapons may even do the same damage per second but the environment, armour, and nature of the opponent can all affect which will be the most effective choice. More than that, the aesthetic and playing style implications will also form part of the player's decision as to which provides an optimised player experience. The role of strategy can get quite sophisticated whether we are talking about the abilities and options which arise as we develop our Wizard or Ranger in a game like Baldur's Gate or what technology we have unlocked at this stage of a game like Civilisation. In such games, decisions unlock new opportunities later in the experience, but at the same time may prohibit other choices which might have otherwise been interesting options and perhaps form a reason to play the game again with a different set of constraints. The importance of understanding the role of strategy is however, as much about providing ways that optimisation decisions need to impact not just the current or next session, but future sessions yet to come. A significant design challenge that this understanding brings up is whether to allow players to reset their decisions or to eventually pick all the options (undermining the choice made in the first place). This works in the context of a game like Civilisation, but in a game like Archero,[14] this arguably served to fundamentally undermine the game's business model.

- **Exchange**: Ultimately, the Optimisation stage is also the point where we cash in many of the elements promised by the progression system. We take assets obtained through play as rewards and use them to obtain the benefits promised through the 'Progression' stage of the Context Loop. The rewards we have gathered need to somewhat match our expectations and take us closer and eventually unlock new status, titles, performance capacity, abilities, and even game modes. That exchange has to feel amazing. We need to feel inherent delight and recognition for our achievements so far, but at the same time, these improvements are enhanced where we can apply some level of choice and where they open us up to new and novel challenges. Designers need to be careful about the risk of power-creep and diminishing marginal utility, so it's important to consider how we can leverage player choice and dilemma into the 'sink' of such rewards through this exchange and remove them from the game economy. Through these methods, we can see how Optimisation becomes the 'engine' of the Context Loop, just as the Resolution stage is the engine of the Core Loop. This is the point where we want players to feel the maximum benefit of the 'Frustration' and 'FOMO' states such that the game delivers a truly meaningful sense of autonomy.

Narrative

The final stage of the Context Loop is a reflection of the reward stage found in the Core Loop. This often forms the longer-term pay-off for the player as we are providing the story of their personal journey through our game experience. Game narrative is a deep and compelling conversation in its own right, but for the purposes of the Context Loop, we want to consider how we can treat the revelation of narrative elements in the story as a form of rewards and how, even in games which don't have a formalised narrative, they still create an inherent personal story rooted in the realisation of the player experience. It would be easy to assume that this is just a retrospective reveal of what has happened, but just as important for our design is the role that the narrative pay-off plays in terms of setting the player up for the next session. This can take a number of forms, including:

Formal Narrative: Just like any medium, games tell stories, and as mentioned above, these are partly about the context of the game but also the experiences we have in those worlds as characters and as players. Each game will have different expressions of perspective in terms of camera and narrative storytelling style as well. By Formal Narrative, we mean the exposition of the game world and how this changes as the player plays through the missions, challenges, and chapters. Whether the player is an observer of the narrative or actually acts as the protagonist, their actions generally drive the plot forward. There are lots of different storytelling methods and models, including famously Joseph Campbell's Hero's Journey, Save the Cat, and the classic 3- or 5-Act plays. However, I think that this approach is often too focused on linear narrative approaches. Games can offer choice and autonomy in ways other media cannot, but also our effectiveness in play forms a central aspect of our experience of that narrative, profoundly affecting the emotional journey as well as making the experience personal and filled with a sense of autonomy. There are other ways we can look at formal narrative elements, and in particular the way soap-opera creates storytelling frameworks that can sustain audiences for decades, not just 2.5 hours in a dark cinema. For the Three Loops model, we have found it particularly useful to apply a variation of the 3-Act Structure[15] for games. The benefit being that this way of thinking goes beyond this specific stage in the Context Loop. It also provides a lens we can consider for the overall flow for every layer of the Three Loops. From Core to Context and Culture, as well as thinking about the flows for motivation and absorption of the player, we can also consider how the experience drives forward the player's personal narrative as well as the game's own narrative arc – building sustainable storytelling from within the game's systems. The four formal narrative stages we are proposing are as follows:

- **Setup**: The opening sequence of the current stage of the story, consisting of the 'inciting incident' related to this stage of the game. This can be expressed as the transitional moment in the Core Loop, between the Start Condition and the Challenge; also, within the Context Loop, this is the transition between Purpose and Progression. Through the narrative, we can define extrinsic meaning beyond the numbers and mechanics that allow the player to emotionally connect with the current stakes and obstacles, as well as our objectives.

- **Confrontation**: This is the spear point of the experience and occurs as the player transitions from the Challenge to the Resolution in the Core Loop and arguably between Progression and Optimisation in the Context Loop where we consider longer-term narrative questions. This is the peak point of tension and requires us to focus on the player's immersion and intense clarity of focus. Importantly, Confrontation doesn't have to be negative. This narrative stage is just as important in Cosy or more sedentary experiences – it's not about the type of emotions involved, rather the engagement level, willingness to suspend disbelief, and connection to the experience.

- **Resolution**: Between the 'Resolution' and 'Reward' stages in the Core Loop, we reach the Climax of the session, leading to our success or failure and eventual pay-off. This is the tilting point between the tension and release as we head into a sense of relief. A similar emotional journey occurs in the Context Loop between the 'Optimisation' and 'Narrative' steps, but this tends to be more about providing a moment where the player gets to feel powerful or prepared after deciding how to spend their rewards or apply their new strategy. This tends to be more about getting ready for the next stage of play and receiving more information about their story arc as much as the story arc of the world and non-player characters.

- **Consolidation**: The 4th part of the 3-Act play for the purposes of our model comes as a 'Consolidation' stage. Triggered between the Rewards and Start Condition for the next session in the Core Loop, this is where the actions, progress, and narrative arc of the game reset or move forward, driving the continuation of play forward. This is often expressed through the reveal of new information, characters, or locations alongside new challenges, constraints, or objectives arising from that reveal. Similarly, this reset process affects the Context Loop, allowing the reset of expectations and potentially even adjusting the players' understanding of their fundamental 'Purpose.'

- **Epistolary Narrative**: A lot of games include items to pick up from recordings, letters, posters, etc., all including some form of information dump, often tangentially related to the arc of the game. They provide a discoverable and collectable form of offering world-building, exposition, and quirky contextual moments, each adding to the tone of the game. They provide a meaningful reward we feel we have unlocked without adding an additional complicated currency exchange process. Their role over time is to build up the wider narrative context for the game as a whole and create an incentive that helps drive players motivated by collection (and completion). Rarely will the game plot be centred on these info dumps, but there are some games where this is an essential factor for longer-term progression.

- **Environment Progression**: One of the keyways we communicate progression through the game is when we unlock new environments and locations. At a basic level, progression includes a change of environment art and/or colour scheme, signifying some underlying change in the experience. This may be trivial, e.g. just a change in difficulty, or significant where the art, style, and context signal to the player changes in the challenges and objectives. When we leave a forest setting and enter a desert environment, we expect there to be a change of enemies, tactics and that some elements of the game rules will evolve. We may use this as a signal that we need to amend our loadout, strategies, or playing style as well. These visual clues provide novelty and can deepen our engagement with the experience, adding to our personal story. Some environment changes, along with audio, can be subtle and yet create deep connections for a player. The Stanley Parable's Broom Cupboard remains a favourite example of this technique.

- **Seasonality**: The rise of LiveOps and Games as a Service has meant that we cannot ignore the opportunities of real-world and in-game seasonal activity. Whether we are talking about Halloween, Valentine's, or even "May The Fourth (be with you)." There are real-world cultural moments that occur throughout the year that games often want to tap into. Don't ignore the local cultural events such as Lunar New Year, Diwali, Golden Week, Ramadan, etc. Where possible, we should explore such cultural events in context with the game world we are building, obviously whilst respecting the real-world traditions! This allows us to form deeper bonds and engagement with our players, and we can use these seasonal activities to introduce new challenges, game modes, and evolving stories which bring our game world to life. We can even leverage clan or factional activity to empower players to help direct the game world's legends. For example, being a member of a colour faction in Pokémon Go means that when my local Pokegym is taken over by my faction, I share in that gain, and likewise when it is lost – that loss is part of my personal story in the game. Expanding on this approach could have significant potential to build even deeper stories in games.

The Narrative stage in the Context Loop done well helps us set up the conditions so the player returns to the 'Relief' state (from Tension) and yet sets the player up with a positive sense of 'Fear of Missing Out' that sustains the excitement about the next stage in play, creating anticipation for the next challenge and to see where our story will take us next.

THE CULTURAL LOOP

Whilst we have explored the 'How' and 'What' we play, we should also consider the 'Why' of play. In this context, we are equating the wider design loop to the Self-Determination Theory concept of Relatedness. Unsurprisingly, we are going to follow the same logical flow as we did for the other two layers, but this time exploring how the game impacts and is impacted by the wider world. This allows us to arguably explore the real concept of a Metagame – the elements of a game that go beyond the core systems of play. However, in reality, just as with any design framework, this is a matter of perspective, and the elements and systems here will indeed end up expressed in elements that you design and build into the game features. However, the difference (if splitting hairs) here is that we are considering not just the inner nature of the game, but the interaction between the players, the game, and the wider community. This approach allows us to take time to also consider other factors related to the playing experience which are too often ignored and which increasingly have a dramatic impact on the potential for a game to be adopted at all, or indeed scale and get noticed.

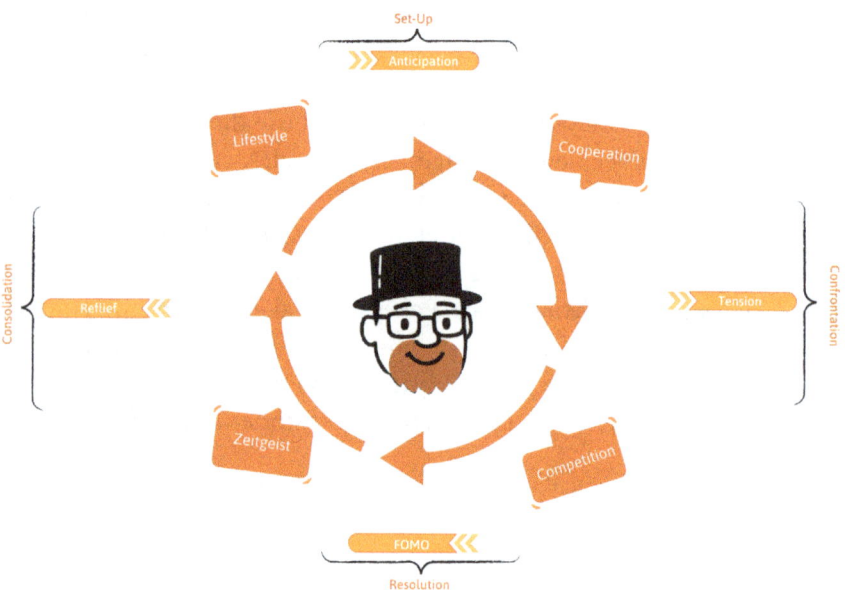

FIGURE 6.4   The cultural loop.

Lifestyle

The first stage for the Cultural Loop is (again) just a form of 'Start Condition' but where we need to consider the player's real-world situation, not just the mechanics of the game. Players have an extraordinary range of choice about the games they may choose to try, let alone those with which they connect and that are a good fit for them to want to evolve into a hobby-like experience. One of the core principles of designers as a whole is that "Form Follows Function," so how can we call ourselves designers if we don't understand the role our games play in the lives of our players? There are a number of characteristics related to the player's social, economic, and cultural needs which we have to an extent explored when we talked about the player audience. However, lifestyle fit is about more than the general function of your game fulfilling a specific 'Player Need'; it is about the positioning of the game as part of their daily routine. There are a number of elements which drive that question:

- **Mode of Use**: Players seek out games not just because of a desire for entertainment within a specific genre, but there are practical realities to the moment of play that affect the selection choice. Mode of Use refers to the specific functional role of the game within the players' routine and the role that the game fulfils for them. This frames the expectations and constraints associated with how the player will engage and what devices/platforms they tend to use at that point. For example, when we are travelling on a train or bus; or perhaps waiting for an extended period of time, there is often a specific set of conditions around the form of entertainment we want. In these circumstances, we tend to reach for a handheld device – often our mobile phone. Players might typically be looking for snackable content which has continual opportunities for breaks so we aren't affected when we have to break our immersion in order to catch the bus or respond to an interruption. Compare this with when players are at home, needing some 'Me-Time' and they retreat to their 'den' or negotiate to take over the family living room to enjoy an extended session on their PC or console. Part of our lifestyle choice here is that we intentionally state to those around us, directly or implicitly, that we don't want to be interrupted. This is something I am personally guilty of and I'm very grateful to have a very understanding family – and yes, playing Skyrim for the nth time is work! Honest!

- **Access**: Part of the lifestyle conditions includes access to the device or platform we intend to play on. This includes whether the player has that device to hand and in mind at the point of decision of what to play; the app installed and enough connectivity, device storage, or power to play. Even not having the device we associate with the game in sight can mean that your game never comes to mind. Too often when looking to play something like Beat Saber,[16] a player may discover their VR goggles are out of power or need an update. Perhaps the furniture in the room is taking up space or the dog wants to jump up on you, making the whole process too inconvenient. Similar problems happen with multiplayer 'couch-coop' experiences, if the players needed to make it happen aren't available at the right moment, or the controllers not charged, or the Wi-Fi is playing up, etc. Any of these things mean we have barriers to play and we won't be able to play that game spontaneously. As developers, we need to understand these potential barriers and think about ways to overcome them, from making the onboarding process quick and simple, to integrating some form of appointment mechanic or other approaches to make it easier to access the experience.

- **Inertia**: Another aspect of lifestyle comes in the form of inertia. Shocking as it seems, players have other things going on in their lives than our games, but even considering this, and all other things being equal, players will not act without intrinsic or extrinsic motivation. We need to create motivational reasons (as we discussed when talking about in Chapter 4 'Why We Play (and Pay)'). The idea of 'Abnegation' or setting aside the other things we should be doing is particularly pertinent as it underlines that players are individuals with different circumstances and motivations. This is why we attempt to build a game through the motivational vectors of Anticipation and FOMO, as well as try to provide positive factors around Autonomy, Competence, and Relatedness. This concept of Relatedness is deeply tied into the ideas of Social Capital (and Social Identity Theory), all of which help us understand the place our game can occupy for the players. If we want our game to maintain a place in the players' subconscious, to be the game that comes to mind when they are ready and want to play, we need to understand what is going on for them better. We don't exist in isolation. There are countless alternative substitutions in terms of other games, other forms of entertainment, responsibilities, and distractions. We can't solve them all. What we can do is build experiences which genuinely delight, concept/brands they identify with, challenges which delightfully frustrate and create compelling reasons to replay. Appointment mechanics can help with this, but external incentives to define times to play can very quickly become counterproductive. No one wants to be 'told' what to play, and if we create a burden on the player if they fail to fulfil certain criteria set by the game, the game itself creates inertia, a barrier against playing. Even a mismatch between our 'mode of use' expectations and the incidents of play (session time, session turnaround, intensity of immersion) can all serve to create barriers for the player to choose your game at that time.

- **Mood**: A factor we often don't consider is how the emotional state of the player can change the way that they present in terms of their behaviour. Players in different emotional states can present as having very different characteristics than we might expect in that cohort or persona of players. The more we understand the role our games relate to the emotional states that drive the player to choose content, the more likelihood we have to encourage them to choose our game, and the better we can focus our experience to respond to the needs that arise from those emotions. In his 2010 paper, Frank Spiller argues that mood regulation is key to sustaining user experience.[17] Indeed, ensuring that your design acknowledges and aligns with the player mood can deepen the connection between the game and the player and help us create an experience which resonates and delights the player. Whilst the extremes of emotion are obvious triggers for engagement and connection, more neutral emotional states are also useful vectors for game design. The way that casual games have for some taken the place of the 'Cigarette Break' is an example of this. More than just the need to satisfy a craving, these moments are often an occasion where we can take time for ourselves, to grab a moment of control in a world where we have little. Having a good understanding of the emotional context that suits your game and that your game can help the player emotionally allows us to connect deeper with them and their lifestyle.

- **Cultural Context**: When thinking about lifestyle, we must not ignore cultural context for that player. There are many factors which affect our responses to stimulus and care needs to be taken to appreciate geographical, national, religious (or none), political, and historical factors that your game may touch upon directly or indirectly through the player's perspectives. This can be a complex process and too often studios revert to a western 'Hollywood' interpretation of narrative and aesthetic needs and the cultural factors, but some sensitivity to wider considerations can pay significant dividends.

All of these lifestyle factors, like the 'Start Condition' and 'Purpose' stages, benefit us when the players enter the experience each time in a state of 'Relief' or relaxation and Anticipation, giving them the mental space to prepare for deeper immersion in play.

Cooperation

The ability to share aspects of an experience can create powerful social connections well beyond the game. This allows the player to feel part of a tribe or fandom. This deepens when we receive or provide information or support within that community. Community experiences are almost the definition of what drives Games as a Service and LiveOps experiences. Without strong community engagement, it's really not possible to sustain games in the long term. By treating Cooperation as a stage in the Cultural flow, we can gain insight into the role it plays in terms of creating a deepening engagement for players and how important it is to maintain and sustain the player's tribal connections in play. Learning from Social Identity Theory, we need to help players feel aligned to those tribes they align with and those with which they use to differentiate themselves. This doesn't mean that every game will have a Cooperative mode, just that we cannot ignore the social connections if we are to maximise engagement with our game over the longer term. There are a number of factors which influence this:

- **Tribal Identity**: Through social identity theory, we have seen how people seek to define their sense of self through an identification with a combination of social 'In-Group' that aligns with their personal attitudes and to use social 'Out-Groups' or distance themselves from characteristics that they reject. The same can also happen within games, and that can be expressed in layers. We can align ourselves as 'Geeks' or 'Nerds' at one level, 'Gamers' at the next level, and even within the game itself, we can align ourselves for or against other subtypes such as 'Tanks,' 'Leets,' or 'Campers.' These groups can be functional, playing styles or perhaps even a Clan or Factional alignment relevant to the games' narrative. Understanding this reality and facilitating it can be an effective way to build a strong community; however, there are significant risks associated to also be aware of. Tribal 'Othering' can very quickly become toxic and damaging for individual players and impacts the perception of the game brand. Some games seem to thrive on toxic behaviour, but they are always capped in terms of their potential as a consequence. Removing toxic behaviour is extremely difficult, and this can seem to arise suddenly as initially the social systems of a game can disguise negative effects as 'just banter.'

- **Community**: Not all games support collaboration within the experience itself, but they will all have some level of online social experience, whether this is official or not. To maximise the potential for the game, the development team (or potentially publishers) should take the lead to establish the tone and provide a space for the community to emerge, share tales, strategies, and insights, as well as generate their own theories about the game and its future direction. Make sure the person doing this is trained properly as a community manager. This is a valuable skill, and having the wrong person representing the team can be disastrous. Too many times, I've seen well-meaning developers missing the tone needed completely, damaging community relations because they didn't have the right communication skills. Importantly, at the point you are developing the community, this is no longer just your game. The game takes on a wider identity, one that is arguably more important than the original design vision. Game communities are essentially the expression of the identity of the game from the perspective of the players, and it is essential to accept that reality. It doesn't mean you are no longer in charge of the direction of new development, or that we have to agree with everything they ask for. But success is tied to how we take the community with us on the journey. We need to collaborate as much as that audience collaborates with each other, listen to, and acknowledge their concerns and issues. But then we need to be clear on what we choose to move forward with (and why). Players are incredibly insightful on what is happening (good and bad) in the game; but they are not usually great at providing workable solutions – they aren't a professional design team.

- **Content Creators**: Increasingly, the role played by content creators is critical to the discovery and engagement process for players. The Content creators provide a level of engagement which can show tips, tricks, and insights into the game. They have opinions, and they can often get things wrong! A lot of players will get information that you failed to provide (intentionally or not) from this section of the community and will generate a parasocial connection with those individuals that can dramatically sway the opinions and reactions of the wider player groups. It is essential for us to understand the scope and perspectives of this aspect of the community and how their content creation provides a level of collaboration with your wider audiences. We will explore this further when we discuss Zeitgeist.

- **Gameplay**: Collaborative play in games can be the ultimate expression of cooperation, with the tools and systems built directly into how we play. That doesn't necessarily mean adding the complexity of building real-time multiplayer. We have games which allow players to create mechanics that can exchange surplus resources, clan systems, as well as shared missions or social challenges. It is amazing how these can trigger emergent behaviour that was not expected. For example, in Heyday, the players were able to offer surplus goods to people visiting their farm. The players on their own created a 'language' for setting up their market stall, which allowed them to communicate an intention to trade much larger volumes of goods than the system originally expected. For a designer, the emergent use of your tools like this, to create workarounds that increase the delight for players, can be the ultimate reward.

Competition

Play has ever been associated with competition, with players seeking some form of status or dominance over others within the established rules. Competition ultimately provides a proxy for the wider role that power and display have culturally and to an extent as a measure of suitability in sexual selection,[18] and games provide an opportunity to explore that without the same consequence. Historically, games have had this role in terms of display and status. Martha Bayless, as part of the 2015 Gender and Status Competition in Pre-Modern Societies[19] noted three games that predated Chess, including the Scandinavian Tafl;[20] the Celtic Fidchell;[21] and Tables Game,[22] a relative of modern backgammon, which provided a kind of competition associated with rulership and warlike prowess. There is a tendency to overly focus on competition as a motivational factor, but when harnessed well, there is no doubt it can be very effective.

- **Personal Competition**: The desire for personal improvement, particularly in the sense of meaningful skills, is deeply motivating, especially where we can see the implications of the changes. Games work exceptionally well to provide instant feedback loops, showing the player the results of their actions immediately and providing a framework for the player to repeat, try, improve, and ultimately 'Win' – whatever that means in the context of the game. Improvement needs to be significant enough to matter, but also attainable in practice – and the application of that improvement needs to be clearly obvious. The First-Person Shooter and Platform games are overt examples of this, where an accurate twitch reaction speed with controllers has real-world application – training hand-eye coordination and accurate differentiation of objects in context. And in play, it's very satisfying when you clear the non-player characters or [mobile] computer-controlled enemies (Mobs) in a scene with ease that previously would have been extremely challenging. This form of internalised competition places the player in comparison with their former actions, separate from the performance of other players active in the game.

- **Direct Competition**: Facing off against other players in a game immediately escalates the intensity of the experience and rapidly increases the enjoyability for most players. There is an immediate rapid escalation of the impact of relative skill which feeds off all the players involved. In terms of design, this removes some significant complexity in terms of difficulty design, but at the same time introduces different complex challenges. Competition is a zero-sum game, literally, there can only be one winner in a simple competitive game. It delivers for those successful players a sense of power and competence and, ideally, the ability to display that to others – even if just as a leaderboard. The players with the best combination of experience, practice, and talent will win out unless there are other systems in place which can balance that out. However, where we provide such balance, we risk undermining the very pleasure that comes from the expression of that skill. Additionally, the greater the number of players, the more unlikely it will be that you as a player are going to find yourself at the extreme 'winning' end of the bell curve of player talent.

- **Matchmaking and Ranked Play**: Dividing up the player audience into relevant cohorts can immediately resolve many of the issues that large-scale games have in terms of competitive play. At a basic level, this can be done through matching players based on their prior performance or rank. A typical model is the Elo ranking, named after its inventor, Hungarian-American physics professor Arpad Elo,[23] that was specifically designed for games which have zero-sum Win/Loss/Draw conditions like Chess. Tournament systems can also help divide up audiences through knockout stages or player leagues which allow participants to gain entry to the upper levels only after defeating the other players in their current level, gaining promotion to the next stage. The UK Premiership Football League uses this model, but arguably the finances involved in the process make it very hard for all but the biggest established teams to ever compete effectively. One of the best applications of a tournament system in games was developed for the mobile game Golf Clash. In this model, every player starts in the lowest level league, but that league is 'sharded' (split) into multiple copies with no more than 100 players. This number is deliberate. It fits well within the Dunbar Number,[24] meaning that it's reasonably easy for us to recognise that number of names. Each time we play, we get a win (3 points) or a loss (1 point). At the end of a few days, the scores are tallied up and the top 10% are promoted to the next higher-ranking group. This means we eventually get promoted to a level where we have other players who have progressed alongside us, and thereby have a parasocial connection to, and that match our level of engagement and skill. Paul Gouge, Alex Rigby, and their team at Playdemic created something that ensures that players benefit from engaging in play, whether they are highly skilled or not, and still benefit further from being skilled as well. It's no wonder they were acquired by Electronic Arts (EA) for $1.4bn[25] having had 150 m installs for Golf Clash.[26]

- **Equipment, Handicaps, and Ghosts**: There is an irony in game development around performance, success and rewards. We expect to get the best items and the most advantage if we are victorious in competition. Performance leads to an increase in power. And it should. We want to feel that we have earned the capacity to be even more successful in games, unlocking the 'Golden Gun' or 'Vorpal

Blade'. This is also an essential factor for the purposes of display: we relish the opportunity to show off our conquest – again the reference to 'sexual selection' and 'prowess' whilst still tangential is very relevant. However, there is a problem. If we only give rewards for beating your competition, where is the incentive to try again if you lose? Our opponents (who beat us) will ever further be distanced from us in terms of attainable success. Our competitive capacity will be further undermined. Matchmaking, Ranking and Tournament systems allow us to split up the audience to mitigate this but only where the audience size is so huge that we don't have to worry about players. This can be a major issue, especially when we start testing. If we don't already have thousands of excitable players desperate to play at every hour of the day, we will hit the 'Critical Mass' problem. This is a way to describe the number of people we need to be online simultaneously in order to ensure that no one will be waiting more than 30 s to match into a game. No matter how innovative, clever, delightful your game is, if you can't get into play in this very tight window, players will churn and NEVER come back. As a result, it's also important to find ways to enable more players to play together without being separated. Team-based games can get away with this by allocating matches based across the whole team to an extent. Extraction shooters and even Battle Royale games like Fortnite can employ alternative success criteria or simply have such a fast reengagement flow that minimises the downtime between sessions. Indeed, the excitement of grabbing a high-power weapon or asset and running immediately to the extraction point, leaving your teammates in the lurch can be super tempting. In general, it's essential to always give players something, especially in defeat, that allows them to gain some gradual improvement. A power-up or shortcut that gets them in a position to better compete. It's important to remember that being too far ahead of the competition is also not much fun. We can redress that by giving the losing players some advantage, such as the 'Blue Shell' in Mario Kart that arbitrarily ruins the leading player's advantage or using some other more subtle 'rubber-band' technique which keeps players in a space where competition remains meaningful. The alternative is to find ways for the higher-ranked players to take on some level of disadvantage voluntarily. Going in with lower-level equipment, in return for a score multiplier makes the game more challenging and interesting, and it's something that can be communicated as a form of power display. Taking on the competitors with "one arm behind your back"! This kind of 'flex' is a quintessential aspect of Golf in the real world where your handicap states the number of additional shots over Par you can take compared to your more skilled opponent.

- **Team, Clan, and Faction**: Beyond personal skill, the ability to play as part of a collective group or indeed to represent our 'In-Group' adds to the intensity of the experience. We become something larger than our own personal ambitions and take on the responsibility and prestige of taking a major role in a collective endeavour. Esports teams are as competitive as any sports team. Indeed, the level of income and celebrity for Esports is rapidly improving and, in some cases, rivals some major sports. Most players enjoy the benefits of engaging in group play and feel a sense of common effort, relatedness, and opposition which deepens the player experience. Faction systems can be an interesting way to scale groups without creating too much burden on individual players. Take the example of Pokémon Go![27] where the player's required commitment to their faction is marginal at best, but this becomes meaningful immediately when the local PokeGym is up for grabs. My contribution to taking that is made more meaningful by the collective efforts of my team – and even if I didn't do anything, I can vicariously bask in the success of my side over the other factions.

Like the 'Resolution' in the Core Loop and 'Optimisation' in the Context Loop, where we think of Competition as a part of a loop experience, we can see its role in terms of the momentum of the game over the longer term. We can see how, especially through the intensity of tournaments and the status importance of maintaining rank, how the timing and performance matter and contribute to motivation through FOMO, whilst the Tension during play reinforces our attention levels.

Zeitgeist

The term means the "spirit of the age" or, in general, the ideas and beliefs of a particular period; however, for our purposes, we will use this term to express the cultural impact and framing provided by your game for your audience in a given period of time. In terms of the Cultural Loop, we need to consider the wider significance of the art, culture, context, and narrative elements of your game from the perspective not just of your player but of your player's audience too. What this means is that our games now, in this world of connected media, streaming, and video essays on YouTube, have become larger in scope, and the consequences of decisions we make in terms of art, playability, and narrative arcs now have an increasingly powerful implication in terms of community development, audience engagement, and ultimately marketability of the game. In short, we need to consider why it will be interesting to watch somebody else play this game, not just whether this game is interesting to play. There are a number of specific ways that we can reinforce the performance capability of our game in order to affect its impact on the social climate.

- **Visual Impact**: The selected art style needs to have a clear resonance not just in terms of the player experience communicating information about the objectives and actions of play but also in communicating aspirational qualities that attract the wider audience when watching the game. When we consider a playing experience, a lot of the core imagination and immersion happens within our own heads. The art, the UX, the visual style need to complement this experience, but they are not the fundamental aspect. As a result, there are many games where, to an outside observer, nothing seems to happen, or at least the setup, challenge, and player intentions are effectively invisible. The viewing audience does not have the benefits of being the one making the choices and performing the actions. They are merely observing the visual impact of what the specific player has chosen to do in that game. As developers wanting to support players' sense of relatedness, we need to communicate the impact of their choices and actions in ways which they can show off. To do this effectively, we can't just think about a fancy 'unboxing' animation for the rewards the player gets at the end. For the wider audience, we must be able to communicate first the apparent available choices, the challenge or dilemma associated with that choice, the implementation of that choice, and finally the results of that choice. In other words, we must convey simply and through visual medium (supported by audio, of course) the experience of the world in such a way where it is understandable what is going on why it matters; as well as how well the person making those choices is performing. The irony is that the visual style doesn't even have to be objectively "good." It's more about the consistency, relevance, and how the art, animation, and UX components fit with the concept the game delivers those matters. Getting this right is like alchemy and almost impossible to define generally, but you know it when you see it. An example of the power of visual feel can be seen in games like League of Legends, where there are extraordinary scales of audience that love to watch competitive play at its highest level. This is almost impenetrable for non-players, and understanding what is happening requires a deep understanding of the abilities and strategic choices at play. This level of advanced insider knowledge, rather than damaging the audience, ends up being an incredibly powerful factor connecting the fan base in their specialist knowledge. Obviously, in a game like League of Legends, the scale is enormous, that doesn't matter as much that they essentially exclude a lot of potential new viewers and players.

- **Space for Commentary**: Whilst this is more specifically a consideration for esports experiences, providing space for the audience to provide commentary is important for any game to maximise the potential for cultural impact. This means we need to think about how the game flow functions in terms of setting the scene for the audiences' expectations of strategy, then the player action, and after that action to round up our conclusions of the implications. These timing questions are usually also important for players themselves, giving them time to frame their engagement in the game. Where those players are streamers, however, this is essential. Content creators are weaving a story for their audiences and where they are utilising our game to tell that story, they need time to predict, choose, act and then debrief. This allows them to provide for their audience a form of 'Start Condition,' 'Challenge,' 'Resolution,' and 'Reward' that also mimics classic storytelling formats such as the 3-Part Narrative structure we discussed earlier. In the esports context, the role of commentary is vital. The 'expert' commentators need to be able to attempt to predict strategy, raise questions or alternative recommendations, then see the action, be surprised or have their expectations confirmed and finally comment on the outcome before resetting for the next moment in the session. This adds a layer of intentionality and depth of engagement that holds the attention and provides insights and alternative perspectives that are inherently entertaining but are not easily implemented in some game design forms.

- **Predictable Surprise**: With a gameplay session, we need emergent moments which derail our expectations as players, but even more so as an audience. These cannot come out of the blue, they can't break established rules but instead need to be emergent consequences. It would be a mistake to assume, therefore, that they must always be 'fair.' Whilst that is generally true, there are circumstances where pulling the rug from player and audience expectations can enhance the experience, but this only works where there was suitable fore-shadowing in advance which both player and audience can use to rationalise that the moment fits into the established context. Surprise also doesn't always have to be huge. It can be an animation of birds taking off when you get too close to an object in the world. They can be the reveal of a storytelling element that the player picks up. The 1970s TV show Columbo is one of the best examples of this technique in television. It is a 'whodunnit' murder mystery, where we see who-did-it at the start of the show! So why do we keep watching it? Well, it's because we are actually watching the detective (a character we have expectations of in terms of character and behaviour and with whom we identify) and trying to work out what Colombo had noticed that helped them solve the murder. This predictable moment also has a time limit. We know the apparently bumbling detective will say the immortal words "Just one more thing" to the murderer about 5 minutes before the end of the show. That's the point at which we have to have made our prediction about how he solved it. If we are right, we are delighted. If we are wrong, we are delighted to see what we missed! This concept, as applied to your tone and genre, can help you leverage predictable surprise in your game from randomised pickups, trigger animations, and emergent moments of gameplay and of course narrative moments.

- **Tribal Context**: Building a community around players and audience is an act of developing a 'Tribal Context'. We are creating a para-social relationship with its own set of norms and mores as well as a common shared history rooted partly in the game world building, and partly in the personal experiences of players in that game. Epic player-driven moments provide the most impactful aspect of that experience. EVE Online has a history of this where players perform underhanded actions leading to massive losses and profound consequences[28] in 2017, a player stripped a corporation wallet and stole an array of assets, including multiple large ships, worth 2.23 trillion ISK (internal currency), which works out to more than $22,300 in real money. This wasn't stopped or reversed – it was seen as part of the game. It didn't overall damage the player base; in fact, this was an important aspect of the legacy of the game itself and part of the legacy of the game. Do not assume that this will work for your game or your community. This approach has considerable risks and implications for the tone and relationships inside your game that need to be carefully balanced with the genre and experience you are trying to create. Instead, take the principles and see what the equivalent could be for your game.

Make no mistake, the moment your game is out there, it will be shares, streamed, and recorded with commentary – well, assuming you have any success at all. This is a good thing. However, if you fail to acknowledge this reality and consider the implications in your design, if you fail to ensure that the gameplay flow supports such engagement and discourse, you will not get the overwhelmingly important community or marketing benefits, which are arguably the most important form of engagement available to us as an industry.

Again, we encourage you to consider the 'Zeitgeist' as a stage in the flow of the player experience. Equivalent to Rewards and Narrative. This maps against the transition from frustration to relief, all the while needing to sustain an element of the Fear of Missing Out, which is essential to create the motivation to play one more time or to come back next session.

The Three Loops Combined

In essence, the basic principle I am trying to get across is that there is a simple flow from the Start Condition, Challenge, Resolution, and Reward. But we need to look at this from the three perspectives of Self-Determination Theory – namely Competence (Core), Autonomy (Context), and Relatedness (Culture). However, what is interesting is when we consider how these elements impact player experiences over time.

The Core Loop focused on 'How we play' and the specific moment-to-moment elements of the experience. The Context Loop focused on 'What the game is' about and how we take those moments of play and make sense of them over time. The Culture Loop gives us our deeper motivation, the 'Why we play,' and this is almost always tied to some extent with how we see ourselves in context with the wider community we see ourselves aligned to – our 'In-Group' as described by Social Identity Theory.

It can be useful to think of this like a clock, with the Core loop as the second hand, Context as the minute hand, and Cultural as the hour hand. Everything is moved forward inevitably from the second hand's repeated cycles but is inevitably made sense of over the longer term by the hour hand's progress.

Within this approach, we have explored how the transition through each stage is also about taking the player motivation from a state of Anticipation to Fear of Missing Out and back; and how we can affect the player attention by understanding the movement from Relief to Tension and back. In the end, how these can help us tell stories in the moment and over the longer term by relating this to the four narrative stages from Set-up to Confrontation and Resolution, with the Consolidation of that to reflect the nature of sustained longer-term storytelling and seasonality that we can learn from long-term story arcs and even soap operas. From this, we can start to explore the building blocks from which we can build our game economy.

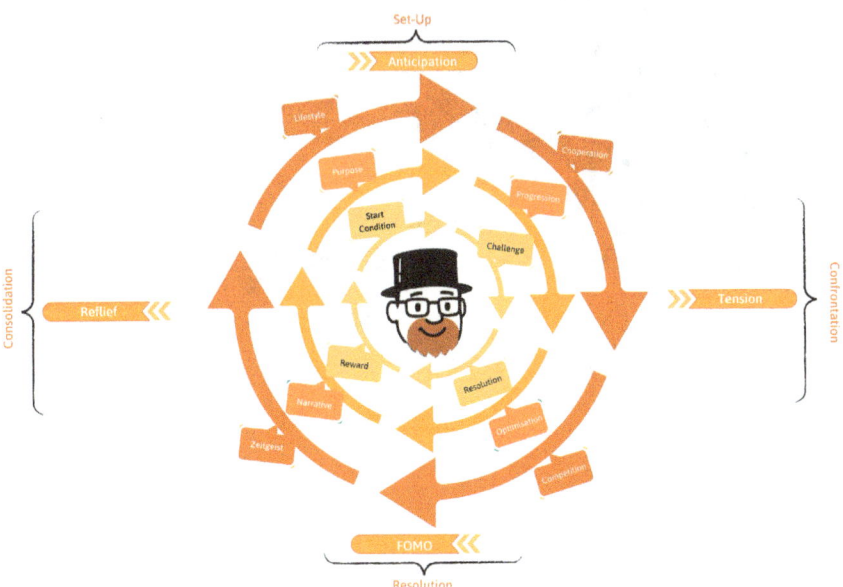

FIGURE 6.5   Loops as layers.

Interview

Thinking about Game Flow allows us to explore how balancing, player psychology, and platform expectations intersect in both core development and LiveOps. I spoke with Laura Warner[29] about her extensive experience working at Disney and EA, as well as Niantic, Bungie, and Nerd Ninjas.

Key to our experiences, Warner and I have both found that the core design principles are platform-agnostic. Warner entered console game design after a career in mobile development, expecting vast differences – but found the fundamentals unchanged.

> "All the foundational things of being a game designer and trying to figure out who your audience is and how they want to experience the game and how to keep them engaged. All that's still true regardless of platform," she said.

Warner acknowledged that there are, of course, important behavioural nuances: players experience mobile games in fragmented sessions, while console gaming is typically more deliberate and scheduled. But at the heart of both, Warner insists, is a shared design discipline.

> Like there are things to figure out, but fundamentally it's the same job, which honestly was a bit of a relief when I made the jump. It wasn't as scary as I thought it was going to be.

One of the key contrasts between platforms lies in when and how games are played. Warner emphasises the contextual nature of player behaviour:

> Mobile gaming fits into your existing life, which is different than [when] you change your schedule for gaming, right? There is a difference there of trying to understand player behaviour and time spent in how they want to engage with these products.

Console gamers are more likely to plan long sessions, while mobile players may only have minutes between obligations. Respecting this difference is vital.

> That one extra screen click might have pushed them out of your game. They might have been like, I only have a couple of minutes. I don't want to spend it clicking through 10 screens.

Designing experiences that align with a player's routine – rather than interrupting it – was a theme Warner returned to frequently.

Working on *Pokémon Go* provided Warner with unique insight into location-based game design where possibly uniquely, the fantasy fits the function. The success of Niantic's breakout hit, she explains, wasn't simply about maps and mechanics – it was about matching theme to action.

> "The fantasy has to fit the gameplay. Right? And I think sometimes people lose sight of that and strip things away, and they just look at the mechanic of it, right?" Warne said.

She cautioned against reducing design to movement tasks alone:

> Put thing at location, ask player to walk to it… but if it's not a thing that feels like I should be walking to it or I care about, I'm not going to put the effort into it.

Even if the IP is removed, a coherent real-world metaphor – such as distinct creatures in distinct habitats – can ground player expectations and support intuitive interaction.

> Different birds live on different continents and things like that… like there's a baseline understanding of the human about that… building on top of something that humans fundamentally understand and then making it fantastical.

Scarcity is central to making collection meaningful; creating a 'joy of the chase' – but it must be balanced across a global player base. Warner articulates the challenge:

> If everyone is special, no one is special. And that same principle applies when you're talking about things like having chase in rarity in the game.

Yet exclusivity cannot override access:

> How do you make sure that while maintaining rarity and chase, you're also being equitable to players and making sure everyone has something exciting to chase?

She highlights that excitement stems not just from rewards, but from the pursuit itself:

> The chase is the fun. Getting it is a good moment and it's a joyful moment when you finally get the thing that you've been looking for. But the true game is in the chase, not actually acquiring it.

Offering everything in a bundle, she warns, might sound convenient but erodes long-term value:

> Then you're done playing. You did it. You're done. You finished the game.

Well-balanced economies can create powerful social incentives, which can be amplified through scarcity. Warner explains how trading emerges when players can't collect everything alone:

> Can we do a trade so we can help each other finish each other's collections? Like the fact that maybe I can't get everything on my own in some of these games forces me to be social and forces me to interact with other players or maybe I wouldn't otherwise.

This collaborative economy deepens engagement – especially in titles that support group mechanics like clans or clubs:

> Being part of a club or a clan will let you help each other out and give resources between each other and those sort of things.

She cites *Heyday*[30] as a standout example:

> Heyday is a beautiful, beautiful game with such depth that I really think it's a brilliant title that I honestly think more of the industry should be paying attention to.

The best-designed mobile experiences are those that respect limited time and attention spans:

> You can go in, play a level, pick my really cute chair, and then move on with my life and feel like I've accomplished something,

but not feel like I am inundated with too many choices for the amount of time I have to give in this moment.

In contrast, battle passes and LiveOps systems must be careful not to overwhelm:

> There almost always arises the topic of like, should we let a player catch up? Should we let a player who hasn't been around for 30 days come in on the last day of the month and purchase their way through everything?

Warner believes framing is critical – players should look forward to the next opportunity rather than dwell on what they have missed.

> You've got to be ahead of them and be able to promise what's coming.

We talked about different methods of framing such player value and methods to allow this to scale without making the game unmanageable. One such approach is 'Prestige' – where players reset some aspect of their progression to the start, often in return for some new capability or status reward. Having implemented prestige systems in *Ingress*, Warner knows the power of allowing advanced players to reset for honour, not progress.

> Everyone will know you're not actually level one, you're level one with a deep prestige to it.

She stresses this only works when players are ready:

> It works oftentimes at its peak when it's a mature audience who's experiencing it… who understood the game, understood what it meant to have gone through what they'd gone to, to get to that point.

Warner draws on games like *Valheim*[31] to explain how players need contrast between effort and reward. She explored concepts like Safe Zones and their impact on motivation; how safety allows experimentation whilst danger provides stakes.

> It's fun to have a safe space that you can then go chase your difficult challenges elsewhere… like that's fun, it's fun to have a safe space that you can then go.

Risk, when tied to a meaningful goal, builds anticipation:

> "If you want those really, really cool looking windows, you have to take out all the bosses to get to those materials... so like there's something you're chasing with those hard moments," said Warner.

We further discussed the role of frustration and failure, echoing the concept of the "FU moment[32]" described by Steinhoff Jelly Splash,[33] Warner reframes frustration as an indicator of deep engagement:

> You're feeling pushed as a player beyond what you maybe perceive as your own skill set currently and it's pushing you to try to figure out how to be better.

She emphasises the need to carefully calibrate challenges so that players feel stretched but not defeated:

> The reason you hopefully don't actually throw your phone or you don't rage quit is because you are so engaged that that moment of frustration is just driving you to keep going.

Rather than push players to spend, Warner believes purchases should feel like an investment in joy:

> I want it to feel like they are investing in a hobby they love... that feels like a fair and reasonable investment into your hobby.

This comment underlines the importance of a focus on ethical monetisation. She cautions against models that punish players for not being skilled enough:

> That feels like I'm being punished for the hobby that I love... it does not feel like a fun way to invest in your hobby.

Free-to-play models, she notes, are evolving beyond early time/money tradeoffs. The goal is sustainable value:

> You're looking for that retention number, right? You're looking for them to want to come back again and again and stick with you for years.

For this reason, Warner challenges industry terminology like 'Whales,' which she feels dehumanises spenders:

> That feels… like it takes all the humanity out of the discussion…
> it feels really different though than talking about somebody who
> is a quote unquote whale, right?

Instead of "whales," she sees dedicated players making thoughtful
investments:

> I don't think that there should be shame in enjoying your hobby…
> if they found something that brings them joy and adds delight to
> their day, good! I'm excited for them to have that.

Ultimately, Warner sees LiveOps not as a monetisation strategy – but as a
retention framework:

> "Live services is about sustained growth… it's about making sure
> your players have reason to return again and again," she concludes.

NOTES

1 https://en.wikipedia.org/wiki/Thomas_Was_Alone
2 https://en.wikipedia.org/wiki/The_Stanley_Parable
3 https://en.wikipedia.org/wiki/AdVenture_Capitalist
4 https://en.wikipedia.org/wiki/Balatro
5 https://en.wikipedia.org/wiki/Don%27t_Starve
6 https://en.wikipedia.org/wiki/Stanford_marshmallow_experiment
7 https://en.wikipedia.org/wiki/Search_and_matching_theory_(economics)
8 https://pmc.ncbi.nlm.nih.gov/articles/PMC5559016/
9 https://neurolaunch.com/does-playing-video-games-release-dopamine/
10 https://neurolaunch.com/video-games-dopamine-depression/
11 https://machinations.io/articles/what-is-game-economy-inflation-how-to-foresee-it-and-how-to-overcome-it-in-your-game-design
12 https://en.wikipedia.org/wiki/Infinity_Nikki
13 Ruth Tomandl discusses how to embrace ambiguity as a producer in game development in her 2017 GDC talk https://youtu.be/4DWdnoLosZ8?si=-fo87QMvuwHScHAc
14 https://archero.fandom.com/wiki/Archero_Wiki
15 https://en.wikipedia.org/wiki/Three-act_structure
16 https://en.wikipedia.org/wiki/Beat_Saber
17 https://www.academia.edu/72769702/Getting_in_the_Mood_The_role_of_mood_in_product_design_and_interaction
18 https://www.frontiersin.org/journals/psychology/articles/10.3389/fpsyg.2022.925842/full
19 https://www.academia.edu/19402338/Gender_and_Status_Competition_in_Premodern_Societies
20 https://en.wikipedia.org/wiki/Tafl_games

21 https://en.wikipedia.org/wiki/Fidchell
22 https://en.wikipedia.org/wiki/Tables_game
23 https://en.wikipedia.org/wiki/Arpad_Elo
24 https://en.wikipedia.org/wiki/Dunbar%27s_number
25 https://altrincham.todaynews.co.uk/business/2024/01/22/altrincham/
26 https://www.ea.com/games/golf-clash
27 https://www.ign.com/wikis/pokemon-go/Teams
28 https://www.pcgamer.com/eve-online-player-uses-obscure-rule-to-pull-off
-the-biggest-heist-in-the-games-history/
29 https://linkedin.com/in/lauramaewarner
30 https://en.wikipedia.org/wiki/Hay_Day
31 https://en.wikipedia.org/wiki/Valheim
32 https://www.youtube.com/watch?v=QctcE3-xTBI
33 https://en.wikipedia.org/wiki/Jelly_Splash

CHAPTER 7

Understanding Utility

DOI: 10.1201/9781003592471-7

WHAT PLAYERS WANT IS "UTILITY"

Or should that read "Utility" is what players want? The term Utility comes from economics, and we will be using it as a catch-all term to help us focus on how to satisfy players. The game economy is more than just an abstract concept in game design. It is the core system that governs how players interact with the game world, how they make progress, and how they perceive value. Without a carefully crafted economy, even the most well-designed gameplay can feel unsatisfying. Players must feel that their time and effort in a game are rewarded in meaningful ways, and a well-constructed economy can enhance their overall experience, motivating them to stay engaged. Delivering Utility is, essentially, the method by which the game delivers on the promise to satisfy the players' 'Need State'; their underlying motivation to start and continue playing.

This foundation provides us with a framework from which to develop a commercial model as well; from the simple Pay-to-Play or more sophisticated models which engage multiple cohorts of players based on their preferences and behaviours. In this chapter, we'll take a deep dive into the practical functional components of game economies. We aim to define some of the tools we have and how they function at a basic level.

What Is Utility?

At the most basic level, all transactions are about the exchange of the expected satisfaction of Utility for time and effort. The value that can be assigned to each element of Utility is based partly on our own subjective expectations (and experienced) satisfaction, the intrinsic functional performance of that element, the social context, and societal agreement on value, alongside factors such as the cost/effort of accessing those items and scarcity. These factors are deeply connected with the experiential benefit from within the game, but also the symbolic benefit gained from the act of acquisition and related status signifiers that they represent.

Economically speaking, most virtual game items can be classified as 'experience goods,' meaning that their intrinsic value can only be assessed once acquired. That tends to mean that these are not substitutable with 'real-world' items, but also means that they won't typically hold the same value expectations as physical goods, which convey the emotional and status benefits.

The fundamental currency of a player is time. How much time a player spends playing, and how intensely, is the principal indication of value we can use. Especially, valuable when it repeats, consistently over time. In the end, many designers would argue that you can use time as the ultimate exchange rate when calculating game balance. However, time doesn't always have a consistent value. Looking for something to pass the time, when the board has a different personal value than when the player is pushed for time due to external issues and still chooses to play. Those moments are precious.

Real money in-game act as a ticket for an experience, either acting as a key to access that playable activity or as a substitute for time and effort spent in a game. Both models are valid, but both introduce complex problems. Different cohorts of players have different expectations from their games, and they will inevitably have to find a different balance between their anticipation of what the game will deliver, their threshold for time available to play, their skill, and capacity to experience progression. Most game designs will manage that balance by bestowing symbolic value to such efforts through rewards, trophies, and symbols of progression and prowess. However, whilst developers can use money to help the player augment their performance in various ways, doing so without care can very easily undermine the very benefits that the player wanted from the game in the first place. You must be careful of the unintended consequences that can happen when you introducing the ability to spend into your game. It is essential to avoid the risk that you undermine the skill, persistence, difficulty, etc., of the game, as it is within those elements that players gain the 'Utility' and fundamentally understand why they value the game experience and what makes it meaningful.

Players are generally not going to be highly motivated to pay to NOT play the game they are interested in – although in the case of idle games I does seem to come quite close to the line. Implementing monetisation design that separates a player from the core experience risks 'breaking the game' and is exactly what players get angry about when they talk about 'Pay To Win', something which gets more critical if the game includes skill-based competitive play. This deeply damages both the game's equivalent of a 'social contract'[1] and indeed the game experience. That being said, there are some contexts where audiences who actually want this in their game. In certain Asian markets, including South Korea and China there are elements of the playing culture that see spending as a legitimate strategic option. This can be extremely profitable. However, if not done carefully and transparently, more often that not this alienates other players and can permanently damage the game's credibility as well as the developer's brand. It is also important to avoid going too far the other way as well. Many developers assume that there can never be any material benefit from real money spending in the game at all. This undermines the point of the role of money as a substitute for time and why they should invest in your game at all. There is a fine balance in how to use real currency, how frequently to trigger a transaction and what proxies to use for real-money itself, whether in the form of soft-currency bundles, Batttle Pass, VIP programmes, or even in-game ads. Ads can act as a very low barrier way for a player to exchange time for money, but where the money comes from the advertiser. We will talk more about exchange later in the chapter.

Types of Utility in a Game

Within a game, it helps to be able to identify the elements of Utility that define the value elements within a game. A designer can use this to help make sense of player motivation and behaviour, as well as to start thinking about how these elements might be packaged within the economy. At this stage, this is not about the exchange (either from time or spend), this is just exploring the components of the game and how those elements can be used systematically. For this, we can break these down into four key types of Utility common in games:

- **Subsistence**: Every game has some methodology to manage access and flow within the game and these mechanisms provide a Utility for the player to be able to satisfy their 'need' to play the game. This can be fuel, health, energy, or other similar mechanisms which are used as barriers to the continuation of play. Players can't continue playing if they have run out of fuel, and it takes time – or some kind of spend – to refresh that resource. Even a 'Cool-Down' period applied to an ability is arguably a subsistence element. Players have to wait (spending time) for the item to next become usable. Similarly, where they have to complete specific activities or collect sufficient resources in order to unlock a new playing area, this could be considered a form of subsistence. The initial licence for a 'Pay Upfront' title is required to allow access to the game at all for what has become known as 'Premium' games is a required item, without which play cannot proceed. Indeed, commercial models which offer try-before-you-buy are identical in terms of Utility type, as they have a paywall – it's just placed after the initial demo experience.

- **Shortcuts**: The elements in the game that can be utilised to augment our playing experience, making it easier for us to complete, survive, or feel otherwise powerful in play beyond raw skill all provide some 'shortcut' in the playing experience to some extent. The selection, timing, and type of shortcut can provide some level of strategic value depending on the game design as well. However, the key to the Utility value for a player is in the practical support to get to our playing goals. There is a fine balance here also, benefits gained from shortcuts may make us feel powerful, but that only happens when they don't make our own choices and actions meaningless. A Shortcut is valued highest when it supports the player experience, makes it visually, narratively, and emotionally more engaging, not when it replaces our choices. A linear approach to shortcuts, such as a +1 sword, can also be unsatisfying. Why would the player still value that item when they later pick up a +3 sword? The design may intentionally make such items obsolete, as a mitigation for inflation, but what if there were other characteristics that mean there was still a reason to use that +1 Sword? For example, if the game had a restricted arena banning higher bonus weapons, a boost to XP for choosing the worse option, or some secondary characteristic that keeps that item valid. For example, if the sword had the 'Fire' quality, that is particularly good against 'Earth'-based opponents and bad against items with the "Water" label, then such shortcuts can deliver additional player choices or strategy, adding to their longer-term value.

- **Social**: Not all items need to have a gameplay benefit to be perceived as valuable. Social goods include all the items which allow us to express our identity and success in the game. The most obvious of this comes from cosmetic items and the rise of Fortnite[2] where the application of self-expression and its function in gameplay has driven over $40bn in revenue. Cosmetics and personalisation go far beyond 'Skins' and include the ability to express your own creativity and tastes within aspects of the game. Players also seek this form of

Utility as a display of our success in play, and even real-world wealth. This need not be a purely narcissistic thing. Social goods allow us to express our identity in context with our 'tribe'. This lets the player demonstrate shared values and even altruism through gifting. However, too many games focus on the development of these types of goods while failing to recognise that for social goods to work, players need space for others to see what they have done. Without social feedback, social goods have more limited intrinsic value; except in terms of creative expression.

- **Strategy**: One of the most exciting types of goods comes where the Utility provides an opportunity for the player to get more deeply involved in the experience. A Strategy good is one focused on delivering playing Utility which allows for meaningful choice in playing approaches. For example, the player unlocks the Vorpal Blade[3] and gets the option to fight a Jabberwocky – a fearsome and undefeatable beast otherwise. This opens a new option and resolution as a moment of play but can also unlock other gameplay strategies and challenges. This becomes more interesting when this type of Utility is used to unlock choice in playing styles. A machine gun offers continuous fire across time but the same overall damage per second over e.g. a minute when compared to a Shotgun but the shotgun does all that damage in one go if it hits. The machine gun lets us score that damage. This can go deeper still with the unlocking of new locations or such as with Metroid games that allow the player to interact with the world in ways which were previously inaccessible. The application of the success matrix behind Scissors, Paper, Stone (traditionally called ick-ack-ock in the U.K.)[4] to strategy goods can unlock deeper engagement for the players by adding an additional layer of competence and autonomy around the selection of our loadout in a game – increasing your perception of control over the playing experience. In turn this delivers increased Utility value for the player, provided the increased complexity doesn't get in the way of the game.

Forms of Utility

The types of Utility that have been described can be experienced in different ways within any game, but in general, the application can be simplified into four principal forms.

- **Consumable**: In many ways, the simplest form is the one-time use item. The 'Power-pill' players pickup in Pac-Man, which transforms our cowardly pizza-shaped icon into a ghost-munching machine, is one of the earliest examples. The core principle is that these items are earned, used, and disposed of regardless of the visual aesthetic or metaphor applied within the context of the game. They are usually of relatively perceived low value individually – although not always the case, and can even be significant quest items that are to be used up at a critical point in the story, such as the 'Elder Scroll' in Skyrim (although it is open to debate if that is a true consumable item).[5] Typical consumable items will be items that will either provide an immediate short-term benefit or be an item for exchange within another system in the game. This can include currencies, resource items used in crafting systems, or unique 'flavoured' components necessary for very specific actions or challenges, and usually the user can collect an inventory of multiple copies of the same item. Consumables are an essential feature when building game economies, as they can be used to motivate the collection and spending in order to drive forward the player journey.

- **Capacity**: How many items a player can carry and store at a time is a key tool in game balance, and a form of Utility that can profoundly impact the gameplay experience. This is essentially a constraint on the player, limiting the scope of items that they can rely on at any given moment in a playing session. How many health potions they can carry affects our ability to respond to damage the player has taken in a fight; how many Iron Ore they can carry can act as a barrier to the player's ability to craft certain items or limits the scope for trade per transaction. It also provides a positive motivator to encourage the active use of collected consumable items, if players can only store ten health potions, they are losing the additional Utility when they have to discard an 11th that they discover, triggering them to use the items more frequently. Capacity is not limited to consumable items. The number of weapons the player can carry has been a feature that can be upgraded in multiple games and genres and shows that Capacity, as a concept, changes not the type of Utility it provides, but helps regulate the application of Utility in play. Interestingly, the sooner players invest in Capacity, the more value they will get in terms of the longer-term experience as this allows them to leverage more value from their consumable items earlier and for longer.

- **Generator**: Almost the opposite of Capacity is the concept of a generator. This is where consumable items are refreshed over time. The form of generator can impact the rate at which your consumable items are refreshed and potentially even the effect of such items in play. This can also be applied to any item with a cooldown period, where the time component is a factor in the way that the player can exercise the Utility in that item or experience. The purpose of a generator is essentially to restore a state for the player where a necessary item in play becomes sufficiently available over time to ensure a good playing experience. This allows us to regulate the frequency and intensity of play and ensure that there is always a reason to return later and play again. Generators can provide an escalation to the stakes at play as the player can access more and more of their resources, creating an engaging intensity in the experience at the time, but with a balancing motivation to encourage players to take a break to avoid burnout – knowing they can come back later with an advantage. Just as with Capacity, the sooner players invest in Generators, the more value they will get in terms of the longer-term experience as this allows them to leverage more value from their consumable items earlier and for longer.

- **Aspirational Items**: For the purposes of understanding Utility, any durable or permanent equipment, upgrades, or similar beneficial items in a game can be considered as 'Aspirational' items. The reason for this is a long-term delivery of Utility – whether a subsistence, shortcut, social, or strategy – is something we as players aspire to and value most intensely prior to obtaining them. However, once the player has them, these items rapidly become a hygiene factor, meaning that they are necessary but no longer intrinsically rewarding, part of our basic functionality of the game. Once the player has the Vorpal Blade and has killed a few Jabberwocky's the sword is just another item and Jabberwocky's are just another form of a 'Bigger Rat'. That doesn't mean that they aren't an important form of Utility, quite the opposite, they allow players to feel that they have a sense of permanence from the assets they have obtained and that they own. However, once they are replaced by something more interesting or with a higher gameplay benefit, they are readily broken down into crafting components or sold for currency and resources where the game permits this. There are ways that can extend the players' emotional engagement with such items, including the ability to upgrade and bestow personalisation on them – including naming them. One approach is to offer systems which mean that using these items actively degrades their capability. In Zelda: Breath of the Wild, the weapons break after a period of use, and the player has to repair and replace them (arguably too rapidly). Encouraging players to use their crafting resources to maintain their items can be a great way to build an investment in their durable items. However, there is a significant issue. Players basically don't like having things taken away from them. Even when it makes the game more interesting. So it's important to ensure such systems are presented positively. During the Beta Testing, World of Warcraft originally had a mechanism which was a penalty for being tired if you played for an extended period. This didn't go down well, although it was well-intentioned. That mechanism still exists. But the way it is presented is instead you get bonus XP for being 'Rested'.[6] It's exactly the same idea and functions identically, only the language has changed.

The Utility Matrix

As reviewing the game economy, designers need to explore the mechanisms at work and identify the specific types and forms of Utility in that game, and attempt to understand how they operate, what they mean to players and how to communicate that value. Not every game will have an entry for each section of the matrix, and many will have multiple entries in the same sections. This may be entirely valid, but can also be an indication of potential underlying opportunities to further optimise the design.

The matrix above is intended to illustrate methods to explore a game's Utility, rather than being a realistic model required for any specific game. Games do not have to have an element for every possible combination; but they may also include multiple variations. The horizontal rows here have been used to explore the relationship between specific examples. Taking fuel as a fundamental subsistence good for a driving game, the player

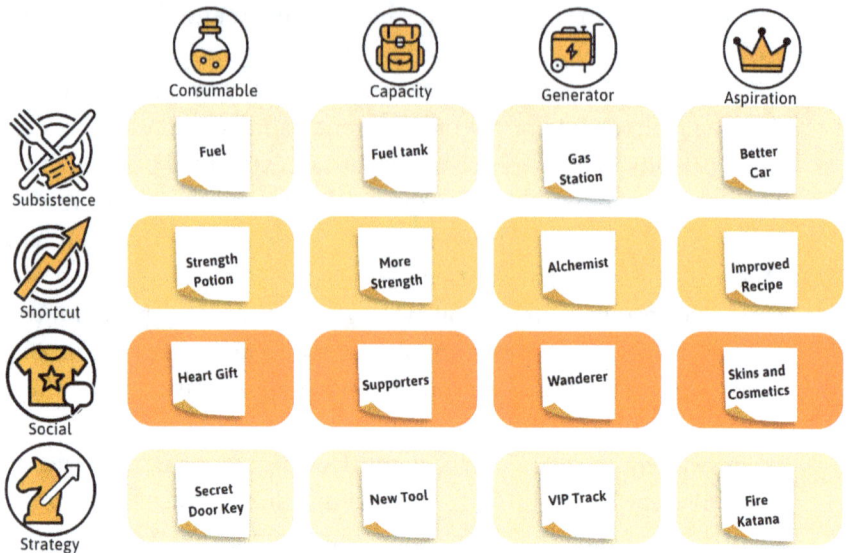

FIGURE 7.1   Types and forms of player utility.

uses fuel each time they race, so they have to have enough available to be able to race at all. They can obtain more through some gameplay method, either waiting till that recoup (via a generator) or via some in-game currency, crafting process, or even a real money exchange. How much fuel they can store at any time is reflected by the size of the fuel tank they have. That can be upgraded as a reward, or again via some in-game currency, crafting process, or even a real money exchange. The rate at which they obtain fuel passively can also be amended through an exchange of gameplay or currency by obtaining some item in the game which boosts the delivery rate – this example includes an item called a 'Gas Station' that represents. The able also includes an aspirational subsistence item called "A Better Car" which would be a vehicle with specific characteristics to make owning it attractive. Whilst typically a player would expect a "better vehicle" to be defined by cosmetic value or improved stats, what can make this a subsistence good would be some factor that makes the aspirational vehicle essential to some aspect of play. In a game like CSR, the ability to enter specific parts of the game, new challenges, or a particular race type requires the player to have a qualifying vehicle. To live up to the concept of aspiration, it also needs those boosted stats, cosmetic looks, and other compelling components, but what makes it a subsistence item is what it unlocks for the player; and occasionally in some games this might be defined by what the player loses access to if that item were to be lost. These aspirational benefits need not only include positive consequences, the design can also reinforce the need for the other subsistence items, such as this new car increasing the rate of fuel consumption or requiring the player to manage capacity or generator upgrades for each individual vehicle – which provides a great scalable "sink."

Taking a different game genre as an example for Shortcuts, consider an RPG adventure game where the player can unlock a Strength Potion which increases our ability to interact in the world and do melee damage. This potion may have a limited period of active benefit, and perhaps even a cooldown period before they can use another. Basically, acting as any consumable item, used and destroyed. The player may have a capacity for the number of potions they can carry. This may be specific to strength potions specifically in some games, but may be a total of all potions, or even as part of an inventory process occupying space in a backpack or weight the player can carry (which of course can be affected by consuming that very potion). The capacity for potential can even be restricted indirectly, through the availability of the crafting items required to make that potion, and the storage capacity for those items, and of course the player can gain related upgrades to such capacity in the usual ways through rewards and exchanges. The generator form of Utility in this example could also take many forms. It could be a separate magical item increasing the likelihood that rewards will drop new potions, it could be access to areas in the world with more craftable resources, or it could be automated, for example, by hiring an Alchemist to make you those potions. Finally, an example of aspirational goods (as well as the magical item that increases the 'drop rate') could be something like an Improved Recipe. This has a permanent material impact on future potions created by the player, with a larger impact on their benefits received whether that means more strength, longer time of beneficial use, shorter cooldown periods, etc. However, at the same time the design could include an increase in the cost of production of such potions, amend the creating ingredients required, and even increase the size of the potion, resetting the Capacity or Generator factors for that Utility.

What this discussion is trying to show is that in understanding the Utility that players value in the game, the designer can better understand the levers to manage engagement. This is profoundly important in getting the design right and forces us to question the playing experience and how to balance the game.

Interview

HOLISTIC BALANCE AND PLAYER MOTIVATION – AN INTERVIEW WITH JAVIER BARNES

Game economy design is more than just numbers; it's about crafting an experience that aligns player motivation with sustainable engagement. In a recent discussion, Javier Barnes,[7] an expert in mobile and live game economy design, shared his insights on how game economies function, the importance of early planning, and the delicate balance between progression, reward systems, and monetisation.

> "In order to be balanced, [a game economy] has to have been designed to be balanceable," Says Barnes.

Many game economies struggle because the foundational systems weren't designed with balance in mind. Barnes warns against introducing economy designers late in development to 'fix' a system that was never structured for balance in the first place.

> The worst situation… is when the game economy and the systems and how the rewards are going to behave are set up, and then you bring in a game economist… who has to create order out of systems that were not made with the idea of balance in mind.

Early involvement ensures that reward structures, taps (ways players earn resources), and sinks (ways players spend resources) are aligned with the game's core design.

It's important to think carefully about how we design reward systems that feel fair. Loot boxes, 'gacha' mechanics, and randomised rewards often generate controversy, yet some implementations are more accepted than others. According to Barnes, poorly designed systems feel punishing because they fail to balance perceived value and enjoyment.

> "Almost no one complains about [Magic: The Gathering booster packs]. We don't even think about it as a gacha system, but they are gacha systems. The way they have been designed, whenever

you open a booster pack, you feel that you got something that was really worth it," says Barnes.

The key difference? Well-implemented reward systems consistently provide a sense of accomplishment and fair value, rather than frustration.

A game economy extends beyond currency – it encompasses everything that can be counted: experience points, items, unlockable content, and even access to missions.

> "I try to visualize games as loop systems... The game introduces elements and removes elements, like I get currencies, and I use the currency for something which transforms that into something else, and that completes the loop," says Barnes.

By structuring these loops effectively, designers can guide players through progression while maintaining engagement.

The most successful economies incentivise player behaviour that aligns with enjoyment, rather than forcing unnatural actions. Barnes highlights the example from Magic: The Gathering Arena:

> "I have multiple accounts. So with the free resources of those many accounts, I have unlimited ability to play drafts. But this is not what the developers would want. I found a way to hack the economy in order to get the most fun experience," says Barnes.

When game economies misalign player desires with design objectives, players find workarounds, potentially undermining the intended economy.

A well-designed economy should direct players toward enjoyable and engaging actions. If the most effective strategy is also the most boring, retention will suffer.

> "The best situation is where the system of incentives makes the players do the actions that are going to make the game more fun," says Barnes.

For example, in RPGs, progression should feel rewarding and strategic, whereas in MOBAs, progression is often aesthetic rather than power driven.

Different games require different types of currency to encourage the right behaviours. Barnes categorises them into three main types:

- **Versatile Currencies** (e.g. soft and hard currencies)
- **Specialised Currencies** (e.g. game-mode specific resources)

- **Progression Trackers** (e.g. XP systems that anchor player advancement)

"Currencies don't matter. What matters is what we want the players to do with those resources. They are tools," says Barnes.

The flexibility and specificity of currency systems influence how players interact with the economy. However, we also have to be aware of the complexity of regional and genre differences; that different audiences have different expectations about game economies. Barnes notes the contrast between Japanese and Western preferences:

"The way the economy and resource system has been designed [for the new Pokémon trading card game] is very Japanese… Japanese players are used to complex economies with very circumstantial resources, whereas Western players find it overwhelming and confusing," says Barnes.

Cultural and genre expectations must be accounted for when designing a game's economy.

Existing models can help frame our thinking, but we still have to implement them carefully. Take the Battle pass. This can be among the best monetisation tools when implemented well. However, they can also feel like grind-heavy chores if they don't align with player expectations.

"Many [players] felt it was very grindy… It was making them play in ways they really did not want to play," said Barnes.

A well-designed battle pass should encourage engagement without forcing players into unnatural gameplay patterns. This applies more generally as effective monetisation has to align with engagement rather than exploiting player frustration.

"Do not assume that because something makes sense on paper, it makes sense in reality… The perception of the player – the real human on the other end – may be completely different," says Barnes.

For example, an overly generous economy can remove the sense of achievement, as seen in Legends of Runeterra,[8] where players lost the excitement of collecting cards because rewards were too abundant.

Final Takeaways

Barnes emphasises three core principles in game economy design:

1. **Intentionality**: Define what player behaviours you want to encourage and structure the economy accordingly.

2. **Perception vs. Reality**: Test and adjust based on actual player experience, not just theoretical balance.

3. **Sustainable Monetisation**: Avoid zero-sum thinking – healthy monetisation models ensure long-term engagement, not just short-term revenue.

"If the game is not enjoyable and if spending is not enjoyable, yeah you maybe can make a certain amount of money, but you are going to eventually burn your players," says Barnes.

By focusing on long-term sustainability and player satisfaction, game economies can become a core pillar of successful game design.

NOTES

1 Social contract – Wikipedia
2 https://www.researchgate.net/publication/347793218_Power_in_Skin_The_Interplay_of_Self-Presentation_Tactical_Play_and_Spending_in_Fortnite
3 https://poetryarchive.org/poem/jabberwocky/
4 https://www.ponderweasel.com/who-invented-rock-paper-scissors
5 https://elderscrolls.fandom.com/wiki/Elder_Scroll_(Dragon)
6 https://www.icy-veins.com/wow/rested-xp-a-detailed-overview
7 https://www.linkedin.com/in/javier-barnes-8b0b5424/
8 https://en.wikipedia.org/wiki/Legends_of_Runeterra

CHAPTER 8

Functions of Exchange

DOI: 10.1201/9781003592471-8

THINKING ABOUT EXCHANGE

Having defined what players want and need in a game, let's consider how players access that value and what they give in exchange. This section will explore the types of exchange expressed in a game and the forms that take, both from a core gameplay perspective as well as in-game commercial elements. For the purposes of our model, the designer needs to be able to take the widest possible view of what constitutes an exchange from the act of play itself to parting with cold, hard cash across different platforms. This chapter will also attempt to examine some of the concerns and risks involved with integrating commercial elements in-game and the controversy this has raised in the wider games community and, indeed, society as a whole, through government and consumer body concerns.[1]

Play as a Form of Exchange

In game design, our principle means of exchange will be focused on what actions in a game unlock the rewards of play. This is about players putting their time and attention into the game itself. This is the most basic form of currency that players trade within the game. Designers create moments of play designed to capture the players' attention, and in return for entertainment and rewarding gameplay, players invest their attention. This includes the intrinsic rewards related to the expression of our skill, creativity, the reveal of narrative, and the satisfaction derived from both the interaction methods as well as the extrinsic rewards from progression and collection, etc. The presence of other players allows the player to express some token of power, status, or tribal belonging in the process.

- **Time**: The fundamental exchange mechanism. The allocation of arguably the scarcest resource, where players have an effectively unlimited range of options as to where to allocate their time. Our aim as designers is to encourage them to choose our game as the place to do that, reward that with player Utility and create reasons for them to want to continue to do that over time, either in this game, through our other games, or indeed to entice others to also invest in our games. This can be tracked by measures such as session length and retention.

- **Attention**: A more subtle aspect of time is related to the level of attention obtained from/delivered to the player. The reflection of the cognitive commitment to the game is a deeper guide to the value players assign to the experience. It reflects the level of engagement in the immersive qualities of the experience, but also the distractions and other compelling pressures that the player is exposed to during the game. Unlike simple measures of time, different game genres fulfil different 'Need States,' and in some games, it is vital that the design does not overly strain the requirement of player focus; in others, it is the most crucial currency. Think about the value proposition of an almost sedative style of play gained from a cosy farming experience and how this requires a materially different level of focus from the player than an elite first-person shooter. This subjective status of focus makes it very hard to directly measure independently from time but can sometimes be estimated from variations in response time and performance optimisation.

- **Skill**: Whilst skill is directly related to attention, it is still valuable to consider it as a reflection on the player's investment in the game. Players will have a natural capacity for performance in the game, but this will evolve measurably as they learn more about the techniques, leverage strategic tools and playing modes, as well as in their performance, especially against others. However, it's also important to remember that this is a messy method of transaction because different players will bring different levels of experience from other similar games, natural ability, and their capacity to learn. Add to that the increase in information available related to tactics and techniques available through content creators, and it can be difficult to quantify or track the investment made compared to the gameplay benefits received. The scope to develop and invest in skill is a critical aspect of building a possibility space that makes the game feel personally meaningful.

- **Grind**: The opposite of skill in many ways, grind is more about persistence and willingness to repeat actions, even when they become predictable and even dull. This repetition is usually vital to the success of a game and necessary for longer-term engagement. Grind provides a route for all players who have the time, not just those with the natural ability. Grind can also become meaningful in its own right. There is a satisfaction in intentional repetition, in looking for the means to optimise. It can become an almost sedative style of play, just as described relating to some cosy games. When alternated with high-attention, demanding moments of play, this can drive the Absorption vector that we explored when looking into the Three Loops model.

Looking at the basic features of play as methods of exchange for rewards and progression reveals more about the flow through a game experience, and how other extrinsic methods can be applied to building a commercial game economy.

Resources as a Form of Exchange

Whilst a basic game may have the player make an interaction and get a result, the kinds of games which retain players long term usually involve some use of resources. These resources can be the cost of an action, a stake, or a tool used to enhance performance. We have talked about the role of this in terms of Utility – players want Subsistence, Shortcuts, Social, and Strategy goods which can take multiple forms. However, it is important to explore some of the specific forms in a bit more detail, to consider how they are used as forms of exchange, and how such resources need to be both earned and spent in meaningful ways to have clear value for players.

- **Soft Currency**: This is typically the most basic resource earned and spent within any game. The term 'Soft' relates to the fact that this is a form of currency readily earned by players through gameplay. It is often awarded for completing levels, defeating enemies, or achieving specific objectives. It is most often spent on activities related to repair, progression, and access to base-level assets and Utility items. Soft Currency usually has high availability, and (arguably) is unlimited if the player is willing to put in the time to extract it. However, Soft Currency has limited purchasing power and is more a signpost to show players that their actions have value and consequence in the game. In some ways, soft currency is more about creating a lubricant to unblock obstacles to get to the next significant stage, making it a way to invest in small amounts of temporary power and not feel stuck in the game. However, more significant steps will require other, more meaningful currency or performance improvement.

- **Resource**: Some currencies are reserved for special use, flavoured for a particular purpose in the game. These include raw materials, e.g. wood/metal/food; items that are used to create other objects, e.g. blueprints, hammers, and even items that are only used in seasonality or to unlock new characters, e.g. Blue Essence in League of Legends. Some games have a small number of resource types used in different combinations across the game. Other games have specific resources used for specific purposes, from personal progression to creating buildings or unit development. The value of implementing resources is that the different uses allow the game design to direct players based on their current gameplay objectives. The game can set 'Go Fetch' missions which rely on the specific type of resource, rather than just reward a universal currency.

- **Hard Currency**: Where a game has in-app purchases, it will often offer a form of premium currency that is acquired through real-money transactions but is also given very sparingly as a reward for significant in-game achievements. Hard Currency is often 'flavoured' to an extent, but not usually in the same way as a resource. Hard Currency is more about access to advanced, more powerful items than possible through soft currencies and other resources alone. It is often used to allow players to unlock rare items, speed up progression, or access exclusive content.

- **Real Money**: Some games also have items which require real money to access. That tends to be limited to cosmetic or collectible items, because unlocking 'Power' or gameplay advantage can be quite problematic and raise accusations of Pay-To-Win. This can be a justified concern and has broken a number of games. Typically, real-money transactions are presented as bundle offers that include a combination of hard and soft Currency, sometimes alongside limited-edition cosmetic items.

- **Anchors**: Some currencies cannot be purchased and are only available through play. This isn't a rejection of monetisation, rather, it is a way for the designer to have a vector against which to simplify the complex balancing of different currencies and resources in a game. If specific meaningful transactions always require this specific currency, then that step is anchored to gameplay progress directly, and players can therefore only progress in line with how much they have actually played the game, thus mitigating against Pay-To-in issues that might otherwise arise.

- **Progression Milestones**: Whilst not a currency, progression milestones such as player level or a stage in the game narrative can be a method to unlock access to a variety of resources and content.

Typically, these are an accumulation of a specific resource, such as experience points (XP) or are achieved by completing a series of in-game locations or tasks.

- **Ratchets**: Often related to Progression Milestones, Ratchets are another method for the developer to simplify the complex balancing of different currencies and resources in a game. Rather than using a specific currency, the player can only invest in or use specific items or content if they have already met the criteria. The term 'Ratchet' relates to how the tool allows motion in one direction only. This applies a restriction which means that only when the criteria are fulfilled can the progression occur. For example, in Clash of Clans, a player can only upgrade their town hall by levelling up other buildings. This enforces a fairly linear upgrade path for the base as a whole, whilst leaving players the autonomy to decide the order in which they resolve each building.

The way in which all these resources are distributed and controlled can significantly impact how players perceive the game and its economy. One of the key principles in resource management is balancing scarcity and abundance, as well as inflation.

- **Scarcity**: When resources are scarce, players must make meaningful decisions about how to use them. For example, in a strategy game, players might have a limited number of actions per day, forcing them to prioritise their objectives. Scarcity can create a sense of challenge and tension, making each decision feel impactful. For scarcity to be meaningful, the activity required to unlock the resources must feel commensurate with its value, and this is likely to adjust over the lifecycle of the player. For example, in Eve Online, mining can be super valuable to get started (unless the player can get help from their friendly local corporation), but it soon fails to deliver sufficient value.

- **Abundance**: On the other hand, too much scarcity can lead to frustration if players feel that they are unable to make meaningful progress. By introducing periods of abundance, such as special events, bonuses, or rewards for completing difficult challenges, players can sense that they are making significant strides, even if only for a short time.

- **Inflation**: The phenomenon of inflation refers to the situation that with the increase of supply of game currency, the supply of money is greater than the actual demand for money, resulting in the depreciation of the game currency and the general rise in prices. This is usually very bad for your game economy, but there can be ways a designer can leverage inflation to rebalance the perceived value and reward obtained from those items. However, this requires great care and can easily run away from you. The best way to deal with inflation is to create a new, alternative use, or reason to spend that item, removing the excess from the economy and effectively increasing demand accordingly.

Balancing these forces is essential for keeping players engaged. If a game feels too restrictive, players may become demotivated. If it feels too easy, players may lose interest due to a lack of meaningful challenges. By carefully managing the availability of resources, game designers can create a dynamic economy that offers players both moments of tension and moments of reward. We will explore how to manage that balance in Chapter 9, 'Sinks and Sources.'

COMMERCIAL FORMS OF EXCHANGE

Where a game includes in-app purchase models, it cannot ignore the function of commercial instruments and their roles in exchange within a game. This can include advertising, referrals, microtransactions, offer walls, and even recurring subscriptions.

Advertising

The majority of content experiences consumed are via some form of promotional material paid for by an advertiser. Games are no exception, and ads do not need to damage the player experience. However, it is important to be careful to work with providers who facilitate methods by which, the game gains most when players engage with the ads. Ads in games are not for everyone, and currently the majority of ad-funded games can be found on mobile. PC gamers have been positively antagonistic about the presence of ads, but there have also been similar negative sentiments from so-called 'Mid-core' mobile games players (games with deeper gameplay and more classic game genres). However, on mobile, ads have unlocked gameplay for more players than ever before and made this sector the single most profitable form of digital entertainment. Ads will remain a key part of monetisation and the player experience, but changes to privacy rules, the actions of certain ad companies, and games platforms have not always been in the best interest of game developers or, indeed, their players. There are multiple ad formats to consider:

- **In-World (Native) Ads**: Branded product placement inside the game experience is not new. One of the earliest examples came with Zool 2, which was funded by Chupa Chups, and was impossible for any player to miss. Splinter Cell: Chaos Theory notably was one of the first that included systems to allow the form of Digital In-Game Advertising, for players to swap assets between brands. Within virtual worlds, brands have innovated in finding ways to connect with gamers. Some of the better examples come from Red Bull, notably the Red Bull Air Race space within PlayStation Home, a genuinely enjoyable arcade flight game. More recently, this has become a little more common with teams offering more simplified propositions such as 'outdoor' billboards that can even make contemporary scenes feel more natural. Brands get 'eyeballs' on their brand, and even some positive cultural association. What separates this format from 'Product Placement' is where they have an ongoing revenue model, where the ad-object can change over time. As opposed to the one-off payment from a static item, n-world ads generally paid out based on the percentage of screen time that the advert enjoys, rather than being paid on 'Impressions'. There are some standards in place with the Advertising Standards bodies on how this can be calculated. Importantly, there is no direct interference with the game, as long as it's consistent with the intended immersive experience.

- **Banner Ads**: The granddaddy of the internet advertising model still exists in games. However, its use is generally limited to either low-quality games, or those where the display isn't unduly interfered with, or where there are few alternative commercial options. This method was very prominent in hyper-casual games, but also common in simple puzzles such as word, number, or picture-based games. Banner ads are generally not very valuable, and pay out based on either impression or click-through. Banner Ads are also fairly notorious for fraud and accidental clicks, but despite the negatives, they do fulfil a role for many games.

- **Interstitial Ads**: Interstitials are ads placed when a player is waiting for their chosen action. It's often used as a block on progress, a means to stop the player for a moment to capture their attention for the ad. These ads can be still images, but in mobile games they are more commonly video. Optimally, this video can be skipped after a few seconds if the player has no interest. Unfortunately, several advertising platforms in the early 2020s removed this feature and even extended the forced viewing time beyond a comfortable 30 s, which can have a measurable negative impact on retention. Even Interstitial Ads can have a useful function and indeed were a positive driving force for the hyper-casual market. When placed well in a game, usually on exit of an intense amount of play, they provide a moment of passive relaxation. This may seem counterintuitive, but for games at risk of burning out the player due to intensity of focus, the placement of an ad can be oddly restorative. However, there are often better ways to provide this kind of relief through game design, without the negative impact on retention that can come from interstitial ads, so it's important to weigh the revenue potential against the impact on long-term retention.

- **Rewarded Ads**: These are typically video ads that have been voluntarily opted into by the player in return for some form of in-game bonus. The optimal experience is short (no more than 30 s) to minimise the risk of the player not returning to the game. As this method has evolved over the decade, the expectations of the type of reward have become more sophisticated. Generally, simple currency offers are not very interesting, instead, more sophisticated offers need to be applied, including:

  - **Unblock**: A targeted reward such as an XP boost, health reset, or power-up which is deliberately positioned due to its ability to help the player overcome a point in the game they are struggling with.

  - **Second Chance**: Usually, a one-time option to continue playing from the moment of failure and keep their progress up to that point.

- **Trial Offer**: An underutilised approach, which is to introduce the player to a new form of play, special skin, or form of power-up that they get to use for a limited time. The aim of this is to allow the player to experience the benefit, whilst establishing that it has commercial value – it's not just free. Often, such use will be followed by a special one-time discount offer to purchase that item.

- **Bonus Rewards**: Another option for Rewarded Ads is where the player can double the rewards they just gained. However, if this is always available, players start to feel that it is a tax and that the real reward they should receive has been cut in half; they feel like it's a commercial trick. When instead there is a cool-down period between the use of such ads (indeed, this can be applied to any of the ad formats described) and players can tactically choose the best time to use the ad, they become a bonus instead.

Rewarded ads remain some of the most valuable commercial instruments, in particular for mobile games, not least as they allow games to monetise a much larger audience for revenue (up to 50% of players in a freemium game). However, the format has not been immune to the negative applications applied by many ad platforms in the early 2020s. These include a series of techniques that can include extending the duration of the ad, then mandating a 'playable' ad immediately after the playback completes (not the game you wanted to play), then after that is done forcing the player to remain on the 'download now' pre-store page for a further 30 s and even moving the exit 'X' around the screen, triggering the player to pull up the store unintentionally. This increase of the player ad journey from a comfortable 30 s to an uncomfortable 90–120 s has a very poor impact on player retention, which is something the player blames on the game, rather than the ad network, who are arguably profiting from this behaviour at the cost of the developer. Fortunately, at the time of writing, most ad networks are willing to change these parameters, but only when asked directly.

- **Playable Ads**: This format is a variation of the Rewarded Ad, where the player is invited to play a simplified version of the advertised game. This can be quite effective for install purposes but has the unfortunate effect of breaking player immersion, asking to play a different game than was desired and damaging retention as a result.

- **Audio Ads**: This is an ad format which, instead of playing a video, plays a radio-style audio ad, often brand based, but increasingly also including games. The advantage is that the player can continue with the game experience unimpeded and get the benefit of the reward as long as their volume is set at an appropriate level. Games should ensure that the provider they work with has tools to ensure that the player can actually hear the ad, or it will inevitably undermine player engagement.

- **Offer Wall**: This is an older form of advertising that has had a resurgence at the time of writing. Players are presented with actions which they are asked to complete in return for benefits in-game (or potentially real-world discounts or such). These include downloading an app and using it for a period of time or signing up to a streaming service account. They require quite a lot of effort for the player to complete and can take the player away from the game experience, but they can be highly profitable, and some players really appreciate them.

Different players will react differently to each of these ad formats. It is important not to let personal bias overly impact the choices of revenue tools used in a game. When deciding if and how to leverage advertising, focus on the feel of the player experience being created, how the application of ads (or indeed any monetisation) delivers value to the player and what is the resulting impact on in-game flow as well as long-term player retention. At the same time, it is important to remember there is always the option to take a more advanced approach in the game design by modifying the player experience dynamically to allow different options, reflecting the different appetites for ads and monetisation methods from different cohorts of players.

If it is not clear, the author is generally positive about the use of ad monetisation methods in games, especially In-World and Rewarded Ads. This is no doubt in part from being the original evangelist for Unity Ads as well as being an advisor for AudioMob, which offers audio-based ads. However, not all games suit this form of monetisation, and each use of an ad has to balance the revenue impact, contribution to the player's engagement with the commercial elements of the game against the impact on the long-term retention of a player – because you cannot control what is shown by the ad company and so cannot guarantee a positive player experience.

Money as a Form of Exchange

The ultimate commercial exchange, of course, comes in the form of real-money transactions, but even here there is much for the designer to consider. Kotler wrote about the role of price as one of the four principles factors in marketing theory alongside Product, Place, and Promotion. The form and focus of payment methods have more consequence than a simple value transaction and can have specific functional and psychological implications. The forms of monetary transaction include:

- **Pay Upfront**: A lot of games traditionally had a packaged upfront price, referred to as 'Paid' or 'Premium' games as a shorthand. These require a commitment from the customer based on their prior knowledge, expectations of delight, and of course significant motivation to act now (e.g. through FOMO). All of that positive momentum has to exceed the combined friction against such a purchase from purchase anxiety from a gap in our information, genuine opportunity cost and substitution goods, and fundamental inertia due to all the other pressures and priorities players experience in their ordinary life. Add to that any friction that occurs in the purchase experience, from initial awareness to building internal desire, ability to select the item, and the payment process itself. All of these elements form potential barriers to purchase. It is what is commonly referred to as a 'Paywall.' And remember, at the point of purchase, the player doesn't yet know whether they like the game!

- **Trial Offer**: Another approach is the 'Trial' version of a game. The player gets access for the first few minutes or sections of a game before they need to pay. This was especially common in the era of physical distribution, where PC magazines would offer discs with free trials of new games. The idea being, if the player enjoyed the game, that would make them more likely to purchase. However, this was not always the case. One classic example was the game Wargasm,[2] developed in the UK, which presented one of the first shooter games where you could alternate between the soldier, the tank, and a helicopter. It predated games like Battlefield 1942 by four years. The game was available on most UK PC magazines and was a recommended game to play on British Telecom's Wireplay Online gaming service. This was one of the most exciting games to play at the time, alongside

Quake 2, Unreal, and Counterstrike. However, players didn't go out and buy the game on mass despite the positive reactions, as the demo provided enough value without needing to spend any money. Despite this observation, the designer, Martin Kendrick, years later informed me that the actual reason for the commercial failure of Wargasm was that the game's name wasn't considered acceptable in the USA. On the wider point of the issues related to trial versions of games, there was a review of titles on Xbox where the game had Trail offers, comparing this with games that instead offered a Trailer or both a Trailer and Trial. Counterintuitively, games offering just a Trailer were generally more successful than those which offered a Trial or both. Only games which offered neither were less successful. The ultimate problem with a Trial Offer is that not only does the experience have to be good, it also has to set up enough anticipation that leaves the player craving more so they will cross that paywall. Trailers allow a player to imagine what the game could be, but a trial leaves no such space for imagination, and the initial experience always requires a player to endure the initial learning process without having already committed to the purchase.

- **Pay in Game**: Increasingly, games are free at the point of access (hence Free-To-Play), removing the initial paywall barrier. There are still barriers related to effort, friction, trust in the game, expectation of quality, fear of being 'manipulated', etc. However, players don't usually pay for playing the core game, but for elements which augment that experience. Good designs avoid creating crunch points that force a payment decision but will communicate meaningful value propositions that satisfy some underlying requirement. That does include experiences which 'frustrate' progress where the player's effort can be readily eased and sped up following an indirect real-money transaction of some kind. These 'In-App Purchases' should be accessed from in-game store rather than occurring in play to avoid any confusion, and on most platforms, there is a second layer of confirmation within the platform's interface to ensure clarity that the transaction is for real money rather than for soft or hard currency. Generally, it is good practice to further isolate real money transactions to specific types of goods or purchases, such as high-value bundles, VIP or Battle pass offers, and exclusive cosmetic items.

- **Subscription**: Reoccurring payments are incredibly valuable for game teams as they deliver longer-term predictable returns and cement even longer-term retention amongst players. As such their impact on a game can be much greater than the price itself conveys. However, there are some significant risks if the implications are not considered fully. First, the initial decision to sign up for a subscription can be a considerable friction point for many players. Just like any paywall, the anticipation, reason to act, and overall value proposition need to be extremely compelling. Once the player has made the decision and subscribed, if the game does not sustain that overwhelming sense of value, frustration may inevitably grow. Therefore, whilst subscribers will often exhibit significant inertia, sustaining payments long beyond the point the player is collecting the value, when they leave, there is the risk of considerable reputational damage. There is also another darker side to a subscription, the temptation to make the offer 'all you can eat,' in other words, the player makes one payment and gets everything. This sounds like a great deal for the player, but it too often ends up being a major issue for both the player and the game team, because a game (or indeed any service) that has a fixed subscription and no upsell will struggle to invest in innovation and risks getting stale and uncompetitive. Justification for innovation requires funding, and funding is only forthcoming from an increase in revenues. If a game can't sell more things to the very audience who has shown their willingness to invest in the game, it is losing a massive opportunity to build a better playing experience. If a game has to increase the subscription price, even if reasonable, it forces a widespread risk of churn. The game's potential revenue is capped by a subscription, capping our ability to make new investments in design beyond the minimum required. Subscription without upsell equals death.

- **External Webstore**: Many major games create Direct-to-Consumer experiences, often via the web, offering a range of commercial items to complement the standard store experience. This can include loyalty programmes, in-app items, or unique digital goods, including short content media or even physical products such as branded merchandise from t-shirts to figurines. In Playtika's Q3 2024 financial report, they showed 28% of their revenue coming from D2C revenues.[3] Most platforms originally had constraints which permitted the game teams from directly 'sign-posting' to alternative stores. However, on April 30th, U.S. District Judge Yvonne Gonzalez Rogers in Oakland ruled that Apple failed to comply with her prior injunction order, which was imposed in an antitrust lawsuit brought by "Fortnite" maker Epic Games.[4] In the EU, similar judgments are expected following the introduction of the Digital Markets Act from the EU, with similar rulings expected from other legislative bodies around the world, signalling an end to such anti-steering rules that appear to be restricting competition and consumer choice. Meta and Apple are appealing these and other related regulations.[5] The platforms, however, do allow users to consume content, such as Netflix and Amazon Kindle Books, on their devices, even though the purchases are not made within the platform. The major platforms such as Apple, Google, and Steam take a significant percentage of retail transactions, at the time typically 30% (although there are variations). This means that there is often a significant improvement in profitability for D2C sales if designed carefully.

- **Crowd Funding**: The rise of Kickstarter and similar platforms in the 2010s was a fantastic innovation which unlocked the potential for indie games to raise awareness and some degree of development funding. This generally was a form of Pay Upfront, but on a more speculative basis. It represents a community's belief in the authenticity and ambition of the project and the team behind it. There is an understanding that not all such funded games will be a success, most will not. But it allows players to feel part of a journey and able to invest in the art of games. However, it is also arguably the most work for the least money possible. Nonetheless it can be very rewarding for the lucky and those teams which have built a loyal paying following. Crowdfunding has proven to be a path for some games which may otherwise have been impossible to make happen using traditional funding models; but only when backed by an active community. It is included here as a form of exchange simply to make the point that even fundraising methods like this are, in fact, a transaction exchange for Utility in your game. In this case, the social capital is in being part of a community that does not just play a game, but who are also critical to the realisation of the game itself.

- **Secondary Market**: The ability for players to take the items they have unlocked through play, or indeed paid for, and then sell them to someone else is, and has always been, a thorny subject, from selling old board games or collections of Magic: The Gathering cards. The author owned a magic card called a Mox Ruby from the original release around 1993. The card was banned from competitive play very early, and he sold it in 1996 for around £60. That same card is worth at the time of writing over $10,000 (around £8,500). This is, of course, the exception, but the sale of MMO accounts, game items, Counter-strike skins, and almost every other kind of game element is common.

The secondary market can be rife with fraud and risk,[6] but where legitimately conducted, it does serve to enhance the base value of items in a game, and even the value of the game itself. There have been many efforts to legitimise the approach from physical retail through computer exchange shops to eBay. However, this is often at the frustration of developers and publishers, not least as whilst the presence of the secondary market probably helps prop up increases in retail pricing, the developers and publishers do not get any direct share. The Blockchain scene has tried to tap into this type of market using cryptography. In particular, in the form of Non-Fungible Tokens[7] and 'Smart Contracts' which allow specific rules and behaviours to be applied to these unique digital assets. However, there is no process to authenticate the person minting (creating the NFT) itself, so the methodology remains as open to fraud and misuse as any other.

- **Grey Markets and Piracy**: Players will ever prefer lower prices, especially FREE. After all, 'What harm is there?' when I reset my region, use a VPN, or even get a cracked version of a game. The answers to this are way too often overly simplistic. Games that offer local country pricing are either attempting to identify a price for the game which more accurately matches the local audience, or more commonly reflecting the requirements of the local platform or legal context. When someone imports from cheaper regions and sells in more expensive ones, this is referred to as the 'Grey Market' – not necessarily illegal but undermining the principles of sale (and grabbing a share of profits along the way). Where this is the player directly (e.g. via change of region on a region-locked platform or use of VPN), they are likely to be in breach of the terms of service and potentially open themselves to a risk of poor performance or even cyber insecurity. However, the effect of these approaches means that more people find out about and enjoy the game – albeit for free, but this has on rare occasions led to significant increases in revenues through legitimate channels. This can, however, devastate game teams where the game uses a 'Pay Upfront' business model. All this being said, some level of Grey Market and Piracy around your game is inevitable and, according to a report by Akamai in 2024, is on the increase[8] especially when a game is successful. There will always be people looking to capitalise on an opportunity. But rather than solely blaming the players, consider what issues in the game's distribution and revenue strategy are causing this to be a problem and what can be done to turn that to the game's favour. This can be in terms of brand development, communications, guerrilla marketing, etc. It can also act as a reason to rethink your business model. For example, where your business model is 'Pay-In-Game', grey markets and Piracy are essentially just forms of distribution. Freemium games benefit when more people play, as long as the access to revenue instruments continues to work. If the game relied on Config, Advertising, In-Game Retail, and Content servers to function, not just the client build, it is possible to preserve the player experience. However, be aware that whilst illegal distribution may potentially be nullified by Free-To-Play models, other attempts to exploit these games have arisen clients with fraud, phishing, and hacking rising to near epidemic levels. This can focus on extracting information about your players, including their private information, using Bots or "Structured Query Language injections" intended to access information on your databases that weren't intended for display. The cyber-attacks can even be more overt, for example, if a criminal can fake being the source of your game, they can modify a build to point to a different server. They could attempt to intercept your servers in a 'Man-In-The-Middle'[9] attack – a kind of hijacking of the communications. Developers should have sensible cyber security hygiene, including the use of secure public/private key messaging between the client and server, never 'trusting' the client using 'Hash checksum' algorithms which ensure that the data has not been altered, and encrypting data – never use human-readable data that could be intercepted.

So far, we have explored the functional methods real money can affect a game and some of the consequences of the way these operate. However, the use of real money as a form of exchange does more than simply provide a transaction process. Pricing communicates additional information about a game or game item based on the context. It tells us something about the relative positioning of the retail item, its attributed value, sets an expectation of quality, and helps communicate a sense of status that the item may confirm, either on the developer or the player.

Philip Kotler[10] argued that price was the most important factor in the market and emphasised the psychological aspects involved in pricing strategies. Most famously, he described a Product Pricing matrix, which explores the role of price setting against quality.

FIGURE 8.1 Kotler's model for Pricing strategy.

- **Premium**: High-Quality Goods charged at a high price – often exclusive or limited-run specialists of luxury items. Note this is the original meaning of the term and should really only be applied to select pay-upfront games but equally can be used to describe select in-app purchases in games such as an exclusive high-quality character skin.

- **Economy**: Low-Quality Goods charged at a low price – often high-volume transaction commodity items

- **Value**: Items offered at a lower price than the expected quality of those items are seen as a high-value good. Making it about the relative status of expected costs versus expected quality rather than any absolute sense of value.

- **Rip-off**: Items where the quality falls below the level expected for the price, create negative experiences, and this can be highly problematic for the developer. But remember this is again about the relative expected costs versus expected quality.

When considering how this affects games, particularly Pay-Upfront PC or Console games, there are many factors which affect these expectations of value. What is the right price for your game may be boosted by whether you are seen as a AAA or III (Triple I – indie) team as being above the levels expected from more mid-range or less experienced developers. The associated trust that your brand conveys is part of that, but so does the quality of delivery in terms of art assets, game feel, and narrative experience implied by the screenshot, trailers, and other marketing materials. The duration of play can further affect that expectation, but it is not always a direct correlation. The game Journey is known for its exceptional quality but actually is around just 2 hours of playtime. That does not undermine the experience or its perceived value but does place the game into a category which frames pricing expectations for the audience based on platform norms.

The exact same logic exists in Free-To-Play games but the contextual triggers used to understand the value proposition are more usually from within that game itself. Our willingness to spend is less about the comparison of costs from other games, but from the comparative value of each item in the game and what they deliver in terms of experience and social capital value. Our framing in this context is often limited to what proportion of disposable income the player is willing to commit to that game as a whole, rather than just the comparison of one IAP item with another.

Additionally, as part of the value proposition aspects of using money for exchange, designers need to consider how they are packaging each offer.

- **Hygiene Bundle**: A collection of assets that is expected to be available in the store of basic currencies or resources. This usually has multiple price points to communicate economies of scale with larger purchases. For example, a fixed number of coins that includes a significant discount at each higher volume/price presented. The use of the term hygiene[11] relates to these bundles commonly being used to present the 'base' level value and items which are expected as necessary, but generally they are rarely intrinsically satisfying, mostly just used to ease up transactions in the game.

- **Featured Bundle**: More complex versions of bundles that usually include some featured or 'Chase' item that has a level of exclusivity or quality status, commonly tied into the current seasonal activity. There will usually be a variety of items with the contents sometimes curated to motivate a specific cohort of players (e.g. new starters or regular spenders) and may even promote a specific style of play or engage with the game. A Starter bundle's focus would be to help the new player make significant early progress, then accelerate their learning process to engage deeply with the game. A Premium bundle may be more about providing the practical assets which support the smooth, optimised playing experience for longer-term committed paying players.

- **Offer**: This is commonly applied to specific bundles but can be applied to individual items as well. Essentially, it refers to some kind of time-limited benefit above the normal, such as discounts, bonus points, "Buy One Get One Free," bonus XP for a period after purchase, or even removal of ads for a period. Offers, in general, mean that the store takes less money for the overall transaction in order to either increase the likelihood of the player making the transaction or increase the new spend that would otherwise have occurred. Either way, the overall value exchange becomes more attractive. The author would not recommend shop-wide offers after managing one of the earliest mobile carrier game stores, he tried a 30% off all games offer.

This achieved a 300% monthly revenue at the time – but subsequently, the audience spend dropped to just 50% of the former levels for the three months after the sale. The net benefit to the store being nil. Whilst this is probably an exceptional situation, more selective store management will be generally more effective than blanket offers.

- **Value Setting**: Sometimes the price that is set is to establish the perceived value of an item, rather than it being a true reflection of supply, demand, and quality. This can be particularly relevant on highly sales-driven platforms depending on the impact on demand when the price is reduced (Price elasticity). Setting a higher price on your premium game, knowing that you will actively be using platform sales to discount the game, may be important to help preserve the revenues derived at higher levels of discount, depending on the volume of players who take up that offer. Over time the sale will continue to drive volumes of sales, but the fact of the reduced price may have more impact on volume than the specific price itself. Sometimes it's a tough call for a developer to decide if they reduce their overall price or instead focus on applying greater discounts during sales as the value setting of the base price and the absolute discount price may be making the impact on revenue greater in real terms.

- **Dummy Pricing**: A variety of Value Setting, but where there is little or no intent to actually sell an item at the Dummy level. This is not about trying to make players feel like Dummies!! No, it's about having pricing packages which are about communicating the value of other packages. Imagine offering 100 Coins for $4.99 and 100 Gems for $6.99 but 100 Coins and 100 Gems for $6.99. The 100 Gems alone price is a dummy price. It's attempting to communicate the idea that 100 Gems are more valuable than Coins and yet there is a package which has both for that same price. However, this approach should be used with caution as it can easily be seen as manipulative and damage the trust players have for in-game and ultimately undermines the overall value proposition; plus it just feels sleazy. It is however important to understand Dummy pricing can be used to guide players to more readily understand the core value.

- **Loss Leader**: Loss leaders are used in physical retail regularly, and perfected by supermarkets. They are goods offered at a super low price, often less than they cost to acquire. These are often items that might otherwise be considered hygiene factors (low motivation), but the proposition value is so overblown that the customer will make a special trip to go into the store – where they will be presented with other items that they need, so they may as well buy here. In games, as these are digital assets which don't lead to a direct financial loss (as duplicating the items costs nothing but bytes), this means offering exceptional value, a cost, perhaps even for free – everyone's favourite price. These offers inspire reciprocation (discussed below) and can give a reason for the player to revisit the shop regularly, engage with a game mode, or take part in some other part of the playing experience which itself supports player engagement and retention.

- **Battle/Season/VIP**: Longer-term compounding experiences such as a Battlepass or Season Pass come in a variety of forms but generally include a range of assets, challenges, or experiences that are unlocked alongside the active period. These tend to be collections of high value that can be charged for a significant cost or as part of a subscription offer. The best examples of this deliver a range of soft and hard currencies, resources in return for completing specific in-game actions – often missions or challenges. They are also combined with 'Chase items' which are high-quality, time-limited (often seasonally) specific items e.g. unique characters, weapons, upgrades, or some form of cosmetics. These items usually convey significant status for players to demonstrate their commitment (and belonging) to the game. In the end, what makes these work is where both Free and Paid (or VIP) players can benefit; and where the most important factor is the more they play, the more they get. If Free players work hard enough, they should be able to unlock any of the associated 'Chase' items but not all. On the other hand, whilst a VIP player can in principle unlock everything in the Pass, to achieve that they also have to play everything! Smart packaging for Passes can create exceptional value for both free players and paying VIPs without undermining the integrity of the game balance, and they can eliminate the 'nickel and dime'ing' of players. Making purchase decisions simpler, meaningful, and something players can look back on positively. Sadly, this has not always been the case. When looking at subscription, one important aspect is to consider further 'Upsell' options such as allowing paying players to purchase items they failed to unlock in the previous seasonal event as a 'catch-up' offer. Additionally, why not offer Free players the chance to convert their incomplete rewards into a Hard Currency that after e.g. three seasons can be used to exchange for a VIP package – without having to spend any real money. This provides a way to increase their engagement and significantly increase the potential that they convert to spend later.

- **Referral**: Another packaging method, this is more about motivating players to engage with others to invite their friends to also play the game. The option to exchange virtual goods and other playing benefits is for players who take the time to recommend the game and help acquire new users. This can be extremely effective but also comes at a risk of burning out your audience. Facebook social games had an extraordinary explosion from 2007, but that market collapsed after just a few years (partly due to the increasing convenience of mobile games). One of the key factors was that this form of referral was at an epidemic level and essentially felt like selling personal social connections for paltry in-game resources. Social trading within guilds or clans has some similar qualities in that players are rewarded for engaging in social transactions, however, these are generally existing players and, as such, less complicated in terms of ethical engagement.

- **Reciprocation**: Humans, as social creatures, want to respond to like-with-like. If a person receives a gift from a person (or service), they will often feel better reciprocating by making a purchase. This intrinsically feels good and makes it easier to see the transaction as not just one-sided. Packaging some transactions with this in mind can be a powerful way to frame other forms of exchange. This is a general phenomenon, and in many industries, marketing teams use this psychological method. However, it is one which can easily be misused. If our design leverages Reciprocation, it must be done carefully, walking a thin ethical line. Creating a positive emotional reaction from offering samples, like Tortilla Chips in a Tex-Mex restaurant[12] makes the customer feel good, special even if they aren't used to it, and upsetting for regulars if withheld. The customer is supposed to be more likely to order more expensive meal combinations as a direct consequence, even if it makes them less likely to finish that meal. That is also deliberate, as it makes it easier to offer more economic value plates (hence more profit); and full/happy customers are more likely to return. Games which seed 'Free Daily' items are attempting something similar, reinforcing reasons for a free player to check out the store, as well as building a habitual behaviour that reinforces a connection with that player, perhaps even a mild sense of obligation to invest back in the game. However, not all reciprocation is balanced. Insurance companies have a long history of offering a 'Free Pen' or 'Alarm clock' or some other cheap 'tat' alongside the customer signing up for an expensive policy. What this demonstrates, and indeed so does the Tortilla Chip example, is that the value of what is offered need not be equal to the expected reciprocation. It is important to be careful that the Player's sense of obligation does not become manipulative, or players will look back on their purchase decisions and their long-term engagement be harmed.

There is one final aspect of exchange that should also be considered. How to fulfil the anticipation that the player expects from the purchase (or rewards) they just unlocked in the game. Key to this is unboxing.

UNBOXING

The post-purchase experience is incredibly important and directly affects the sense of satisfaction. We know this from regular everyday transactions, think about how a fast-food server handing over the meal can impact our feelings about the food. The period from when the player completes the purchase to their first experience of the product is an opportunity to communicate, reinforce, and foreshadow reasons for the player to both enjoy the Utility of what they have acquired and to be open to making future purchases. There are a number of factors that should be considered, including:

- **Signalling**: The act of unlocking a purchase is a moment to signal to the player that the transaction has completed and that they now possess the 'Utility' they were expecting. Failing to confirm leaves the consumer confused and often unnecessarily frustrated. This moment can deliver more than a cold, simple confirmation; it can help reinforce player engagement with the game overall. If the player feels special, powerful, and that they have received some commensurate status benefits, this will positively impact their attitude about the game. Think about how pleasurable it is to enjoy the physical extraction of a mobile phone from the box it came in. Apple transformed the value perception of their devices arguably as much by how pleasurable it is to open the box as by the device inside and its integrated UX. In games, it is also important that when a player exchanges their hard-earned "soft," "hard," or real money currency, they feel they are getting something that matches their expectation of value. Beyond value exchange, it is also essential to clearly communicate to the player how they actually benefit from that Utility in play. Too often, game purchases bury the actual functional benefit behind layers of the User Experience (UX) or just assume that the player will notice the stat changes (or whatever that item offers). It is important to ensure that the (UX) flow actively helps to communicate how the new Utility item works. This does not necessarily mean that an explosive confetti animation or arduous tutorial flow has to happen every time a purchase is made or a reward unlocked. Over-the-top signalling, especially where it creates friction for the player to be able to get back into the experience can in itself be harmful to retention and even cheapen the experience. Different players at different stages in their lifecycle (experience in the game) need different types of signalling.

- **Delayed Gratification:** Holding back on the delivery, by creating some space between the moment of transaction and the realisation of that Utility can be harnessed in the reveal process to intensify the satisfaction. Take a 'Treasure Chest' reward object. There may be some uncertainty over the details of what it contains, perhaps because the contents are scaled to your performance in the session. Taking time to reveal those results, building tension through that delay intensifies the experience and makes a big deal of the results. Anticipation is magnified when we know the results of our actions are recorded but we have yet to see that communicated. This is the reason every TV gameshow host will wait a ridiculous amount of time to tell the contestants (and audience) the result. It creates space to speculate about the results and the associated rewards that this might deliver. This intensifies the player's emotional experience and heightens their satisfaction from the process. But where this becomes overly used, adds too much delay or becomes tedious, especially where the results don't have sufficient variety, 'incomplete information' or otherwise fail to create meaningful suspense. Sometimes it can just become too much effort and players will churn.

- **Loot Crates:** We can't talk about 'Delayed Gratification' without mentioning the much-maligned (and too often misused) 'Loot Crates.' These collections of randomised rewards have in some locations, notably Belgium and The Netherlands, been banned when used as purchasable items. This follows poor designs and bad actors using manipulative practices that have created accusations that they mirror gambling-like behaviour. The UK has sought consultation and, at the time of writing, this remains 'Under Review.'[13] The concerns are mostly focused on a couple of core questions.

First, there is the random uncertainty of the value of the contents, and whether this constitutes the definition of a stake which can later be cashed out. Secondly, the transparency of information about the contents and the ability of that player to keep track of their associated spending. These issues are amplified by concerns over the use of games by children and other vulnerable people. There are methods to alleviate these issues and indeed these approaches are already required by law in several jurisdictions. In the United Kingdom, these have been outlined in the Advertising Standards Associations 2021 "Guidance on Advertising in-game purchases."[14] This requires designs to ensure that the contents of the bundle are clearly communicated; that there is no undue pressure contained in the promotion of these items; that the payout does not vary with multiple purchases; etc. Additionally, where players are unable to exchange or 'cash out' their unwanted items, we can also reduce the negative non-play-related motivations. There are valid revenue opportunities when offering 'loot crate' like items, and players often desire them. However, we have to understand (and mitigate) the risk that speculation becomes a more significant motivator than play. It is this speculative element that can magnify the risk, especially for vulnerable players who may not have the capacity to appreciate the consequences. Ethical monetisation does not mean ignoring the attractive qualities that randomised rewards offer players; but we need to treat the process with care, communicate effectively, and especially respect vulnerable players. Good practice means we authentically focus on the value for gameplay, pay attention to possible unintended consequences, and ultimately respect our players over the long term.

- **Visibility**: When players acquire new goods, there is value in their being able to see that item immediately in context and to be able to put it to use. This is not the signalling process described above, this is more about players providing context for the purchased Utility alongside other elements of the game, such as unlocked sections of the world or other previously purchased items. This can be used to communicate power, status, or functional benefits, but it can also show acquisition history in a way that conveys a sense that those prior transactions had purpose and sustained value. This is not something that is useful or even realistic for every game, especially for a game which has a large number of consumable items or where each new item intentionally replaces (sinks) the previous, however, it can be a powerful way for players to show status and engagement.

- **Foreshadowing**: Showing players what they can unlock through exchange/purchase in the near future can be very motivational, tapping into collecting behaviour but there are limits. Such items need to feel attainable with a reasonable level of effort, and be intrinsically attractive; e.g. this season there are a number of desirable 'chase items.' The game can present them with clear information or use ambiguity to make them more enticing, but it has to be clear that the player has not yet acquired them. For example, it is common that such items are presented as 'unfilled' or blank spaces for the player to fill – just like a collectable sticker book. Other options can also be applied to communicate such future value. The items can be mentioned in narrative, art, trailers, or even offered as trial experiences. Creating a 'legend' or intrinsic game lore context for aspirational items can help communicate the perception of value, especially when presented in contrast with the items the player has already acquired.

- **Replacement vs. Collection**: New items often simply functionally replace existing inventory items. The player gets a better sword which replaces the previous one. The player unlocks a faster car. There is no benefit to the old car, indeed, we never see it again. This approach to new items has the benefit of providing an immediate 'Sink,' removing the effort to unlock the previous item from the economy, and usually this also resets any upgrade paths with this new item. However, it does create a linear path for items and generally means the game both needs more volume of content assets, with less personal connection to those items, in order to have longer-term progression. Items often ends up just become progression markers rather than having any inherent value or reflecting any sense of choice or autonomy. The alternative is to create a collection of that type of asset, whether they are heroes, weapons, cars, etc. This requires that each item of the collection type has some unique features which can still offer value even where there are 'better' items. Combining the use of secondary variables and the logic within 'Scissors-Paper-Stone' can be extremely useful. A "Fire" sword will have more useful effects against an Earth-equipped opponent than a water-based elemental weapon. If a tournament restricts access to players with only Tier 3 weapons, it will be useful for the player to be able to dust off one of their old favourite weapons. Taking the Collection mindset translates the process of acquiring new items into a strategic opportunity for the player.

- **Degradation and Prestige**: Whilst not really an unboxing element, it seems logical to outline another aspect related to the use of acquired items which is not necessarily part of the core experience but relates to commercial exchange. When players use an item in some games, like swords in "The Legend of Zelda: Breath of the Wild,"[15] they degrade in quality. Wear and tear, when established as a fundamental principle of play, can add to the strategic experience. This makes the choice of which items (especially where there is a collection mechanic) very meaningful. Degraded items often can be refreshed through crafting and consumable items or may be exchanged for resources themselves, e.g. sold for gold or broken down for Iron, Wood, or Hide. The mechanism provides a superb method to sink resources and effort into maintaining your equipment, providing an engaging, relaxing variant of play. Getting this right, however, can be complicated. Crafting and repairing are available in The Elder Scrolls V: Skyrim[16] but the economy is so overblown that there rarely is any benefit to putting in the time for that crafting. Degrading items as a concept affects the tone of the game and tends to have a negative resonance as you are taking things away from the player. This works brilliantly in a game like The Long Dark[17] but it can be a reason for players to churn in other games. This can be addressed in exactly the same way as World of Warcraft approached their "Rested" bonus XP method, just by turning the language on its head. Talking about temporary benefits from 'buffing' your items rather than just breaking the items. There is a variant of this approach used in idle games (and across other genres) known as 'Prestige.' With this approach, the player opts to reset an item that has reached its current maximum progression back to a basic level so it can be upgraded all over again. Why would a player do that? Well, in practice it means they get to play again in a pattern that fits our preferred style (and not constantly harder). They also usually get both a status benefit and some mechanical advantage, including a faster generation of coins, gold, XPs, etc. Prestige systems allow players to reset their progress in return for new rewards or challenges. This gives highly engaged players a reason to continue playing even after reaching the "endgame." These are also great systems for designers who want to find positive ways for players to 'sink' resources and reset or reframe player experience.

What we have tried to express in this section is that there is more to the process of an exchange in a game than whether the player is choosing to invest just time or money, as well as how much. There are consequences and advantages to building an engaging player experience when we pay attention to the method, the packaging, and even the unboxing of the results of that exchange.

EXCHANGE AS FRICTION

Every interaction which takes the player out of their immersion will have an impact on their engagement and hence retention. Each player will have a certain level of tolerance for such interruptions, and indeed at different stages of play they may even welcome interruptions, or at least such interruptions may avoid the player from burning out by playing too intensely.

Factors which affect this include the degree and positioning of the offer or blocking behaviour but also the complexity of the decision required or steps necessary to complete the exchange path.

- **Hot Cold Empathy Gap**: As we discussed in *Chapter 4 "Why Do We Play? (And Pay?)"* George F. Loewenstein showed that human understanding is "state-dependent" and a consequence of that is that the decision-making process is affected by the intensity of the emotional state the individual is in when presented with such choices. If a player is in an intense playing session and a pop-up is presented which asked them to spend money, such as with the old arcade games like Gauntlet[18] needing another 100 Yen, Quarter or 50 pence piece if you want to carry on playing, but you only have 10, no 9, no 8 s to put the coin in the slot. That was extremely compelling and in 1987 on the last day of the season at Butlins Skegness, the author and three fellow waiters spent what felt like several hours playing that game with holiday-maker guests constantly throwing in more coins for us to continue. No one was thinking about the purchase decision, opportunity costs, or anything other than the spectacle of a group of players trying to finish the game together. Whilst time pressure itself is one of the behaviours prohibited today, this experience demonstrates the fully encompassing 'blindspot' that players can find themselves in. I have no regrets over that experience, it was a moment I will delight in forever even though I have not seen any of those people since. But we have all been in the situation where we deeply regret the impact of a heated spending moment. Once the player eventually stops, they can quickly regret their choices and once in the 'cold' rational state they simply can't put themselves in the mindset they were in when they made those decisions. Instead, they will either try to retrospectively rationalise it or they will end up angry and frustrated, feeling cheated by the game. That can lead to them choosing "never to do that again" at least until the next time. If you put purchase decisions in the middle of a flow, it can become manipulative and each time players are pushed under these conditions, there is a significant cumulative impact on our trust and frustration. Ethical purchasing processes should always present players with an opportunity to reflect on their choices reasonably; with clean breaks from the flow.

- **Relief vs.s Frustration**: Some game revenue models (especially on mobile) have focused on creating some barrier or interruption to progress. The use of energy or health forces an end to the current session of play, unless the player tops up that subsistence resource.

This doesn't even have to be subtle. Players may have an (interstitial) advert forced on them and have to experience (or potentially skip) it in order to return to play. Every time this happens, it is immediately frustrating and can create a reason to churn. Some games will allow the player to pay to remove these ads, something players often state that they want. However, this can be quite unsatisfactory because at the core the player is simply playing to remove a barrier to play, rather than gaining a specific positive Utility and may lead to them burning out as there is no competing method to regulate the flow of play and create moments to break out. This is because energy and health often have intrinsic functions that help manage progression and player session engagement, they can force a change of pace to bring a player back into the 'Relief' from 'Tension,' hence avoiding the burnout. That also means that they help keep players attention for longer and even provide reasons to return later. Too much intensity of interaction creates longer time-sinks and mental effort, which can become overly demanding. A surprising example of the benefits of interstitial ads came when you reviewed how players engaged with Hyper-Casual games, especially at the peak of that market just prior to COVID. These very simple, short-form titles have an intense loop of activity which is inherently compelling. The placement of an interstitial ad ends up providing a short, forced break from that intensity and a moment of relief before the player dives into the next round. These principles apply more generally, but in games with longer-term engagement it's helpful to consider gameplay alternatives (not just ads) to provide those breaks or changes in pace. Think about how Relief and Frustration affect the players' motivation and attention, not just in play, but also between sessions to reduce the fatigue that comes from both unhelpful and restful interruptions. However, make no mistake, whilst ads and similar interruption techniques can have a positive impact on engagement and retention, they have to be considered holistically in terms of their impact on long-term retention.

• **Path to Utility**: The effort that a player has to take from awareness of an offer, time taken to become interested, and even design is a step-by-step process. It is rarely instantaneous, and each evolution towards assessing the desirability of an exchange requires the player to digest what there is to anticipate, fear missing out, and what there is to gain in terms of power or status. Even then, the process requires that the player understands how to make the exchange and has reason to act at that point. Anything which gets in the way of that process increases the frustration and anxiety involved. It is essential for the player to be able to immediately understand what they are choosing, why they benefit, and exactly what they need to do and expect from the results. However, too often, the process to go from gameplay to see an item to purchase, whether that requires real money or in-game currency, where I can obtain it, and how I get to use it is often obfuscated. This is where packaging and unboxing principles become super important. However, it is also valuable to ensure that you consider factors where you have less control, such as how the platform store operates, what happens in the UX if there is an issue with payment methods, or if the ad platforms you work with are unable to provide the fill-rate levels you need and, as such, cannot deliver a suitable ad. If an ad network (as has been the case at the time of writing) unfairly increases the duration of the ad, forces a secondary playable experience, and holds the player longer than necessary on the store link, perhaps by moving the close button, all this will create a greatly increased level of frustration. Players at different life stages are going to have a different tolerance for barriers and delays caused by issues in the path to Utility.

Interview

Ad-based monetisation has long been a cornerstone of mobile gaming, offering developers an alternative revenue stream to in-app purchases. However, the complexity of ad networks, demand-side platforms (DSPs), and player segmentation often leaves developers struggling to optimise their monetisation strategies. Felix Braberg,[19] an ad monetisation expert with over eight years of experience, breaks down the intricacies of this system and provides insights into how game developers can maximise revenue while maintaining a positive player experience.

The rise of mobile gaming was accompanied by a significant challenge: discoverability. With millions of apps flooding the App Store and Google Play, developers needed a way to attract users efficiently. Braberg recounts how this problem led to the emergence of mobile ad networks:

> One of the things that went horribly wrong when the app stores launched was actually discoverability. How do you actually build a company on the app store? And basically, how do you get users?

Google's acquisition of AdMob in 2009 marked a turning point, introducing the concept of ads inside applications as a primary mechanism for user acquisition. Today, approximately 45%–50% of app downloads come from paid sources, underscoring the dominance of ad monetisation in mobile gaming.

To grasp how ad monetisation works, developers need to understand the roles of DSPs and ad networks. Braberg explains the difference:

> A DSP is something called a demand-side platform. That means that they don't own the actual relationship with the publisher or the game developer, but they buy it on open RTB. Networks, on the other hand, have direct developer relationships and take about 36% from an impression.

In simpler terms, DSPs operate as intermediaries that purchase ad placements programmatically, whereas ad networks establish direct partnerships with developers. This distinction is crucial because it influences the revenue share that developers receive from ad placements.

There are three primary ad formats that drive the majority of ad revenue in mobile gaming:

1. **Banner Ads**: Small ads that typically appear at the top or bottom of the screen.

2. **Interstitial Ads**: Full-screen ads that appear between gameplay segments.

3. **Rewarded Ads**: Opt-in video ads that grant in-game rewards upon completion.

Braberg highlights their respective earnings potential:

> Rewarded ads have the highest eCPM because they're the longest and also show intent. Typically, rewarded eCPMs tend to be around $30 in the U.S. and $15 worldwide. Interstitials are around $15–$20 in the States, while banners are significantly lower at around $1–$3.

Understanding these variations helps developers design their monetisation strategies effectively.

One of the key challenges for developers is maximising ad revenue without negatively impacting player experience. Braberg emphasises that mediation – using multiple ad networks to bid for inventory – ensures high fill rates:

> If you have maybe 10,000 DAU and you set up mediation with five to six networks, you will sell 95% of your inventory. That's no problem.

Fill rate, the percentage of available ad impressions that are successfully filled with an ad, used to be a major concern. However, with modern mediation platforms and real-time bidding, developers can optimise eCPMs and maintain consistent revenue streams.

"Different networks have access to different data that they can use to estimate how much a user is worth. Google uses 94 different factors. Temperature of your location is one of them. So basically, all these things factor into the eCPM," said Braberg.

All these data points profoundly affect how much the advertisers are willing to spend on your game's inventory of course.

"[Platforms look at a] rolling seven day average of what the inventory they see in your app is doing. …how often a click through has happened from their ads in your app; the amount of unique users they can reach, how many impressions have been served to that user before on the day," Braberg states.

However, this is not a static factor, as Braberg further explained, there is the Recency Effect, which also plays an important factor.

So basically, networks assume that if it's the first impression of the day, a user has more attention than if you're serving the 12th impression. It goes down linearly. Usually after five impressions, you start really seeing a per unit cost decrease. …So the only thing you can really do on this is kind of design a game that has a lot of unique users or basically it has a lot of purchasers and that will increase your eCPM, says Braberg.

The removal of IDFA by Apple had profound implications for mobile ad monetisation. Braberg argues that this move was less about privacy and more about market control:

Apple got rid of the IDFA not because of privacy. They more did it because they wanted control and basically shifted people from using third-party networks inside of their app store to charging these themselves and having Apple search ads.

This change has made it more difficult for ad networks to target users effectively, leading to higher user acquisition costs and lower ad revenue for developers. In turn, it has forced developers to explore new strategies, such as segmentation and personalisation, to maintain revenue.

Not all players respond to ads the same way. While some users prefer an ad-free experience, others are willing to watch multiple rewarded ads. Take for example the use of interstitials which is not something we have actively advocated in this book, preferring Rewards Ads. However, Braberg rightly challenged this assumption.

> But Oscar is different from Felix, right? We're different people. And essentially what kind of one of the hottest topic has been recently in ad monetization is segmentation. And that means you show different types of users, different types of experiences. So while Oscar might have that opinion that he doesn't want to annoy the user, Felix who likes interstitials doesn't mind it.

This led Braberg to emphasise how important segmentation is to improving monetisation:

> Segmentation and designing that in a clever way is a better way of thinking about it. For example, if an IAP campaign brought the user, you don't see banners or interstitials for the first three days. But if an ad ROAS user comes in, they see them after the first level.

By analysing user acquisition channels and tailoring ad experiences accordingly, developers can strike a balance between ad revenue and player satisfaction.

Offer walls, though often criticised for their intrusive nature, remain a powerful tool in ad monetisation. They allow players to earn significant in-game rewards by completing high-value tasks, such as downloading apps or signing up for services. Braberg highlights their growing popularity:

> Offer walls have eCPMs between $300 to $600. If you get 12% of a user base to even go to the Offer Wall, that's considered very good.

Beyond offer walls, developers must also contend with increasing ad durations and complex exit mechanisms. Braberg explains how this trend started:

> A genius team at IronSource realized that if they made rewarded ads 50 seconds long and added difficulty with end cards, they would generate more clicks and thus more revenue. Now rewarded ads can be upwards of 120 seconds long.

This escalation underscores the importance of striking a balance between profitability and UX.

The Future of Ad Monetisation in Games

Despite declining eCPMs and rising user acquisition costs, ad monetisation remains a viable revenue stream. Braberg shares his outlook:

> The smartphone and the app store market as a whole is not going anywhere. Until iOS and Android go away for some new thing, ads will be a thing on mobile and they will be extremely effective.

He also suggests that developers should embrace ad monetisation as a core component of their business models rather than treating it as an afterthought:

> The key is that you need to have a lot of users that watch a lot of ads. If done right, rewarded ads don't just generate revenue; they also enhance player engagement.

Ad-based monetisation has evolved from a supplementary revenue stream to a sophisticated system requiring strategic planning. From understanding the nuances of DSPs and ad networks to optimising ad placement and leveraging segmentation, developers must navigate a complex ecosystem to maximise their earnings. By embracing new trends and prioritising UX, game developers can create sustainable revenue models while delivering engaging experiences for players.

NOTES

1 https://www.sciencedirect.com/science/article/pii/S0747563219302602
2 https://en.wikipedia.org/wiki/Wargasm_(video_game)
3 https://www.globenewswire.com/news-release/2024/11/07/2976462/0/en/Playtika-Holding-Corp-Reports-Q3–2024-Financial-Results.html
4 https://www.reuters.com/sustainability/boards-policy-regulation/us-judge-rules-apple-violated-order-reform-app-store-2025-04-30/
5 https://www.reuters.com/legal/transactional/apple-files-legal-challenge-eus-digital-markets-act-2023-11-17/
6 https://rusi.org/explore-our-research/publications/rusi-newsbrief/gaming-system-money-laundering-through-online-games
7 https://en.wikipedia.org/wiki/Non-fungible_token
8 https://securitybrief.co.uk/story/cyber-threats-surge-in-gaming-industry-through-2024#:~:text=According%20to%20recent%20data%20from,%2DService%20(DDoS)%20attacks
9 https://en.wikipedia.org/wiki/Man-in-the-middle_attack
10 https://www.toolshero.com/strategy/kotler-pricing-strategies/
11 https://en.wikipedia.org/wiki/Two-factor_theory

12 https://freakonomics.com/podcast/theres-no-such-thing-as-a-free-appetizer

13 https://commonslibrary.parliament.uk/research-briefings/cbp-8498/#:~:text=They%20often%20appear%20as%20chests,can%20encourage%20children%20to%20gamble

14 https://www.asa.org.uk/resource/guidance-on-advertising-in-game-purchases.html

15 https://en.wikipedia.org/wiki/The_Legend_of_Zelda:_Breath_of_the_Wild

16 https://en.wikipedia.org/wiki/The_Elder_Scrolls_V:_Skyrim

17 https://en.wikipedia.org/wiki/The_Long_Dark

18 https://en.wikipedia.org/wiki/Gauntlet_(1985_video_game)

19 https://www.linkedin.com/in/felix-braberg-7a732b51

CHAPTER 9

Sinks and Sources

DOI: 10.1201/9781003592471-9

WHERE DOES IT COME FROM; WHERE DOES IT GO?

So far, we have looked at the anatomy of a game and the way that games can be described as loops with utility goods which can be exchanged through a variety of mechanisms from play, to view, and, of course commercial instruments.

These are the bones and muscles of the game, but to understand how these all connect, consider where in the game each utility good is acquired (referred to as the Source, Tap, or Faucet) against where they are utilised in the game (a Sink or Drain). In the end, what we call utility still needs to be rooted in the game experience at some level, and for a game to be 'balanced,' these must be designed so we can maintain a dynamic equilibrium.

Sink & Source Analysis is a form of systems thinking designers can use to understand the rate at which players can acquire each good, and how we regulate the scarcity and spending of those items. It is literally about developing a model to help understand supply, demand, and the value of each exchange.

Mapping the Game

We have talked about mapping the game in terms of the Core, Cultural, and Context loops, and we can use that model to think about where each type of utility is acquired or utilised by the player. Different designers and games will look at this differently, so to minimise bias let's explore this generically. In this generic game, there is a core loop where the players invest their 'Time' to play, and in return may have some form of 'Energy' to represent the volume of activity they could complete in a session.

When considering the challenge, they face they commit to a level of energy (the price to enter the scene) in addition to selecting a loadout of shortcuts (which might be consumable power-ups or selection of equipment for that session. The start the Resolution stage of the game by completing the necessary actions and losing health during the process. However, if they also gain some experience points to progress that character, they typically gain more if they are successful than if they fail. Then, at the reward they gain some kind of resources and usually some form of currency to facilitate future progression or crafting.

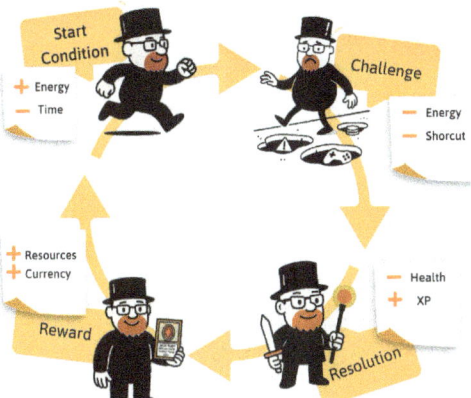

FIGURE 9.1   Core loop.

Taking the same approach for the Context loop, the generic game might allow the player to exchange XP for an increase in level. This example assumes that level progression is key to expressing the 'reason to play,' but different games will see this differently. This example game assumes that progress is represented by the player increasing their relative power through some kind of crafting process which uses up resources and currency. The allocation of those utilities within the Optimisation stage allows players to invest more of their time and generate Shortcuts; the consumable and aspirational goods to improve their relative power. Players then gain a social pay-off in status or narrative rewards in the narrative stage.

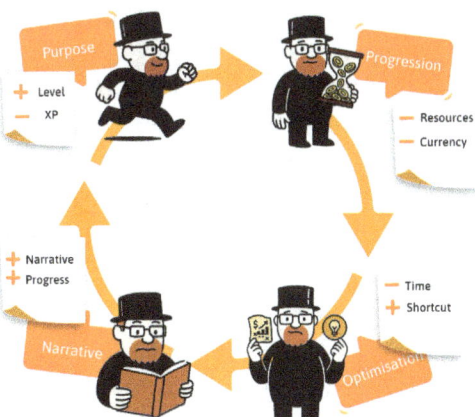

FIGURE 9.2   Context loop.

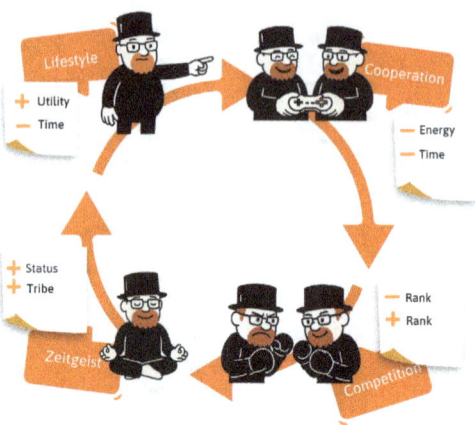

FIGURE 9.3   Culture loop.

The Cultural loop can be a little more complicated as there can be more abstract forms of utility which don't quite follow a Sink/Source model, but this can still be a useful exercise. At the lifestyle stage, the player seeks to maximise Utility generally, but in this example, the player decides to exchange time in this game as opposed to some other form of activity (abnegation). In this example, the Cooperation stage also assumes a further sink of energy (such as players sharing access to levels with members of their Tribe/Team/Clan) as well as a further sink in Player time (based on shared planning and engagement with the Tribe).

Under Competition in this example, the Utility 'Rank' has been added. This is intended to show that players are competing for a specific kind of skill-based status and that can both be gained and lost through play. Remember that at game time, the player will also gain from any Core mechanic loop Rewards every session, so we don't have to represent that twice. This is just for the designer to consider the Cultural pay-off comes in terms of Status and Tribe (representing connections in your team/clan/guild). This often includes cosmetic and personalisation. The example has focused on competitive play, but this can equally be applied to games which feature user-generated creative expression and the social capital that this can deliver.

Alternative Ways to Map Utility

Using loops to understand where utility can be derived is very useful, but it also has its limitations. Loops tend to reflect how different layers of an experience interact as systems. They tend not to cleanly translate to how a player might perceive their linear experience. A player will have a personal journey through the game where the different loops repeat at a different rate. Like the hands of an analogue clock showing seconds, minutes, and hours.

An alternative way to review the games sinks and sources is to think about the game as a linear flow for a typical player – indeed, there are good reasons to consider the linear flow for multiple player types or cohorts. Another way we can do this is to draw the flows that players might experience elements through specific features of a game. This can take the form of literal levels, step by step, and we can put numbers against each of these levels to represent the output.

The following image shows a different, generic example intended to map a smooth power-level progression:

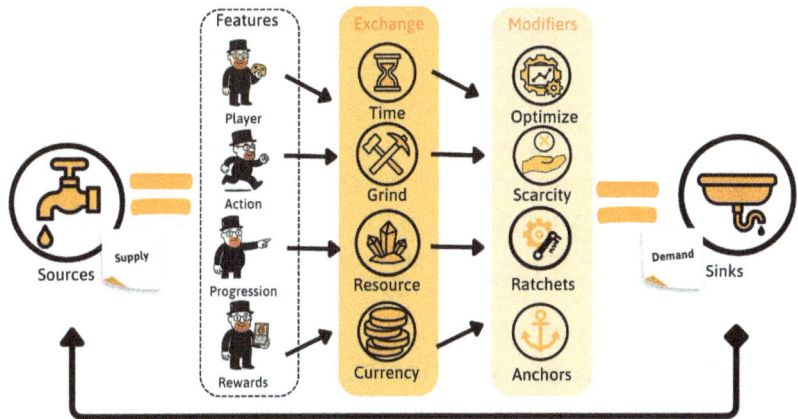

FIGURE 9.4   Sources, exchange, modifiers and sinks.

For this, let's focus on the flow of the player experience through the game as a whole; considering the overarching experience rather than how the loops deliver motivation in layers. For every feature, try to understand the role they play in terms of Source or supply of utility items, as well as how these systems act as Sink or generators of Demand for those same items. When a player gains a reward and then exchanges that for an increase in power, that shows an action of Supply as well as an action of Exchange driven by demand and its associated value to the player.

Before creating such a document, first assess each feature, form of exchange, and any modifiers that happen in the game:

Categories of Sinks and Sources

In this approach, we have included four high-level feature categories, as a designer you may use less generic approaches. These are intended to explore the following:

- **Player**: The Utility pertaining directly to the player, including 'power', abilities, health, and inventory items. This is about what the player themselves bring into the playing activity and therefore is partly about the individual but also about the data assigned to that person and their character(s), environment(s), or interactions. The player brings (Source) these elements into the game to empower their activities, rewards and progress are often added (Sunk) into this category.

- **Activity**: For the purposes of this example activity encompasses all the things that the player does in the game, the act of play in its wider sense. This often will be a one-to-one match with the Core Loop but may, in some games, have components from other loops if they map to explicit forms of interaction. Players invest (Sink) elements they have obtained into ways to improve their performance but also receive as an output (Source) utility (currencies, rewards, resources, items) from such activities. Those utility items may be directly usable or that need to be exchanged for rewards, progression, or offers. Items invested in an activity may be consumed or retained based on how they are designed.

- **Progression**: For the purpose of this model, this is the mechanism which allows the player and the game world to evolve over time. Whilst generally this is a one-to-one match with the Context Loop it may be useful to treat this slightly differently, blurring some activities and optimisations with rewards or offers. Players might spend (Sink) XP and increase (Source) an improvement in our Player Level as part of progression or instead they may spend (Sink) resources and currencies against Blueprints to craft (Source) improved equipment or resources. Progression as a category can also be used to frame systems to maintain the player's status and power, not just advance it. So, degradation of assets and 'Prestige' systems as discussed previously can be effective Sinks; renewing the benefit of the original sources.

- **Reward**: The systems which release rewards are usually mechanisms used to support delayed gratification but also include premium offers and even the rewards from rewarded ad systems. They are included separately from the other features as it can help to focus on how the player experiences that process but use features which match the game being designed. Rewards usually include utility goods which improve the scope of the player, which directly impact the performance of activities, even increase the rate of progression (although avoiding duplication with the progression feature). Rewards can be released directly from completing actions, but for the purposes of this example we will assume that instead they exchanged for tickets/tokens that are provided as utility items after game activity. Examples of such tokens can include keys or treasure chests obtained at the end of a successful game session and players sink these 'keys' in exchange for the rewards contained inside those chests. Such exchange mechanisms may also come from progression so even where there is no explicit exchange good for the player, it can still be a useful exercise to treat rewards as its own category. Offers, are effectively just rewards which include some form of commercial exchange even if simply 'reciprocation' in the case of a free daily item. Cosmetic items are a typical example of a reward which are sourced as rewards and then (sunk) by assigning them to the player inventory.

Building a Sink/Source Map

Please note that these 'Features' are just generic examples, and we may need to add more to help map out our games' use of utility and exchange. One common option is to consider 'Seasonality' as a category which works well to independently track Battle pass Sink and Source patterns as well as tracking access to unique items. However, it is usually sensible to keep the number of categories low in order to help you avoid getting confused and missing things.

In Figure 9.6 (Sources, exchange, modifiers and sinks), we showed different exchange factors, in this case, we are just showing four: Time, Grind, Resource, and Currency all of which were discussed in *Chapter 8: Functions of Exchange*. Think about what those exchange mechanisms mean in terms of the form, function and flow of the game. In thinking about the characteristics of the utility items players have obtained, we can go further and consider how those exchange transactions can be further modified by their role in the design. Anchors and Ratchets (again discussed in *Chapter 8: Functions of Exchange*) help us frame the elements which derive from play alone, versus those elements which come from offers and other commercial transactions. There may even be some form an exchange rate applied between these different transactions and that might affect ideas like Optimisation and Scarcity? Especially where there are substitute methods to make that exchange within the design perhaps to motivate different styles of play. Mapping out the game by identifying the relevant features, exchange systems, and modifiers helps, and their role in terms of acting as a Source or Sink solidifies what balance issues the game may have and the tools, we have in place to manage that.

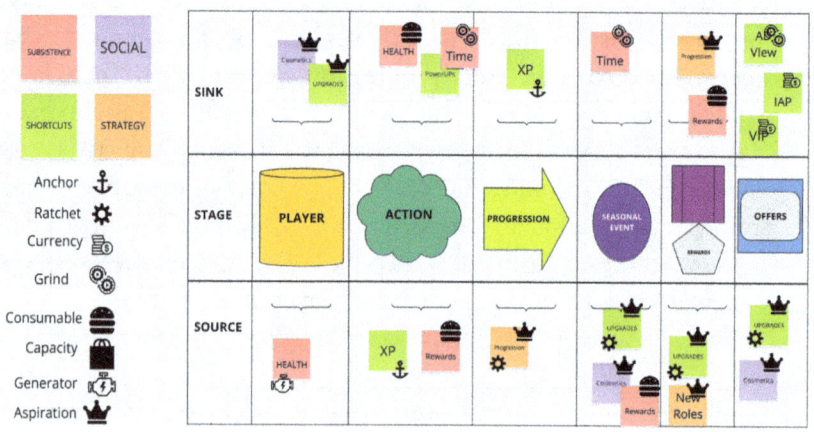

FIGURE 9.5   Example sink/source map.

To make that practical, one useful technique is to create a table with a set of columns for each feature and to use sticky notes to show each utility item in terms of its sinks and sources. In the diagram below is an example game and colour-coded virtual sticky notes to represent utility types with icons to reflect forms and exchange types. If you do an exercise like this ensure that there are at least two sticky notes for each individual utility item. There MUST be at least one sink and one source (although there can be more of each). This is essential in order to avoid inflation – although there is an argument that there generally should be more sinks than sources for each item to drive 'Demand.'

Regulating Flow

The level of detail this should be taken to is down to the complexity of the game, and the patience of the designer. For the purposes of this example, the intention is to ensure that what players value (Utility), the form that takes, how that is acquired (Source), and how it is used (Sink) has been properly assessed. Once the flow of these items is understood, it's possible to start to assess how best to regulate that flow to ensure satisfying gameplay.

We regulate flow for a number of reasons:

Complexity: Different games have different levels of complexity in terms of the currency or resources that help deliver player utility gradually over time. Some games have a few simple characteristics, sometimes linear, sometimes orthogonal in terms of their ability to impact the resolution of gameplay moments. Some of these resources will be consumable, such as a 'hint' or a strength potion, others will be more permanent, such as equipping a 'Hat of Wonder.' In either case, our capacity to hold or apply such items at any time has a significant impact on our choice of action and our effectiveness. Other games will have complex characteristics, rarely linear, almost always orthogonal, where it is not simply about the application of currency and resources now, but how that choice will affect the next, and the next, and the next. The ability to consider ahead is at the heart of optimisation. When looking at our Sinks/Sources, consider the emergent properties that arise with the way utility items interact and how this can be applied to the mechanics. Predicting the interactions between multiple utility items, each of which may have an orthogonal relationship with each other is a problem that could be compared to the classic astronomical conundrum known as the 'Three-Body Problem.' The mathematics to model this can be beyond most games designers and indeed potentially be unsolvable. However, there are some tools available to us to help mitigate that such as platforms that attempt to model systems, such as Machinations or to use a Monte Carlo Simulation, a mathematical approach which uses randomness and repeat samples to simulate the impact of multiple inputs for deterministic systems – such as a game. However, there are two ways Designers can do this more hands-on. We can build something as a guess and playtest it (this is generally the essential way we make games) and we can use anchors. As described in *Chapter 8: Functions of Exchange* we can define a small number (perhaps just one) currency or utility which can only be obtained through play and fix the value of all other utility items against that currency. This method leverages a concept once common, but no longer used in real-world economies, known as the Gold Standard. For games, this mindset is useful as it allows us to minimise complexity and ensure that our focus remains on gameplay and hence the core value players want from us.

Scarcity and Constraint: The rate at which players can access the utility items we have identified through our Sink/Source analysis is critical to the effectiveness of our design and there are multiple factors which affect this. We can consider the effort versus drop-rate of items or currency; we can scale the volume of those resources needed for exchange as we progress, or we can specialise those items in some way. We will explore Drop Rates and their implications on difficulty design later but in terms of scarcity we need to consider the effort required to gather specific resource and how that is affected as the player's power increases on the availability of that item. Scarcity is a critical as defines the value of any utility item. Supply, Demand, and Value are directly connected as discussed when exploring Price Elasticity of Demand. But Digital goods basically have no natural limit; they are essentially just a database entry and therefore free for the development team to produce. Indeed, a player dedicated enough can get as near to infinite volume of any given resource that will break the game's economy if there are no other constraints. Grind-playing behaviour is essential to sustainable game economies but are also a huge contributor to game item inflation, as poorly designed systems and retail bundles can simply undermine the value in the game. Even where with systems designed to scale the volume of resource or currency items needed for exchanges as the player levels, that ability to grind tasks can undermine the perceived value of progression. Indeed, increased player power tend only to them obtaining ever more reward volumes and further reinforces such inflation. Providing constraints on capacity or available volume that can be collects can mitigate this. How many of those items can the player carry? can the source only be used to extract a finite volume of the currency or resource? or is that resource specialised so it is only useful for very specific circumstances? A specialist resource that has no sustained value after you have built the items or completed the progression path that needed it, becomes valueless (Sunk). Take the example of a crafting system. The game may define a bunch of specialist resources they may have a type e.g. herb, they may have a specialist use or effect category e.g. fire magic and a unique effect e.g. Protection for Fire damage. Our 'Fireweed' could be used as an ingredient in low-level potions but is most highly sought for making protection from fire potions. If it is only found in specific locations, e.g. beside a volcano and that there are only 15 plants accessible each day this creates a 'natural' sense of scarcity, opportunity cost in terms of collection and utility which can be fed into the narrative. Add other ingredients and a requirement to use an anchor currency can help manage scarcity and help maintain the value of those items and still deepen player engagement.

Optimisation: Another aspect which can modify the acquisition and use of resources comes with optimisation, which can take multiple forms but in its simplistic form can be thought of as an exchange rate. A player may choose a particular set of actions which generate a specific set of resources. These may then be exchanged (at different rates) for the alternative assets the player needs to produce, unlock stages or generally progress. As designers we don't need to limit ourselves to a simple one-to-one relationship between time and reward. The game can adjust the pay-off ratios through missions, tasks, and challenges methods to motivate players to experience the game in different ways. Allowing those focused on skill to access those resources differently than those focused on grind or, indeed, social interactions. To avoid this becoming hard to manage it is possible to tie these motivations into Anchor currencies as well ensuring that there has to at least have been some consistent level of gameplay and even to require some of each mode of play from the player in the order for them to achieve he next stage of progression. Games like The Long Dark and Fallout 76 significantly increase engagement through the use of resources and depreciation of assets. This means taking the time to explore to collect and craft resources in order to get ready for the next mission or challenge. Taking easier, more grinding tasks with less inherent meaning, in order to prepare for the task the player really cares about. There is a parallel to the concept of "Hotdog Economics." In the United Kingdom we buy hotdogs in packs of eight and buns in packs of six (In the USA its more usually ten dogs to eight buns). There is an imbalance in these goods despite their consumption being deeply connected. This means that there are now extra dogs and that imbalance can be addressed if more buns are purchased. However, buying more buns leads to having an excess of that bread. Of course, buns can be utilised for other foods, but being focused on hotdogs leads to a motivation to get more dogs. The key point is that the acquisition of hotdogs does not immediately satisfy the balance with the hotdog buns and although it is easy to calculate the optimal number, for most people the effort is just above the level of instinct so there remains a level of ambiguity and motivation to optimise. This imbalance in Hotdog economics is useful to explore other profound questions about emergent properties, notably Paul Krugman in 1997[1] used this to explore more general principles about implications related to productivity. The reason we focus on Optimisation as a stage in the context loops is that it scratches an itch that is deeply satisfying. The ambiguity between the Source and Sink of utility goods in a game obtained by different actions and strategies is an intrinsically enjoyable activity that is inherently rewarding for players and at the same time helps us to sustain our game economy effectively.

Feedback Loops: Feedback loops are a vital factor in systems thinking, especially in the context of Macroeconomics, which we very briefly discussed in *Chapter 2: Defining an Economy*. Any system where there are actions which can either add supply to a system or alternatively remove items from a system has to consider the implications of feedback loops. The game design attempts to positively reinforce player behaviour by providing rewards for success and tapping into negative feedback loops when requiring earned currency/goods to be exchanged for progression. Even the concept of a Source is fundamentally a positive feedback factor. Players take an action and increase the supply of a good in the game economy. Similarly, a Sink, by definition, delivers negative feedback, removing the exchanged or degraded asset from the supply in the game economy. The term positive in this case is purely mathematical not a value judgement on the process and failing to balance this well is how systems create inflation or deflation accordingly. These impacts can be emergent, not just related to the specific assets involved. For example, a positive reinforcement such as allocating the best rewards only to winning players can have a detrimental impact on a game, creating an ever-expanding gulf between the naturally skilled and motivated players and everyone else. This can lead to players being unable to enjoy the game with their friends and even reinforce a toxic community climate. In another example, not providing any positive reinforcement rewards to players who repeatedly fail against a difficult opponent, cannot increase their power level and may never achieve the necessary skill to continue playing. On the other hand, negative reinforcement can also be the players' friend, even though an instinctive response may make them feel off. However, if over time the game requires an ever-increasing level of effort to achieve further improvements in terms of power and progression, the experience can feel even more meaningful; allowing the game to retain the player longer. This is despite having effectively reduced the relative exchange rate of effort versus benefit.

- **Supply, Demand, and Price**: In the end, all of this comes back to the principles of Supply and Demand discussed in *Chapter 2: Defining an Economy*. We attempt to map the value of each exchange based upon the supply and demand of goods within our systems. Unlike the real-world economy, we have a lot of control in a game over what resources are available, how they are used and where they are applied. This means we can map and monitor through our Sinks and Sources how we can maintain the player experience. Understanding this 'Price' is vital to commercial game design in order for us to appreciate what monetary instruments are going to shift behaviour, deepening player engagement as well as optimising our revenues. Where we are offering bundles of currency or resources, we need to appreciate how this increase in supply (Source) affects scarcity as well as other exchange methods. Time-poor players spending cash on Soft or Hard Currency in order to compensate for their lack of disposable time to play and to maintain a level of satisfaction in terms of progression, is a good thing. It will remove friction inherent in the exchange of time for progress. However, when this undermines their need to play, we often find that the exchange in fact can undermine the inherent meaningfulness of their in-game actions. Paying to NOT play is rarely a good experience. This is why it helps to define Anchor currencies to minimise this risk as well as to avoid accusations of "Pay To Win" (something which I would personally define more seriously as a broken game). However, like all rules in Game Economy Design, context is everything and there are cases in, for example, Idle Games and games like Monopoly GO![2] where paying to skip the game is in effect, seen as a positive. But this is rare and not generally applicable.

In the end, it could be argued that the purpose of an economy at all is to provide structure to manage the progression of a game and mapping that economy out in the context of both the playing loops and the vectors or categories of interaction allows us to better understand what is going on when we build systems. It allows us to use tools such as spreadsheets (See Following Example), Monte Carlo simulations, or Machinations. io – even paper prototypes to experiment and test the balance in a game. However, we cannot get away from a quintessential factor which is common to all game design, including board games, card games, and of course computer games: Game Feel. Understanding balance is not just about what the maths says about the game we cannot separate the experience from how it makes us feel and how we interpret the complex interaction between playing actions, rewards, progression, and retention.

In the next chapter, we will explore how we take the principles of this mapping further and consider the implications for player progression and difficulty.

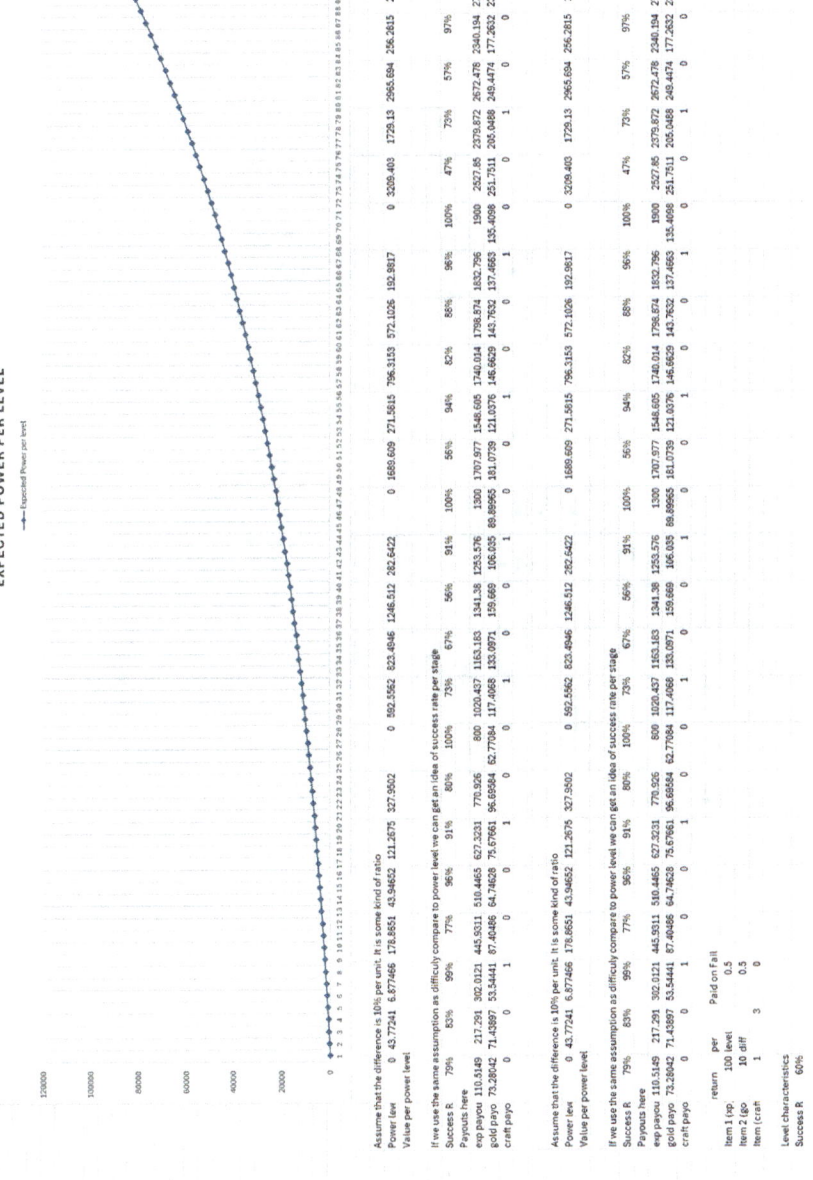

FIGURE 9.6   Expected power level example.

Interview

THE ART AND SCIENCE OF GAME BALANCE –
AN INTERVIEW WITH HUEL FUCHSBERGER

Game balance is one of the most crucial yet complex aspects of game design. It dictates the pacing, difficulty, and overall experience of the player. Whether in level design, progression mechanics, or monetisation strategies, achieving balance requires a mix of data analysis, iteration, and intuition. In this discussion with Huel Fuchsberger,[3] Senior game designer at Next Games, we explore the nuances of level design in match-three games and how balance influences engagement and monetisation.

Fuchsberger's journey in game design spans several renowned companies, including Wooga, Rovio, and Next Games, where he has primarily worked on level design for mobile games.

> "I have never really done a lot of games from scratch, except for now, for the first time and Next Games I'm doing this for the first time. But typically, when I joined the team, it was about the fundamental building blocks for the core, the toy or the core game," said Fuchsberger.

Level design serves as the foundation of player interaction with the game. In match-three games, levels are handcrafted, ensuring a human touch in the puzzle-solving experience. Unlike procedurally generated content, handcrafted levels allow designers to structure the player's journey in a meaningful way.

> "The nice thing about handcrafted levels is that another human being feels that another human being has created this puzzle for them, and they're trying to kind of re-step your traces, and that makes it interesting," said Fuchsberger.

Designing levels in match-three games follows a structured approach that incorporates a beginning, middle, and end. This progression mirrors traditional storytelling structures, ensuring a smooth yet engaging experience for the player.

"We have like some sort of beginning phase, a middle phase, and then a kind of wrap-up phase, an ending phase to thinking," said Fuchsberger.

The beginning of a level introduces mechanics, the middle phase allows the player to develop strategies, and the ending phase ties up the experience – ideally with a sense of accomplishment. The Nintendo method of game design, which involves introducing a mechanic, allowing mastery, and then subverting it, is also a key approach in level progression.

"I introduce a new concept, I play around a little bit with this concept, and then I put a twist on that concept," said Fuchsberger.

Difficulty balancing is a crucial part of level design, particularly in casual games like match-three, where the goal is to provide a challenge without overwhelming the player.

"We try to always avoid making you feel stupid or dumb. It's a broad audience. It's also supposed to be a very relaxing experience," said Fuchsberger.

This balance is tricky because different players have varying levels of experience. Some players will find the game too easy, while others may struggle. Over time, game developers have moved from static difficulty settings to more dynamic balancing techniques that personalise the challenge based on player behaviour.

"When I started out my career, then it was all about static. So there was like one funnel, and everyone got the same level and the same configuration. These days, it's fully dynamic where you can react to what the player is experiencing and making sure that the experience is consistent throughout," said Fuchsberger.

The expectation of difficulty must be carefully managed. Players should feel like they are progressing based on their own skill rather than external constraints.

"I think a good example in match-three of that is how labels kind of affect people's expectation of levels. And that's in most of my games, we really tried to always label them accurately because we found that it is more helpful to players to know, 'Hey, this level is going to be a little bit more difficult,' because it also manages the expectation," said Fuchsberger.

One of the biggest challenges in game design today is keeping players engaged over the long term. Match-three games often rely on live operations and constant content updates to maintain player interest. However, this creates an ongoing content treadmill, where designers must continually produce new levels and mechanics to keep the game fresh.

> There's only so many ways that you can rearrange five game pieces to keep it interesting.

To counteract this, developers introduce progression systems, events, and live operations to provide additional motivation for continued play.

> "The progression systems, your events, your live operations should be taking over and bringing people and keeping people engaged and giving them more high-level goals beyond just reaching the next level," said Fuchsberger.

But this also introduces its own set of challenges. If side content becomes too dominant, it can overshadow the core experience and lead to fragmented player engagement.

> "The more and more the side content gets, yeah, if it eats up more and more of your time, then yeah, then the saga content and the spiral continues because the other content is not getting better, and then you're putting more and more side content, but then people are not onboarded to it correctly," said Fuchsberger.

Monetisation in free-to-play games is closely tied to game balance. Players need to encounter the right level of friction to feel compelled to spend, but not so much that they become frustrated and quit.

> "Just taking away that friction, just giving you Candy Crush[4] with an unlimited bank account – I don't think that would be a satisfying experience. That friction is part of the experience," said Fuchsberger.

Effective monetisation relies on well-timed challenges and valuable purchases. Fuchsberger points out that the appeal of spending is often tied to the sense of reward, particularly in unlocking or upgrading mechanics.

> "When the player does use real currency and they go through the flow of purchasing, the game recognizes that and rewards you at

that moment already. It's reinforcing you doing a good thing," said Fuchsberger.

This principle extends to collection mechanics and other systems that enhance the reward experience.

"With collections, you can bring that gacha-like excitement in a way where it's not necessarily gameplay-influencing, but it still provides a nice experience and creates moments of reward and wonder," said Fuchsberger.

Designing with Intent

Ultimately, effective game balance comes down to designing with intent. Every aspect of the player experience – from level structure to difficulty and monetisation – must be carefully considered to create a compelling and sustainable game.

"We are designing with intent, and you need to make sure that your intent is clear and comes through as well. Otherwise, if it's muddled, then it will feel muddled as well to the player," said Fuchsberger.

For aspiring level designers, Fuchsberger offers a final piece of advice:

Don't underestimate how much you can do in level design and try to dedicate yourself to that. Because for me personally, it was not necessarily the work itself that didn't keep me interested, but it was just an opportunity to move something else forward.

Game balance is an ongoing process of iteration and refinement. Through careful design, meaningful progression, and fair monetisation, developers can craft experiences that keep players engaged for years.

NOTES

1 Paul Krugman's thought experiment of the hot-dog-and-bun economy in *The Accidental Theorist* (1998, pp. 18–23)
2 https://en.wikipedia.org/wiki/Monopoly_Go!
3 https://www.linkedin.com/in/huelfuchsberger
4 https://en.wikipedia.org/wiki/Candy_Crush_Saga

CHAPTER 10

Balance

WHAT DOES BALANCE MEAN IN A GAME?

At least we come to probably the part of economy design where the 'rubber meets the road.' So far, we have been trying to establish the components and flows that exist within the game at each of the three loops of Core, Context, and Culture. Great-feeling game balance comes from how we adjust these flows to match the player lifecycle, and it starts with the playing experience itself.

Balance Does Not Equal Fairness

Let's get the obvious stuff out of the way. Game balance refers to the process of adjusting game mechanics, rewards, challenges, and other elements to create an engaging gameplay experience. This is typically associated with the game being seen as 'fair.' There is some truth to that in so far as designers need to ensure that players do not feel that there is no bias (pro or against) towards any single strategy, item of equipment, or character that will unduly affect their success or progression in the game. Players are often highly sensitive to perceived imbalance, especially where this impacts personal skill or willingness to spend. However, it is important to appreciate that these are subjective concepts.

- **Fairness**: A balanced game often strives to ensure that all available options (characters, items, strategies) have a reasonable chance of success, preventing any single choice from dominating the game. However, there are games where the design must accommodate different skill levels and playing styles, which may not be as compatible. There may be narrative choices, where we deliberately press the thumb on the difficulty scales. That being said, when players feel that the game is unfair and that they failed a level because of the mechanics rather than because of their skill or choices that can very quickly lead to "rage quitting" the game. As an obsessed player of Slay the Spire[1] there are moments where I "know" that the specific level was "overbalanced" and unfair (obviously I don't actually know but I strongly suspect). This works for that game and a player like myself, as this forces me to consider alternative strategies across my next run. This only works because I continue to believe that success is obtainable.

- **Intended Player Experience**: Balance is often experienced more as the complex expression of the feelings of challenge, reward, and satisfaction for players. The sensation of meaningful impact where the player's skill, choices, patience, or ability to grind eventually results in the aspired results is often included in what players consider a balanced game. Ambiguity can also be an important factor. An experience can be heightened when we don't know the results and the reveal of the rewards, narrative, and next challenge all contribute to the sense of engagement and what players respond to as a 'Balanced' experience.

- **Ongoing Process**: Game balance is rarely constant. A game which is always 'in balance' is generally not appealing. Just as we discussed in *Chapter 5: What Is a Game Anyway* to deliver both the Motivation and Absorption Vectors in a game is dynamic, a shifting flow through emotional states. This means for that to be in balance the design has to itself be dynamic with an ongoing process of adjustments and refinements. This also changes over time, and over the player lifecycle which we will explore below.

To further explore balance in the playing experience, let's explore four concepts: Game Feel, Perfect Balance, Player Lifecycle, and Power Curves.

Game Feel

As we have taken a theoretical framework for this book, we have deliberately avoided going into the specifics of how different games function. Indeed, there are as many forms of games as we can imagine, and we are

FIGURE 10.1   Steve Swink's game feel.

already trying to cover more than enough. The balance between contemplating an interaction, the nature and duration of that interaction, the sensory responses as we interact, as well as its impact on the world or our opposition and the lasting change we trigger, all contribute to Game Feel. The cognitive connections between expectations and experiences are critical when it comes to response time, impact, and a sense of relative 'power'. A player's response to a game is deeply tied to their prior experiences in other games and the real world. Despite this, designers can find it hard to articulate exactly why a specific game's feel is off and what should be done instead, but through repeated and diverse gameplay experiences and extensive playtesting, it is possible to build 'design muscles' that help us identify possible models we can draw upon to rebalance the experience. Steve Swink explores the experiential element in great detail in their book "Game Feel: A Game Designer's Guide to Virtual Sensation".[2] A simplification of their premise could be described as how game feel comes between interconnections from the player intent and how their interactions with the physical gaming devices (with their inherent latency) in the real world provide an interface into the game world. It is in the game world that players suspend their disbelief and experience the gameplay and social elements. These are affected by the game systems, either intrinsically in the build or derived through server interactions which calculate the in-game responses. These responses are represented through the visuals, controller reactions, haptic feedback, audio, logic, narrative, and sensory responses the player experiences. All this sensory feedback is subject to the player's cognitive processes (and its inherent latency), and in turn, that informs the next stage of their intent, repeating the cycle through the gameplay.

Perfect Balance

There is no such thing as perfect balance. There is no simple mathematical formula to understanding how mechanics translate to power and status. In fact, trying to use simple mathematics often backfires and fails to "feel satisfying." Take a random number generator. We have a system that pays out 1 to 50 gold each time. In a truly random experience there is a chance, however low, that one player will get one gold every single time, yet another will get 50 every single time. The more players you have, the likelihood that this will happen to one individual will necessarily increase. This is obviously not balanced in terms of the experience for the affected individuals and will damage both players' experience of the game. Instead, it is important to use pseudorandom numbers, payouts that feel like random, but that avoid the downsides of clustering. Perfect balance is also in the eye of the beholder. Every time a new League of Legends update comes out, there will be some change to some of the character's abilities, and yes, much of this is about the developer making stat changes to mix up the experience. However, quite often there can be an uproar of anger from the community who feel that one character is now overpowered, and another has been "nerfed." These complaints can come even when the changes are largely cosmetic, or which have in fact been balanced by other changes elsewhere in the game systems. The gap between player skill, grind, understanding of systems, and their application leaves gaps in the information available to a player and their expectations of gameplay behaviour. That can fundamentally affect their experience of the game and may end up being described as a failure of balance; even when it is nothing of the sort; just a misunderstanding. Folks new to design will also assume that all options available to a player within the game should be equal and workable. However, that quickly becomes boring. In a previous example, we talked about players being able to choose between a machine gun that does the same damage per second but with an orthogonal (completely independent) application in terms of how that damage was applied. Without the nuance of the choice between maintaining aim versus the timing of damage, the weapons would have no advantage and thereby whilst balanced they would be boring. And even with this, players who have their own playing style preferences still will tell you one or the other is imbalanced! If your choices e.g. exit the location using Stealth, Combat, and Hacking, are always truly equally balanced, it can feel like a pointless choice – especially if both end up with the same reward. There needs to feel like a dilemma with a cost vs. benefit when we make that choice. If I use stealth to take out enemies (which should feel harder and unforgiving if I fail), then I expect to get the benefit in terms of increased rewards – unlike in The Last of Us (yes, it frustrates me that you get less ammo dropped from enemies when using stealth than shooting in that game). There is another perspective to take away from this. All the energy of the angst and anger about imbalance hides a dirty secret. Despite the outraged reactions against imbalance, players still get a thrill when they find some level of contextual advantage by choosing the right option in a moment of play. Especially if there is an opponent who doesn't know about that 'arcane knowledge.' It makes the player feel powerful and is part of the learning experience. Intentional nerfs and buffs to the experience can indeed help build interesting game feel and develop players' sense of autonomy, letting them feel clever for working out how to use skills and tactics in innovative ways that others have yet to work out.

Player Lifecycle

As if understanding balance is hard enough because of the subjective nature of the player experience, it is not static. Expectations change over different player life stages, and the approach that players at each stage engage in the games is also affected by the differences between products and service experiences.

The Product Lifecycle tends to have an initial peak, where the engagement has to exceed any barriers to entry (such as a paywall) and then tends to sharply decline. Pay Upfront products tend to benefit from the sunk cost that the player has already paid for the game, so they are more likely to stay playing through onboarding. However, they don't benefit from renewed engagement that comes with sustained experiences. Instead, these games have to focus on traditional product management, looking after maximising the 'Long Tail' audience. This is typically includes sales and offers such as Steam Sale discounts, as well as introducing infrequent DLC packages or other forms of out-of-game promotions.

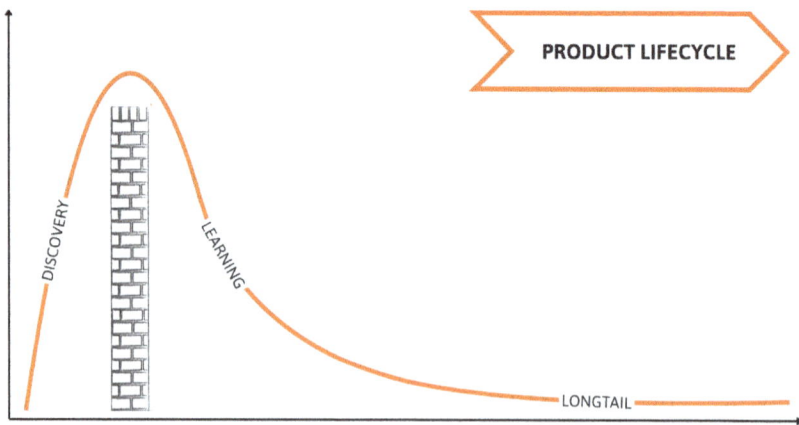

FIGURE 10.2   Pical product lifecyle.

On the other hand, service games lifecycles are more deeply tied into player engagement and retention, with in-game activities playing as much a part as any community or store offering. This includes the Discovery, Learning, Engaging, Super Engaging and Re-engaging stages we will explore below.

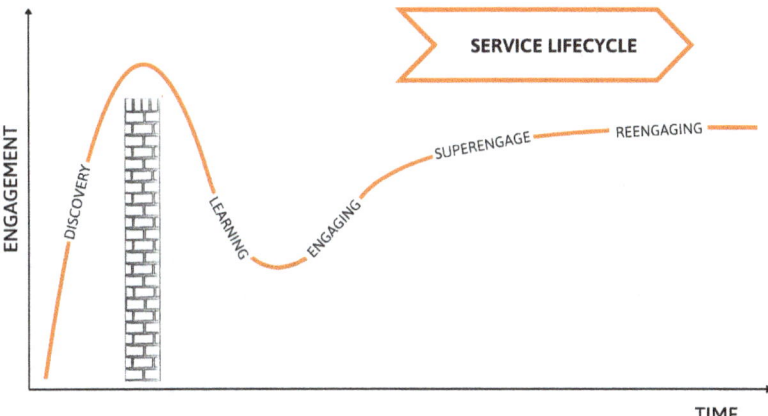

FIGURE 10.3 Typical service lifecyle.

Both models require the developer to deliver excitement and engagement to get players over any barriers to acquiring those players. Indeed, teams with portfolios of products are increasingly using the same techniques as service game teams.

These concepts are explored in more detail in the book Games as a Service,[3] but for the purposes of understanding Lifecycle in terms of its impact on economy design for service games, it is possible to break down the experiences into five life stages. These are:

- **Discovery**: Players find the game and need to decide if they will install and perhaps try the game (not guaranteed – just look at your Steam Library or mobile device and consider the games you have installed and not yet gotten around to playing yet!). Their desires and expectations are fairly binary: 'I will play now' or 'I have other things that are more urgent.' There is little room for any nuance or explanation in this stage. However, too often game developers waste time with burdensome splash screens shouting about partners or tools, or even exposition about the game world, rather than letting the player get straight into play. Audiences recognise that it is bad for a movie to spend time telling you about the world rather than showing you, and yet games too often require players to press 'X' to continue countless times rather than letting the player get on with the play. One of the worst examples of this in 2024 was Infinity Nikky where after the install you have forced registration flow, before a 10 GB (around 40 minutes download time), then another 20 minutes on-rails of onboarding exposition. Games like that which have an existing sizable, supportive community from previous titles seem to get away with it, but unfortunately these are survivor stories that leave too many game developers with the impression that this doesn't cause major issues. The reality is that this sort of thing kills most games. Our role as designers at the Discovery stage is to think about how we 'Activate' the player to get through to the Learning experience with as little friction as possible. But at the same time, we must ensure that the player can see the value in becoming engaged in play.

- **Learning**: Once the game is installed and the player has decided to play, the next stage is all about 'Learning'. This is not just about learning the game's systems and controls, but also where it fits into our real-world routines. At one end, games can be short-form precious personal moments or opportunities to clear your mind (a mental Coffee/Tea break), at the other extreme, we find games where we commit more deeply not just time, but part of our identity, becoming hobbies with significant commitment. The First Time User Experience is critical during the learning stage. It literally is the difference between players engaging longer term or churning. We need to communicate not just how to play the game, but why it will continue to matter. We need to demonstrate sufficient value that means they choose our game against all the other competing options for their entertainment. This is vital to build engagement and retention as much as it is vital for building revenue models. In service games, especially mobile, the majority of players will tend to quit within 24 hours of installing the game, often never to return. This presents a huge challenge given that revenues rely on retained players. However, when we step back and compare the freemium acquisition experience to other retail experiences we see that this happens all of the time. Potential purchasers will look at the items they desire and decide if that item is something for which they are willing to push the button and convert to pay. The only difference is that with freemium experiences we invite people into our game before they convert. This allows them to properly assess what our game experience has to offer. And we start counting the audience at this first engagement. If that excites them, they will stay to enjoy the "goods" and hopefully pay for elements that complete their "need" states. Most retail items don't have this opportunity, and in the case of Pay Upfront games, they can't even count the people who were interested enough to try, but not ready to pay, and therefore how many were 'churned' before they even tried? The key difference for me is that Freemium games are both the play experience and the shop directly. This gives those developers more capacity to tailor the player journey to their audience in order to maximise engagement, retention, and of course monetisation. These games are not limited to the capacity of the retail platform to present the game's value in the best light, and it matters to the team to sustain the player experience over time; investing in the player as much as their own success. Even if that seems an idealistic way to look at it. The Learning stage is an opportunity to explain to players why they will love coming back, and if the game team fails to rapidly and immersively help them understand the method and value of gameplay they will fail to retain and convert them to spend. There is an aspect of balance necessary to consider during the Learning stage because the developer's goal is not necessarily to convert the player just to spending, but more to 'Activating' them to engage with the game. This can be as simple as getting the player past the uncomfortable early stage where the player has yet to understand the context of the game and why it fits into their routine. We have to get across reasons for the player to care about the game; at least enough to start the process of making it a part of their routine. Part of that will always be teasing the potential longer-term excitement. Foreshadowing to generate anticipation about what is to come (often by leaning into the ambiguity of what comes next) and building 'Fear of Missing Out.'

- **Engaging**: Determining the point that a player gets through the learning stage can be complex to determine, rather than being the completion of a specific tutorial step, this really only occurs at a point where they can be seen to have started sustained, habitual patterns of play. When a player has genuinely reached the Engaging stage, for them the game is no longer about the experience the developer created, but more about how that player uses those systems to satisfy their ongoing needs. This is not necessarily tied to a conversion to spend at the same time; although there are games which attract a category of player who chooses to 'Front-load' or spend a significant amount early to get a significant advantage at the early stages of play. More common in a mobile game is to see players start to convert to watching rewarded ads as a method to mitigate against friction in the game as well as to start to learn the value of paid-for items. It can take a few days of repeated play for those who will convert to spending to start that process, whether that is with microtransactions or committing to a subscription option in the game. However, this is not the only measure of success to track, early in the Engaging stage, the more important success measure comes from a consistency of return to play (usually measured in D7 to D30 retention) as well as session frequency and duration (a good measure of engagement). The Engaged user, whether paying or not, will share important commonalities in terms of how they satisfy their playing needs in the game. Commercial engagement for players at this life stage will often be focused on lubricating their progression path and perhaps some limited social expression. The game developer should focus on mitigating frustration and continuing to foreshadow future value in ways that keep the play feeling meaningful. Designers have to be careful not to let players feel that they are wasting time within loops that they have already completely understood or Grok'ed. We still want inherently rewarding mechanics that players choose to repeat continuously where the grind benefit is compelling; but ideally they should feel continually relevant with pathways that can be optimised. We can think of the flow of the game here almost as a form of 'Second Time User Experience' or STUE, where rather than teaching the player about how the game works, we are looking to help the player hone and optimise their experience, encouraging them to benefit from repeating the systems of play. Too often this aspect does not seem to be fully considered in many game designs, but it can play an important part in maximising players' evolution to the next life stage. Converting a player to spend real money is a critical aspect to commercial success, but it comes out of engaged players being retained and exciting them through anticipation, social capital, and FOMO to act to spend money. Repeat revenues are critical to scaling your games business and that will not happen without sustaining longer term player engagement. What we need once we bring players onboard is to deepen their commitment and focus our efforts on converting them to becoming true fans of the game, i.e., 'Super-Engaging' users. Interestingly, it is the Engaging player who tend to be most fairly active in community and social media aspects, rather than Super-Engaged players themselves; who can tend to be more insular.

- **Super-Engaging**: The big fans of your game who are most willing to spend large amounts of money in your game are NOT 'Whales.' That term was a shorthand used to help monetisation designers talk about high spend behaviour but this was arguably built on a mistaken comparison with the gambling market. Whales are a term used by Las Vegas casinos to describe the very biggest spenders who will turn up at a resort with a very large amount of cash that they intend to sink into their time off. They often stay until they spend all of that money; including any winnings they gain during that time. They rarely leave having made a profit from gambling. Instead, Super-Engaging users (or Super Fans) are players who adopt your game experience as part of their identity. Their behaviour and commitment to the game is as deep whether they have the disposable income to drop $thousands or simply a small regular $1 per week. Designers have to understand that the capacity for Super-Fans to commit for the longer term is more scalable and sustainable than any strategy that were to target Whale-like behaviour. This is because the focus is on developing a sustainable committed audience. That audience delivers value and support beyond just financial considerations and at the same time can deliver more predictable revenues over time. A community of SuperFans brings sustainable returns closer to how compound interest works (building and building value in our game) rather than individual peaks in income generated from a small group of very wealthy individuals. The unfortunate reality is that very often Whale players tend not to be all community focused. Their needs and behaviours can even be contradictory to sustaining the wider audience of players necessary for sustainability. Relying on a small number of fickle players who may churn at a whim is extremely risky. Understanding why players fall in love with your game and how to deliver that value consistently and authentically to them is necessary to scale service games. An ethical and player-focused design philosophy is always more effective for the longer term. By the time a player becomes a Super-Engaging user, they will often have come to value game-related status, skill, and power, including ways to communicate their identity through the lens of that game. This tends to tap deeply into tribalism, not just expressed in the game but in their general life through collectibles, clothing, and digital forms of personalisation. Interestingly, focusing on our SuperFans often shows that a key aspect needed to sustain their engagement is providing social visibility of their actions and status. This feeds back to positively reinforce 'Engaging' life stage players who aspire to their capabilities, features, and cosmetics. This can help feed meaningful community experiences. Another reason to focus on SuperFans who value shared experiences rather than Whales, who tend to have a more internalised focus.

- **Reengaging**: Players churn, even those that were once Super-Fans, and even if we see incredible loyalty from our audience so far, to ignore this reality is to risk the sustainability of your game. Real life sometimes just gets in the way. As a result, it's always important to understand how we reduce the barriers for players to return after an extended break. The needs of these players, like each of the life stages we have outlined, will be different. In the case of a reengaged user, we have some stark elements to consider. Reengaged users are likely to not correctly remember how to play, which means they can get frustrated, especially when they are required to go through the original first-time experience. This can feel like an intolerable barrier to them. The Legend of Zelda: Breath of the Wild[4] is a game which I admire greatly, but as a player I have found myself not finishing the game, and every time I try again, I am profoundly frustrated by having to restart as I simply can't remember all the actions needed to play. As designers, we need to consider options, offers, and motivations to get back into playing for lapsed players. They are considerably cheaper to re-acquire than new users and have the potential to engage and convert to spending much more readily, however, every update, every release after that lapse means that the player has already missed out on vital information. The gap in their knowledge of the game expands, and the idea of starting again can easily seem unassailable. Finding a way to create what could be called a Lapsed

Time User Experience to optimise the user journey for this kind of player can be extremely beneficial.

- **Sideways Funnel**: A way to look at life stages is to think about it as a sideways funnel or "Lifecycle Pipeline." There are generally more people who enter the funnel than who reach the end. But unlike a traditional 'sales funnel,' we need to think about the role that ongoing engagement plays as a pipeline moving the player along the path to deeper engagement. We can think about how we activate, convert, and reengage our audiences from those just in the Discovery stage all the way to SuperFans and how we build on the inherent virality that a strong, active community can help deliver.

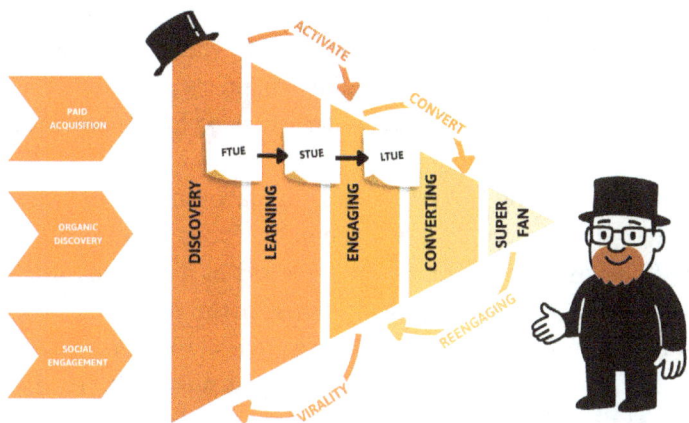

FIGURE 10.4   Lifecycle as a funnel.

Power Curves

Power in games usually refers to the multiplication of the effectiveness of basic player actions through some factor related to progression, situation, and equipment. As such, they are intrinsically linked to progression and the difficulty experienced by the player. These are actions which can be broken down into basic numbers and where the game can apply modifiers to them. The numbers on the roll of a dice modified by some variable are very common to anyone who has ever played a board game. Tabletop games, from classical miniature wargames to Table Tops Role Playing Games (TTRPGs) like *Dungeons & Dragons*, have made dice modifiers central to the experience. The basic principle that my +1 sword is not as effective as a +2 is obvious, but when combined with other numerical factors, the implications of incremental increases can become more complex. For example, if a player character has armour this can affect their opponent from effectively striking them, this will affect the ability of that opponent to successfully hit at all, and even when hit, the level of damage that the player character might take. These factors scale as the player progresses in the game, and they may see a commensurate increase in the difficulty they experience when facing a 'bigger' enemy. We might start out facing a Rat at first, but later we encounter a more dangerous enemy, a spider, then a wolf, and later a bear. The difficulty we face increases each time, but so does the players' skill. However, if the game doesn't also increase the modifiers available to the character, the game will quickly get too difficult – no longer feeling fair. To reflect this, we provide modifiers through rewards and progression that help make the player feel more powerful. However, as soon as they progress, they can lose interest in the earlier content. This reflects the concept of diminishing returns we also discussed in Chapter 4.

There are several elements to consider when exploring power curves:

- **Natural Learning Curve**: Players will have a natural learning curve as they start to comprehend the games core concepts, interaction methods, as well as the specific nuances of using equipment, techniques, and the specific interactions in the moment – e.g. a particular enemy's patterns or vulnerabilities. This tends to take time to start, then rapidly increase before plateauing. Players have their own skill ceiling, which can make it challenging to set difficulty in a way which will be seen as fair to everyone. Put this in context with a multiplayer game, if the game just provides linear progression for skilled players only, that will leave less skilled players behind very rapidly, rapidly dividing the audience and potentially making the game dull for everyone – as they can no longer play fairly with friends. Managing the sensation of power, as well as avoiding inexorable increases, is vital to game balance and ensuring play remains interesting over the longer term.

- **Scaling progression**: Making each incremental step to increase power levels requires increasing levels of effort and exchange to obtain, which can slow the progress. This helps to minimise the differences between players and to reduce the net impact of power versus skill. A significant risk in many games is too much Power escalation that can undermine the game experience by removing the challenge and, as a result, the consequences (and indeed meaning) of playing. In multiplayer games, power escalation can unduly split the audience into segments which are each too small to sustain the critical mass needed to ensure we always have access to competitors who can offer a meaningful challenge.

- **Grind Rewards**: Linking rewards to effort and time engaged with play as well as success is important to ensure that less skilled players can still progress and compete on a relatively level playing field. However, these have to be carefully considered to avoid completely undermining the value of skill in a game. Multiplayer Online Battle Arena games are very focused on skill, and players can be very sensitive to power rewards; potentially why successful new Multiplayer Online Battle Arena titles have been quite extremely rare. Even outside the world of multiplayer, 'Grind Rewards' can be super important to avoid players rage-quitting games. If a player is coming up against a significant boss in a game like Archero, they don't expect to succeed the first time. They will lose the 'big rewards' but will retain lower-level rewards, allowing multiple attempts to not just help in terms of practice to hone their skills, but also to 'buff' their abilities.

- **Short Term Buffs and Nerfs**: The terms Buff and Nerf seem to have originated in the MMO Ultima Online and refer to ways to amend player and monster power improvements (Buffs) or limitations (Nerfs). Whilst often used to describe permanent changes, time-limited or single-session power modifiers can contribute to engaging gameplay. For example, a potion, spell, or power-up token triggered by the player as consumable items can make all the difference in that moment to success. These moments have a visceral impact on our excitement, as whilst we understand that they are temporary, players attribute the results to their skill in using them. Scarcity is key to making consumable items interesting to players, but that can be managed in different ways. First, making them inherently rare, of course, can work; however, additionally the design can adjust the level of modifier, the costs to access, duration of benefit, cool down periods after their use or even simple capacity (how many we can hold) limits. Additionally, what other dilemma factors apply, such as can these consumables be stacked with others? And can these produce emergent or additive effects? The ability to upgrade Buffs and Nerfs can be linked into progression and may include other conditions such as cost of ingredients, actions required to prepare (crafting), or even some conditions which restrict access to those upgrades (ratchets), such as having to have unlocked a contact, built a particular building or be a specific level to access the 'recipe' needed to create the upgraded version. A fascinating exercise that has been used in interviews for game designers is to ask, "How many different types of health potion can you devise when the only variables you have are Time and Health points?" One example might be a simple 50 HP potion. But by adding time variables we may also have one that delivers 10 HP per 3 s over a 15 s period. That is meaningfully different from the simple version. How about one which gives 200 HP immediately but then takes away 100 after 30 s has elapsed – killing the character if they have fallen below that threshold. That has a profoundly different playing impact. Oh! And the minimum pass rate for this as an interview question is to have at least ten distinct variations!

- **Randomness**: Adding a random number generator to an activity has a levelling potential, especially where our power is applied to that variable independently from our personal skill. This provides space and ambiguity, mitigating the inexorable effect of progression. However, getting the range of variability right is vital in order to not make our actions feel pointless. Skill still matters. Additionally, as has already been stated, true randomness is not always great and it's important to ensure that we use pseudorandom models where possible instead. Gauging the random number range and associated scale of incremental power values can be very subjective and can directly affect 'Game Feel.' This is most clearly seen when considering different dice used in TTRPGs. In *Dungeons & Dragons*, we tend to use a D20 with proficiency bonuses and statistics adding +1 for each increment. In Chaosium's classic game, Call of Cthulhu,[5] players use two 10-sided dice to create a number between 01 and (1)00, with player scores which often start very low and when we progress it is usually just a few points at a time, if at all. As a result, we quickly feel somewhat powerful after just a few sessions in D&D; but in Cthulhu we often feel quite incompetent and vulnerable – we also tend to lose our characters to 'Insanity' before we ever get to feel powerful. These approaches to randomness directly create key elements of the different emotional experience of each game. There are additional lessons about how to apply conditional randomness across traditional dice, TTRPG, and board game systems that can apply to any game design. For example, the maths behind the concept of rolling multiple dice and choosing the best (or worst) used in character creation of Advantage/Disadvantage in DND 5e[6] informs how we might minimise extreme variations of randomness without removing the possibility entirely. Mathematician and comedian, Matt Parker, covers the probabilities involved in Advantage roles in exquisite detail in one of his videos on YouTube.[7]

- **Orthogonal Design**: Games often have multiple independent systems which do not directly affect each other and provide separate benefits for gameplay and progression. For example, a game may have a system for climbing when exploring a 3D environment and a crafting system for making equipment or potions. These moments are totally independent and each may have its own set of progression, or they may be tied into the character's general progression. Systems in games may have some level of interaction with other systems to different degrees; for example, this may include:

  - **Mutual Exclusivity:** Each choice, Fighting, Crafting, Climbing, is distinct and does not overlap in function.

  - **Circular Counterplay:** Each option (Scissors/Paper/Stone) beats one and loses to another, ensuring no dominant strategy.

  - **Equal Power Dynamics:** There is no option that is outright stronger than the others across all matchups, but there may be differences in application. Driving a car or a motorbike can cover the same distance on the road as effectively, but the driving feel is different.

  - **Diversity of Choices:** Each option can be utilised for different scenarios, but some will be a better fit in a particular situation. Choosing to fight, try stealth, or hacking may all be options, but they have different costs, benefits, and outcomes. The use of dilemmas usually adds to the playing experience.

- **Emergent Systems:** The combination of different systems can create unexpected benefits or conditions which unlock new ways of playing the game. This can be the simple 'twist' of rules needed to make a puzzle game more interesting or layers of improvement such as taking an "Eldritch Bolt," adding the Fire Element, then a 'Sniper' ability and "Multibolts" power-up. How different would this be in terms of use if it were the "Water" element or if instead the ability to "Grapple" were added?

- **Prestige Systems**: *Chapter 8: Functions of Exchange* introduced this principle where players actively choose to reset a progressed item in return for further gameplay. This, as mentioned, is an excellent way to help sustain the progression path through games. Players voluntarily decide to sacrifice their progress; it is a significant sacrifice, but one which such systems reward through visual signalling, performance improvements, as well as offering the chance for players to enjoy again the steps involved in rebuilding that item. Where these benefits are orthogonal to the core systems, this can be particularly helpful to sustain longer-term playability without introducing too much power escalation.

Game Economy as a Story

There is another lens to consider when we think about balance, which is the role it plays in revealing the game narrative. Games are stories where we are the ones acting and play an important role both in terms of acting as a kind of 'reward' mechanism in the Context Loop, but also in how we think about the journey of the playing experience more generally, as explored in *Chapter 5: What Is a Game Anyway*. Here however we want to explore how narrative thinking can also add an additional dimension to economy design as experienced by the player.

- **Narrative Unlocks**: Communicating the impact of changing power dynamics is something we can deliver through the use of the game and personal experience narrative. Demonstrating the increasing power of the enemies we face can be part of the player journey, we can communicate an expectation of a change in difficulty as we enter new regions or levels of the game, or as we progress in a specific run during a session. We can communicate the unlocking of new levels of power or new options for ways to play through story moments, reveals, and 'unboxing' moments when we obtain rewards (or indeed make purchases). Where we illustrate the mechanics of play through visual, narrative, and audio elements in the game, we deepen the immersion and avoid a 'Dragon' being seen as just a bigger 'Rat.'

- **Missions and Challenges**: The way a game communicates the short- and longer-term game missions and challenges has both a world-building and framing function; helping to define how players experience the game. Part of what helps a game feel balanced is how the game presents such challenges and manages any queues of these elements; including how integrated that is with the game's narrative as well as UX/UI design. This includes the information we leave out, and the possibility space that allows for players to set their own expectations of challenge. Such expectations can also be reinforced with the mission configs, narrative, and reward payout. We can even chain together missions and challenges to create a narrative arc. For example, imagine a mission in a sandbox game like Baldur's Gate 3[8] where there are some thugs who kidnapped a servant from a castle (Challenge 1), the player goes on the mission and faces an initial group of guards, gets the rewards but in the process learns that this servant was an important person and they have been captured by a Gang Leader who knew their real identity (Challenge 2). Thinking about the management, release, and context of how we signpost to players the next task can be powerful and does not have to railroad the player but provides an effective lens to maximise the player experience. The spawning of the thugs can start slow, but then a building opens, and more enemies pour out (Challenge Stage 3). We may even see the Gang Leader holding the servant with a pistol pointing at them, perhaps they leave with just a few of the gang to take you out… (Challenge Stage 4) Throughout each challenge stage, difficulty and reward levels can escalate through each fight, up to the boss fight with the gang leader. Those stakes can be reset for subsequent missions or ratcheted against the players' overall progression.

- **Emotional Texture**: One of the most impactful talks at GDC for the author was the talk at GDC 2014 by Florian Steinhoff.[9] In that talk, he explored how important the emotional impact of play is for engagement. Opening with the statement that 'Anger is a very powerful emotion,' he went on to explain that even in a cute, supposedly casual experience like Jelly Splash, emotions are part of the 'played experience' and indeed the personal narrative we experience in a game. We all know that moment in a game where we are super engaged and then we lose. We did something not quite right, didn't have access to the right move, or just hit a time limit. And we lose it! We explode with rage and frustration. However, this kind of anger is not one of aggression. This is not directed at a person and is not harmful to our own sense of identity or those around us. We may have a passing, instant desire to throw our mobile device out the window or our controller through our TV screen, but this explosion of energy is, in fact, engagement. Immersion is deeply connected to emotional engagement, and this is not always just cosy and clean, this involves the whole range of human responses. Key to this approach is realising that the game experience needs 'emotional texture'. Players need moments of "Peaking difficulty" (what Florian referred to as the FUUUU moments) of intense frustration which are noticeably harder to play. These are moments that show players that they can fail and that their actions in the game matter. The level of peak difficulty needs to be sufficient to make the challenge meaningful, frustrating, and importantly deeply satisfying when they eventually win. Players may have to retry multiple times, but they should never feel that it is impossible to succeed. Additionally,

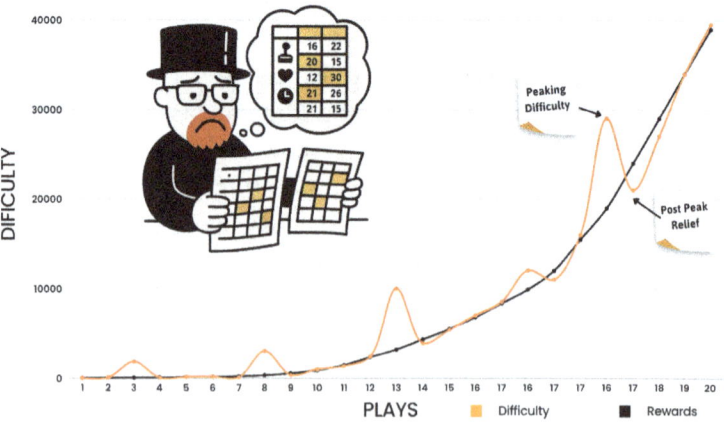

FIGURE 10.5 Spikes in reward and difficulty.

it is important that each attempt has some (reduced) reward so they can feel that despite the set-back we continue to progress. The moment of victory should be intense with an appropriate level of pay-off in terms of rewards, narrative, and satisfaction and also ideally followed by 'post-peak-relief' level. This is often a much easier moment of play where the player gets to relish the newfound power they have unlocked. This often is a good time to introduce new playing techniques or obstacles. A time to teach new rules without too much pressure. When the game has this kind of 'pressure-build' moments throughout the progression of a game we create the emotional texture needed to deepen emotional engagement in the game necessary to help convert users to spending. Florian defined a FUUUU factor mathematically as a ratio of Attempts to Play versus 'Nearly Won.' That description is critical to understanding "emotion texture." To Fail completely is not emotionally interesting. To succeed is not emotionally interesting. It is when we believe we should have succeeded that drives this positive form of frustration, especially where we 'know' that the potential to win was there if only we optimised our strategy.

Interview

GAME FEEL AND ECONOMY BALANCING –
AN INTERVIEW WITH LUNA JAVIER

Game economy design is not just about numbers; it's about understanding player psychology and creating an experience that feels engaging, rewarding, and balanced. In a recent conversation with Luna Javier,[10] former Design Director of Altitude Games, we explored the intersection of game feel and economic balancing – how the emotional experience of the player interacts with resource flows, progression, and monetisation.

Javier brings a unique perspective to game design, describing herself as a 'feels designer' rather than a 'math designer.' This distinction underpins her approach to economy balancing, focusing not just on spreadsheets but on how players emotionally experience progression, failure, and success. Throughout our discussion, she shared her insights into balancing game mechanics, designing for retention, and ensuring that monetisation enhances – rather than disrupts – the player experience.

Javier's career in game design spans more than 20 years, beginning with Anino Games,[11] where she was involved in making CD-ROM games – literally burning and delivering the physical discs herself. Over time, her experience evolved through Boom Zap Entertainment,[12] where she worked on Hidden Object Puzzle Adventure Games, before cofounding Altitude Games in 2014. This transition from small indie projects to large-scale mobile and web-based free-to-play games has shaped her understanding of game economies.

When developing a new game, Javier highlights the significant differences between working on self-published titles and client-driven projects. "For the starting years of Altitude, we did just self-publishing. So, it was really a bunch of friends who wanted to make our own mobile game for ourselves and not for anybody else," she explains. "And then obviously that didn't turn out very well. And then we switched into Work for Hire."

The work-for-hire model introduced a structured approval process, where publishers like Pikpok,[13] Kongregate,[14] and Big Fish[15] would request pitches that ranged from reskinning existing games to developing entirely new concepts. Javier describes the challenges of working with different publishers:

> "Some partners are more creatively controlling... Others are much more open. Like it's literally, 'We trust you. We'll check once in a while, but you make all the decisions and we're hands off,'" said Javier.

Before any development begins, the pitch process plays a critical role in determining whether a game concept moves forward. Javier explains that pitch formats have evolved over time, particularly in different genres.

> "We did hyper-casual for about a year and a half during the pandemic. And the pitch format there was literally one slide, with one image and a few bullets," said Javier.

Regardless of the format, the goal remains the same: clearly communicating the core gameplay concept, market viability, and development risks.

> "The pitch isn't just the game idea and why it's cool and the features, because that's kind of easy. We would do market research, competitor research, everything from the scope of the project. We would put in the pitch already the project plan," said Javier.

An interesting addition to this process is the use of early marketing tests, producing ad creatives to gauge player interest before full development. However, she acknowledged the exhaustive nature of the process:

> "We just made ads from Unity recording. It was gruelling because we would make like two or three game ideas a week just hoping to get CTR rates that were high enough. And sometimes something would go through, but most of them don't," said Javier.

Whilst gruelling, this approach does at least provide an indication of the viability of a given concept.

Once a game idea has been approved, the focus shifts to prototyping the core loop. Javier explains their approach:

> Right after the pitch, we do the core loop prototype, which means that you need rewards feeding in and some kind of progression, but we're not strict about the numbers there.

Rather than meticulously balancing values at the prototype stage, she prioritises proving that the loop itself is engaging.

> Just rig the amount, it doesn't matter. Just make sure they're earning some coins and spending them on something.

However, the balancing process becomes critical once the first-time user experience is designed.

> "The first couple of minutes, you need to be able to see the progression and feel some of it," she explains. "You start getting some power, but still, it's very smooth and easy, and you feel good and it's rewarding."

At this stage, her team transitions from instinctual game feel to structured data analysis.

> "We iterate on this process all the time, but right now, after our core loop prototype, we have a first-time user experience prototype. Then we go for day one retention and day seven content," said Javier.

One of the most fascinating aspects of Javier's approach is the balance between numerical design and player perception.

> I have a team of game designers right now and half of us are feels designers and half of us are math designers or systems designers really.

Systems designers start with a spreadsheet, mapping out numbers, progression, and level balance from the outset. Javier, however, works in the opposite way, trying to understand the player experience itself.

> "One conversation I had recently with a systems designer... he described how he imagined players progressing: playing two or three battles, unlocking a base, upgrading something, and so on. And I said, 'Okay, your game does not play like that at all,'" said Javier.

The numbers had been carefully mapped, but they didn't align with the actual player experience. This is where game feel overrides pure data modelling. The player experience has to come first, and the numbers need to match that – not the other way around.

With the rise of games-as-a-service, ongoing balance adjustments have become necessary. Javier outlined that they have a team that monitors games that are live and uses the data from that to back up their assumptions as they refine in future releases. This iterative process allows them to refine economy balancing after launch.

> We just release in very, very small chunks. So we don't even have to worry about the rest of the sheet yet.

Javier stresses that testing with real players is vital and that for game balancing whilst numbers are important, you need all of that. It remains essential to put the game in the hands of real players and understand what they experience and how that makes them feel.

Monetisation is a natural extension of game balance.

> "For our mobile games, we only do rewarded ads and IAP," Javier explains. "So we don't do interstitials, which automatically solves some problems."

Her team prioritises making in-game purchases feel natural rather than forced. The reward has to be something that the player really wants. Players only watch rewarded ads or indeed engage in any form of exchange for benefits they actually value.

> "You want them to give you their money willingly because they like something so much and they want it again." Said Javier.

Javier's approach to balancing and economy design ultimately focuses on the player's journey.

> "Get a draft of your numbers, plug it in the build, and test it right away." Said Javier.

Numbers matter, but they need to serve the emotional experience first and foremost. Whether designing for game feel, balancing progression, or introducing monetisation, the goal remains the same: ensure that every action in the game has meaning and impact. It is all about understanding what the players care about and what motivates them to play.

Interview

DESIGNING NARRATIVE INTO THE GAME ECONOMY – AN INTERVIEW WITH VALENTINA TAMER

Too often, the role of narrative in how game systems function, especially the economy design, is missed by designers. We explored this aspect of design by talking to Valentina Tamer,[16] Narrative Designer, and Writer at Ubisoft. Tamer explores how storytelling connects intimately with the economy, player agency, and design balance. Narrative is not merely text or lore, but a dynamic system that shapes everything from challenge curves to progression to emotional pay-off.

> Narrative systems need to be balanced just like other gameplay features and it is so deeply entwined in all aspects of the game that it is impossible to ignore it.

Challenge, she adds, is itself a narrative:

> It's also narrative, it's drama basically. You decide that the player starts with a tutorial... then things start to ramp up... they get stronger and they can overcome these issues, and so this dramatic curve has these fluctuations so that the result is a satisfying game experience.

The principles of narrative expand even into the environment and visual aspects of gameplay, and as Tamer points out, even sandbox games carry narrative through design:

> "The environment holds a story in itself... things get destroyed and rebuilt and you see that history in its elements very often. Just the geometrical shapes that we are navigating and the light and how it falls onto these shapes influences how we perceive an experience," she says.

Tamer explains how games can be arranged on a scale of player agency when it comes to story. Interaction doesn't necessarily negate the role of linear narrative, and branching narrative does not always escalate to hundreds of alternative endings. There are endless variations.

> [When] We give more storytelling agency to the players... but the level design, game design, and writing... have to collaborate to develop these dramatic arcs.

A lot of game developers fixate on the parallels to movie storytelling, trying to transpose a roughly 2-hour film script format into a game that might take over 40 hours to play. This often fails to acknowledge how we consume game materials differently from film content. Players tend to apply their agency to take their time and explore (and loot!) every possible aspect in a scene. This can suck the urgency and drama out of the moment. Something which movie-goers simply don't have time to consider as the next impactful moment arrives. Writing structure from other formats can often offer more useful ways of thinking, from TV series or serialised narratives to the overlapping arcs found within soap opera writing. But trying to force these writing structures from other media onto games can sometimes crush player autonomy.

> "When I played [this one game] ... I ended up in a concentration camp and I was like, my god, I didn't make these decisions at all," said Tamer.

In this example, she didn't see her own decisions reflected in the development of the story, diminishing her sense of agency as a player. However, agency is not without limitations, and it is also important to think about expectation-setting:

> It's always finding about a balance of setting expectations and fulfilling these expectations respectfully so that the players get what they think they were promised.

Building the narrative structure not only creates the context that players engage with in the game, but it also plays a fundamental role in shaping economic systems and vice versa:

Game economy and narrative should always be tied together very closely, because the economy of what we do to earn what... is also story. This is also drama.

Games benefit from building on coherence, which means that every creative decision needs to stem from the same core... one that fits the mechanics, narrative, world, and the character. This means that narrative consistency needs to influence every decision at some level:

If you give me a list of rewards... different types of military weapons named exactly like they're called in real life, I know this is a [realistic] military shooter or something [with similar intent].

The core principle at play here is the role that narrative plays in providing a framing structure. World-building and narrative arcs provide a foundation which can then be reflected in player action, purpose, progression, and social engagement.

"Narrative framing of what you do and what its consequences are in the game world give players a sense of power and agency. ... When you do a repetitive action in order to help out an NPC that you like... that is emotionally rewarding even though the action itself might not be that complicated," said Tamer.

Discussing player progression, Tamer highlighted that storytelling itself should match the game's natural learning curves and challenges.

"Overcoming the odds... is a very dramatic thing in terms of storytelling, where somebody starts out in a position of powerlessness... and then they can come out victorious. You have a super tough enemy... and then afterwards you don't have boss fights for a while, but just normal enemies, and suddenly they're super easy... I actually am more powerful now," she says.

Thinking about narrative as layers can help game designers make more use of these techniques Tamer suggests:

I often think of narrative in games as like a Russian doll structure where you have the small arcs... then on top of that... the game's chapter... then the biggest arc is the entire game experience.

Each episode needs to be its own satisfying arc… but the season builds up to something bigger.

Designing for LiveOps and Seasons raises questions about sustainability and ongoing costs of content creation, but using narrative can come to the rescue:

It's called seasonal storytelling for a reason because they are seasons just like TV shows and it needs to be treated similarly.

However, live games, she argues, require planning and flexibility:

You always have to plan ahead a little bit. But that reactivity to players is something that can be done in live service games.

The key difference between games and other storytelling formats comes down to the principle of empowering Player Choice, even in more directed, linear experiences, Tamer emphasises agency and delivering on your promises:

Even the most linear video games still give the player the agency to navigate that story space. They decide the pacing, they decide the exact movements. If you set up the expectation that they can deeply influence the story and then it's all fake… chances are that players are gonna stop caring.

Tamer concludes with a clear takeaway:

Narrative should always be used to frame whatever is happening inside of the economy… to motivate players, to give meaning to what they're doing… and what that reward does to their character and their place in the world. Without narrative framing Players are going to stop caring about it or it's gonna feel like a chore.

NOTES

1 https://en.wikipedia.org/wiki/Slay_the_Spire
2 https://www.taylorfrancis.com/books/mono/10.1201/9781482267334/
   game-feel-steve-swink
3 https://www.taylorfrancis.com/books/mono/10.4324/9781315849102/
   games-service-oscar-clark

4 https://en.wikipedia.org/wiki/The_Legend_of_Zelda:_Breath_of_the_
Wild
5 https://en.wikipedia.org/wiki/Call_of_Cthulhu_(role-playing_game)
6 https://en.wikipedia.org/wiki/Editions_of_Dungeons_%26_Dragons
7 https://youtu.be/X_DdGRjtwAo?si=87kKnnL7SZEWmyFG
8 https://en.wikipedia.org/wiki/Baldur%27s_Gate_3
9 https://archive.org/details/GDC2014Steinhoff
10 linkedin.com/in/lunacruz
11 https://en.wikipedia.org/wiki/Anino_Games
12 https://en.wikipedia.org/wiki/Boomzap_Entertainment
13 https://en.wikipedia.org/wiki/PikPok
14 https://en.wikipedia.org/wiki/Kongregate
15 https://en.wikipedia.org/wiki/Big_Fish_Games
16 https://www.inkedin.com/in/valentina-tamer-9907009b

CHAPTER 11

Validating Your Game

DOI: 10.1201/9781003592471-11

VALIDATING GAME IDEAS WITH DATA

Making video games is one of the most complex endeavours imaginable. We combine narrative, logic, animation, art, audio effects, and music with visual storytelling, applied psychology, physics, lighting, and within both client and server technology. All of these components and skill sets are required to deliver a (sometimes) convincing simulated experience that our audience will not only judge against its functional delivery, but more importantly, on their own eclectic subjective personal taste. I have lost count of the number of times I have heard a player dismiss years of work from dozens of talented people with the simple phrase, "That Game Sucks." To make matters worse, as developers, we have to invest significant sums of money to get the experience to a stage where we can either release it ourselves or convince publishers and investors to hand over even more money to market it. That marketing activity requires its own set of skills and magical delivery (often underappreciated by the development team); and even once released, that's not the end. We then have to continue to support the community, potentially for decades of play! Despite this insanity games, as we have said, are the single largest form of digital entertainment on the planet. But how is it possible for any game team to pull off this superheroic feat without destroying themselves?

The reality is that games fail.

The key is testing them and iterating, and for that to work, we need data.

Test early, test often, and focus your designs using data insights.

Defining Vision Means Understanding "Why?"

Before we can validate any concept or game, we have to start by defining what 'Good Looks Like'. This isn't just a bunch of people getting together because we want to make 'this game' – although that's often how it starts. If we are making games, we will need to build a common understanding within our team about what it is we are planning on building. However, this is less about the technology, perhaps more importantly we need to understand why. In a podcast for GameDevLocal[1] Graham McAllister,[2] former Founder of Player Research, says that a clear Game Vision is central to the success of a team, and it's almost never about the talent of any individuals in that team. He argues that defining a game is not about the technical delivery, it's a psychology question. Who are our players? What do they care about? And what is it about our game that satisfies those needs?

Only when we truly have a common understanding of the "Why" of the game can we know that the art, gameplay, progression, rewards, and economy work together.

However, building a business around a single game vision is not usually enough. To turn our vision into a strategy, we must understand what we, as a team (founders), consider to be success; and not just for the one game if we want the team to be sustainable. This can't just be about revenue; we need to include other factors which help us to define what we value, our shared mission, and an honest understanding of what level of risk is acceptable.

There are several considerations:

Money: What is the scale of expectations for the business in terms of revenues that can realistically be expected to be delivered? And what might be possible if the business were to be explosively successful? This has to be grounded in a deep understanding of the following elements:

- **Total Addressable Market** (TAM): The total value in the market for your type of games product.

- **Serviceable Addressable Market** (SAM): The proportion of that market your games can realistically acquire.

- **Serviceable Obtainable Market** (SOM): The proportion of the serviceable addressable market which your business model could acquire – basically your targets, investment, and market power.

Values: People who make games, indeed people who make companies, have a set of core principles which drive their ambition forward and which glue them together in a shared identity. These factors deeply impact the sense of 'Tribe' within the organisation and help define the flavour of activities that the organisation delivers. They must be authentic to have any meaning, and if they are not 'lived' by not only the management but also any intermediary management, they quickly become meaningless or even counterproductive. Values should not be considered as an afterthought, or a set of five random words painted on an office wall. When they truly express the identity of a team, they communicate the culture of that team and help empower individuals to act. This means that the business can develop the following:

- **Shared Endeavour**: Creates a shorthand for the wider team to instinctively interpret and execute on requirements, steering the organisation to a common mission.

- **Prioritisation:** Helping management make strategic decisions on what is most important for the team and the agility to rapidly take the team as a whole with them.

- **Relevance:** Allows the team to focus on decisions, delivery, and communication consistently in ways that connect the leadership, team, and audience.

Expression: Effective teams recognise and own the passions that are driving their design vision and sense of purpose as an organisation. What is adding meaning to what you are trying to deliver beyond making money? This could be about sharing some conviction about profound issues affecting humanity at one extreme or something as simple and uncontroversial as how much we like cats. This includes:

- **Communicate Ideas**: To matter to an audience, every medium needs to convey something that the creators have to say. Games are no different from books, TV, and film in how they need to convey some 'truth' from the profound to the profane. These ideas can be in the mechanics, art, narrative, audio, or any combination.

- **Add to Genre**: For many designers, there is something they want to bring to a form of play or game narrative style, which comes from a deep love of previous experiences. This could be to 'correct' issues they experienced or to focus down on a specific mechanic and show how it can deliver alternative experiences.

- **Peer Recognition**: It is important not to underestimate the significance of the desire to gain respect from other game developers. This can be through formal awards, sales, or even just reviews from people who matter. Defining what peer recognition you are seeking (if any) can also help frame how you tackle a game and what success looks like. This might be based on Metacritic reviews, winning awards, or having your game trailer released during the Super bowl.

Market: Finally, it's important not to ignore the market itself and to deeply understand the forces at play. Whether your game is a new entrant or an established player, it's essential to appreciate the competitive landscape and the conflicting demands for attention of the audience. The commercial issues that made 2024 so difficult for many developers demonstrated not only the impact of societal changes from the recovery from the pandemic and general economic stress, but also that the industry has now reached a mature stage requiring more strategic thinking to ensure success.

- **Market Gap**: From your analysis of the competitive, political, and community trends can you identify underserved audiences or changes in trends, such as formerly dominant games losing traction to newer entrants. What player needs are not being served, and that your game can deliver?

- **Innovation**: From understanding the substitute products for your game in the market, can you identify specific new solutions or approaches which can radically change the experience for the better. This could be engaging mechanics, new forms of story, or simply ways to reduce established friction in the market. Rewarded Ads was one of these innovations in 2014 and led to mobile games becoming the dominant format not just because it unlocked revenue from more players, but it also provided a new discovery method. Scott Rodger's[3] 'Triangle of Weirdness'[4] warns about trying to introduce too much change, advising developers to only change one thing at a time.

- **Addressable Audience**: One of the key issues affecting the industry at the time of writing, and likely to continue, is our ability to target players who might be interested in our games. One of the side effects of how the privacy debate has played out is the consolidation of data amongst a handful of companies, and this has led to increased costs and reduced effectiveness of games marketing. As a result, when considering the market, it is necessary to fully embrace the audience not just in terms of the values they have, the needs (Utility) they seek from our game, but also the channels through which they can be reached and the messaging which will motivate them.

It's quite common for teams to use Design Pillars, or single unmovable phrases, to define these aspects as 'What Good Looks Like' as solid immovable principles. Whilst this can be helpful to anchor the core of what you are trying to build; it can also be a barrier to adaptability and iteration. That is kind of the point of pillars, things which the designer considers to be a sacred cow. However, having sacred cows creates blind spots and can prevent adaptation to what better suits the needs of the audience. As an alternative method, there is the concept of Vectors. This means that rather than just stating that we are making a "Stealth" or "Crafting" game, instead we establish how we measure what makes these categories important to us in terms of driving success. Is it that we want to make a 'Stealth Game' or that we have identified that the target audience responds to stealth mechanics with deeper engagement? Or even that the 'Stealth' subgenre (needs) presents a market opportunity?

Science and Design

Going beyond what we want to make and focusing on what the audience responds to can greatly improve our chances of success. Adding a method to measure this creates a chance for us to test our ideas with that audience in meaningful ways, which can help us make the game even better than if we just rely on our own 'Genius'. We can learn from the scientific method to help us escape our own bias. This means creating our design as a hypothesis, setting out our expectations for what we think that will deliver, and then testing it and seeing if we hit those goals. This takes nothing away from the creative process; rather, it focuses it into something powerful, minimising our own bias.

Central to this way of working is the Key Performance Indicator (KPI). This term just means what metric will be used to validate the result we predict we can achieve. There are many metrics that can be used, and at different stages of development, there will be different combinations and scores. Using numbers and various methods, data capture is mandatory, but there are different approaches to gather information of different types; but this breaks into two fundamental types.

- **Qualitative Research**: Used to consider the quality of elements, usually based on human reactions and emotional responses. They can be conducted as individual interviews or focus group sessions even ethnographic studies (although that is usually for categories rather than individual games). The results are usually gathered through surveys or based on observed behaviour and assigned a score. The Likert Scale[5] is a common method used to ensure some consistency in responses with either 5 (offering a symmetrical choice) or 4 (which forces the interviewee to take a stance).

- **Quantitative Data**: Based on numerical data and statistical analysis to identify the scale of response and significance of outcomes within predesigned experimental structures. Game teams have the capacity to collect on various aspects from Attribution (how players are acquired and what targetable characteristics they have in common); Gameplay (actions performed during the process); Conversion (spending habits within the game); and Sentiment (social engagement and tone of responses). This should always be done responsibly, and there are considerable fines in place for privacy breaches. The author helped produce the UK's Information Commission Office to develop a set of best practices for data collection for game developers.[6]

We can use both approaches to decide how we are going to measure our KPIs, but key to making this effective is to ensure that our 'experimental design' is solid. This means that the experience must be consistently testable, that variables are significant (of a sufficient scale to be representative), independent (not manipulatable by the researcher), and as far as practical 'double-blinded,' meaning we cannot influence or be influenced by the

FIGURE 11.1 Failure is Always An Option.

participants. And it's important to remember that "Failure is Always an Option,"[7] and that is important to know the reality and kill a game early, to avoid investing more money into a game which is not going to be successful.

Game testing often compromises some of these factors due to budget constraints and external factors (such as not wanting to damage marketing launches by sharing with too many players too early). These compromises will affect the validity of the results, but early in development, such testing can still be helpful to set the development on the right track for confirmation later. It's also worth noting that research doesn't always (in fact, rarely) show a binary success/failure. There are often unanswered questions, especially as we attempt to diagnose the data further in order to understand what the key causes of issues were – such as significant increases in churn at specific stages of the First Time User Experience (FTUE). Deciding whether to give the game another chance, to fix, or to be brutal and kill those games takes courage and insight. Usually, it's worth planning in at least a second test before killing a game to confirm those results weren't a mistake or coincidence from some external factor (such as a massive increase in both cost per install and Churn during the weekend where Baldur's Gate 3 was released – true story!). However, you should also avoid being too forgiving of your data, if the second test doesn't show a positive rate of change (which you should define in advance), then be prepared to kill it and move to the next concept.

Typical KPI factors used by game developers include:

- **Platform Ranking**: e.g. Top 10/100 in Apple/Google/Steam games

- **Revenue**: Regular (e.g. monthly, quarterly revenue targets)

- **ROAS**: % Return on Advertising Spend over a period (e.g. D30/D60/D90)

- **LTV**: The lifetime value of the player in terms of their cost of acquisition and support versus their net revenue, usually over a period (e.g. D30/D60/D90)

- **Retention Levels**: The % of players who remain layering over a period (e.g. D1/D14/D30/D60/D90/D120)

- **Engagement (Game)**: Intensity of play is usually measured through session duration and sessions per day

- **Engagement (Socials)**: The volume and proportion of interactions to posts/updates on social platforms compared to the followers

- **Net Promoter Score (NPS)**: The proportion of players who would recommend it to a friend

- **Metacritic Scores**: The average review scores for the games over multiple platforms across professional critics and consumers

- **Awards**: Public recognitions of quality, usually from events, trade press, or public institutions

- **Press Coverage**: The volume and reach (number of views) of external mentions driven by review/press releases/announcements and wider interest in your game

- **Sentiment Analysis**: The proportion of positive words (compared to negative and neutral) expressed in social and community posts relevant to your game

- **Cost Per Install**: The average spend in specific campaigns or across all marketing for each acquired customer download.

- **Stream/Content Views**: The level of engagement (e.g. minutes watched, total views) by the (CPI) audiences of content creators using your game as the focus of their material

- **Players**: The total number of players in a given period which can be broken into Daily Active, Monthly Active, and Concurrent. Additional characteristics include New, Returning (usually within seven days), and Resurrected (returning after more than e.g. 30 days).

Whether you are part of the leadership team or an economy designer trying to improve the performance of a game, understanding the vision for the game as a vector with specific KPIs is exceptionally powerful and will become extremely helpful when considering interventions to modify and drive solutions to improve any game.

DEVELOPMENT LIFESTAGES

Applying validation for your game changes at different stages in the development process.

Concept Development

Economy designers rarely get involved in developing the initial concept for a commercial game in a studio, however, it is important to

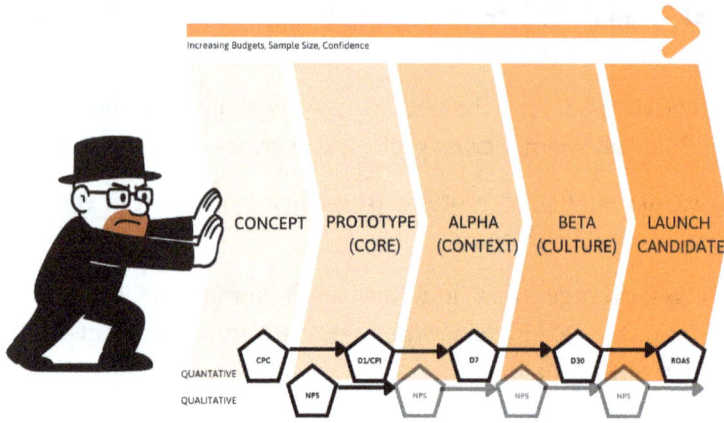

FIGURE 11.2   Rethinking milestone development.

understand the principles and concepts from which the game you are working on emerged originally. Although this is reductive, it is possible to break initial game design approaches into one of four types in terms of describing their origins – although in practice all games will include some element of each type.

- **Market Driven**: The design came from an analysis of player needs, from an understanding of the audience and an appreciation that they were underserved in the market at the time of development. Games which are designed for specific audiences will also tend to have some concept of how to target those audiences and focus on commercial principles. However, this means they can fall down if too little attention is paid to the emotional engagement and intrinsic delight within the mechanics and loops.

- **Experimentation**: One of the lessons from the surge in the Hyper-Casual market from 2016 to 2020 was the power of low-cost rapid iteration and development. Creating frameworks where a team can execute and test multiple designs after just a few hours of experimentation increases the understanding in the team of what works, hones their development skills, and provides more 'shots at goal' as cheaply as possible. However, it is important to retrospectively understand where those mechanics fit in terms of market reach and longer-term engagement to avoid the downward fate of the hyper-casual model.

- **Instinctive**: Every designer has heard random people telling them that they "…have a great idea for a game." Most designers I know have moments of ideation like this at least daily. What is hard for people who don't do this professionally to understand is that, usually, an idea is not valuable in itself. Success comes hard after solid planning, testing, iteration, and execution. That being said, a lot of games do start out of an original ephemeral concept that caught fire in the designer's imagination. The development of the game design that emerged from an instinctive spark to evolve along with the team and in response to audience interactions can be magical. This instinctive inspiration should not be ignored but can also be the source of tension when it comes without an appreciation of the market needs. The industry loves to celebrate the auteur designer and their magnum opus; but in games, it is very rare that one mind was solely responsible for the title's success.

- **Reconstructive**: There are arguably no totally new formats of games developed in practice. Play is such an established concept where the derivation of the mechanics, interactions, logic, rules, art, and narrative can be seen to have evolved from previous experiences. Developers often crave to reproduce a formative experience they had in their early days as a player, and this can provide the focus for their own development. To do this successfully, it is usually necessary to consider the influences and circumstances which led to the creation of that original game, rather than just how it felt to play the game that resulted. Designers must also consider how a modern audience will themselves have evolved in terms of expectations in terms of audio/visual quality, game player expectations, and narrative context. One effective method comes from simplification, deconstructing the game into base principles, reducing the scope, and then developing what remains into a unique game in its own sense. Another approach would be to take the principles of the game and reset them in a new context, often in audio/visual style, narrative, or genre. However the game deals with this, it's rarely good to simply clone a game you love and hope that it delivers success.

Core Production

Traditional development approaches require the design team to make assumptions about what will work for their audience. They will often be operating through different stages, including:

- **Prototype**: An initial expression of the methods of play using usually primitive elements or off-the-shelf assets to demonstrate how the core play experience will work.

- **Vertical Slice**: Usually, a delivery which includes all the core functional stages of play – showing the range of interactions and levels but not yet fully developed. This approach is often necessary for publishers to have confidence in the game but has critical risks as it requires a lot of expensive development before the game can be usefully market tested.

- **Alpha Build**: The first really playable version of the game, usually very buggy, and used internally (usually) to ensure that the end-to-end experience matches the vision. This is usually the first build which can be effectively market tested.

- **Beta Build**: This is the first publicly playable version of the game, often used for market testing and even 'Early Access' where players may even confirm their willingness to pay for playing that game.

- **Early Access/Open Beta/Soft Launch**: A light version of the launch process with some form of constraint on the ways players can access the game, but in essence, this is a live game and a fully realised game release which has to be of merchantable quality.

- **Launch**: The 'final' release of the game before it goes into LiveOps mode.

A more modern way to approach development takes lessons introduced from innovations in the Hyper-Casual market and the application of the principles of 'The Lean Startup.' This has been referred to as Test-Driven 'Development' and includes the following stages:

- **Paper Prototype**: Rapid ideation of the game concept through short paragraph descriptions up to e.g. one-page design documents, whiteboard diagrams, and even simple physical game elements (cards/

dice/blocks/modelling clay). The aim is to explore as many variations as possible and retain only the best-fitting concepts.

- **First Trailer**: Where only sufficient development time is spent on the winning concepts to develop a trailer of the experience the designer has in mind. This model uses only low-cost pre-produced assets from the game engine stores or known artists (the use of GenAI is becoming common, but this has some ethical and legal constraints which should not be ignored). Typically, such testing needs a solid experimental design, such as comparing the performance of trailers showing off, for example, two game mechanic variations with two art style variants. Especially early in the process, perhaps as an internal process for a concept to be progressed into development at all, to use ultra-low spend User Acquisition testing; spending as little as possible to get a remotely significant result. The KPI for these tests has to be 'Cost Per Click' engagement as there is nothing to actually play. The intention here is simply to get a feel for which variation has the best potential for audience interest.

- **D1 Test**: Having selected the variation (game mechanic and art style) which seemed to most appeal to our target audience, then build the game's Core Mechanic, ideally to the extent where there is at least sufficient for 20 minutes to an hour's worth of play. Ideally this would be via an endless loop with some rewards (but without progression elements). This needs to be rapid development, if the game fails to connect with players, we need to be prepared to throw it away and try again. Testing requires an updated trailer and a release to the relevant App Store or early-access platform; for example, Android and Itch.io. This is effectively a real launch of the game, where we recruit players again with an ultra-low-cost User Acquisition campaign, which gives us a chance to confirm our Cost Per Click is consistent as well as giving a "Cost Per Install." Because this is playable, it is also possible to measure Day 1 retention (D1). Ideally the game should include at least some basic data collection in the process including attribution and some method to track player behaviour. Additionally, at this stage it helps to run usability testing. This can be done through specialist researchers within internal testing labs, but generally it is not a good idea to run these tests personally as that introduces significant risk of bias. Online testing services like Antidote[8] and PlayTestCloud[9] are a fantastic way to get the scale, rapidity and generally bias-free analysis needed – arguably at least as effective as a biometric testing lab. Usability testing provides strong qualitative feedback from players – what they like/dislike and observations on how they engage in the user experience (UX), which is shown in recordings from the testing. This is invaluable to show where players get stuck or misinterpret instructions in ways that the development team (including QA) may never notice. Additionally, participants are surveyed and given a set of questions, which can give us the Net Promoter Score, helping us assess how engaged they are with the game – and an indication if they would recommend it to a friend.

Each variable that is tested for must have a predefined metric defining what KPI levels we expect for the testing to be effective, eliminating the option to fudge the results. Where we fail those success criteria, we should seriously consider discontinuing development. Retesting is an option (as above) where we can see how to resolve the issue rapidly. However, there must be a significant positive rate of change in the data in the follow-up test, or we risk going down a rabbit hole. Games which cannot iterate rapidly and that aren't brutal in their decision-making will escalate their costs and even sink too much of their funds into projects that are just going to fail later anyway. Developers following this approach need to move fast, take the lessons from game testing, pivot, and live another day to develop a more marketable experience before spending all of their investors' money.

- **D7 Test**: Once the team has evidence that they have a solid Core Loop, it is time to move onto the Context Loop – including the purpose, progression, optimisation and narrative pay-off. Just as with the D1 test, that means running relevant ultra-low-cost UA tests, but often this will need us to spend slightly more to ensure more statistical significance to our results. Ideally, tests at this stage include tracking a complete FTUE to ensure that it transitions the player from 'Learning to Engaging' as effectively as possible. Repeating the Qualitative User Testing is also ideal at this point where the budget allows. This helps with understanding the emotional impact we are trying to deliver through the player journey, as well as confirming that we have maintained our previous NPS levels. Small, rapid development remains very important, and it is recommended to repeat the testing process regularly as new gameplay systems are developed to ensure we are building improvements in layers, building confidence in each stage. Games which take too long, or which add too many new elements between tests, will not fully benefit from the approach.

- **D14-D30 Test**: After building confidence in short-term retention for the game, the next stage is to confirm the delivery of longer-term retention. Different teams and games will have to consider how they resolve not only D14 or D30 retention but also how specific aspects of the Cultural Loop are integrated. Indeed, the developer may decide to delay some elements of the experience until post-launch. Social play can throw a spanner into the planning of these kinds of tests. Multiplayer games require a critical mass of players available to play on demand. Success is as much down to the availability of other players as it is to the game experience itself, as players don't get to enjoy a game if they can't find someone to play with; and many testers will bail if they have to wait more than 30 s at any time. Getting the scale of testers necessary can be extremely expensive, and although 'Bots' can be far from ideal, they are necessary to manage lower volume testing. There are other elements of the game which may need to be implemented in order to ensure that the testing reflects the final experience. This can include showing off store-page designs or where relevant ad placements. Commercial revenue is not usually the main objective at this stage, but as developers, we need to know who such elements might affect player engagement positively and negatively. Some teams will use this early access stage to test pricing and even generate some initial revenue. This might be ads where relevant or some kind of initial 'Founder' offering. Once again where it is possible use ultra-low spend UA and User-Testing to get the additional information, but again it may make sense to increase UA spend at this stage to get larger audiences that will increase confidence in the results; but spending too much can negatively impact the initial launch impact. This stage tends to be where it is important to start building an engaged community through various social platforms and often is where we are actively running the game almost as if live. That includes early-stage versions of running LiveOps, DevOps, and Community management and transitioning the development process from classical product delivery to something that delivers sustainable, predictable regular updates.

- **ROAS Testing**: Having confirmed D30 retention, developers should turn to making sure that their monetisation models deliver the required levels of return and what impact this has on retention. This stage is all about working out the 'Return on Advertising Spend.' Terms like 'Soft Launch' are also used to describe this stage, but effectively the game is live and launched (although full-scale marketing has yet to be kicked off). This is the first point where we would start to use larger levels of UA spend to recruit a sufficient pool of players to have statistical significance in our results. Done well, this process also helps build momentum for the successful commercialisation of the game as well.

- **Launch & Scale**: Once we have confidence in both our retention and monetisation, we are basically ready for full Launch. As mentioned, the operation of the game is usually already in full Live operations mode by this point, but now that your proposition has evidence that it works, the brakes on marketing can come off with the confidence that the game can succeed and can start scaling! Except with the simplest games (ones usually with a Start/Middle/End) developers will need to sustain more development, more releases, and ongoing testing to sustain and continue to grow the game. How much and how frequently varies between games and genres.

Post Launch

Developing a solid marketing strategy is the topic for another book, but for an economy designer, the release of a game is generally just the beginning; especially for LiveOps games. Post launch we will need to focus on ways to deliver deeper engagement, retention, conversion, and importantly, sustaining the lifetime value of each player. Each season is effectively a new launch, and a new opportunity for testing and importantly, integrating lessons from previous releases. We need to continue to develop insights and integrate them into how we continue to deliver player value. The same techniques we use are often called for when a team is looking to review the performance of other existing games, not least when we are reviewing the market and trying to evaluate potential gaps in the market for new games as well as for content for our live experiences.

Some key techniques we can leverage include:

- **Player Insights**: As well as keeping track of the obvious KPIs for Retention and Revenues, it's important to keep track of other metrics such as session length, challenge completion, Win/Loss ratios, rate of content changes, engagement with crafting, etc. Indeed, anything that can help you understand what players are actually doing in the game. Tools like funnel analysis or heat maps showing the movement of players through each location can help us understand how effectively the game is communicating through narrative, visuals, and gameplay challenges. There may be whole features or gameplay locations that players are missing out on that contain key pickups or trigger specific encounters. Players not experiencing all of the intended gameplay can potentially create imbalance in terms of the power curves – i.e., later encounters may be too hard if the player doesn't unlock the extra XP to level up because they missed either too many lower-level fights or didn't collect enough resources. It is vital to understand the difference between how game elements should function versus what players actually do. This does not just help improve the UX but also can help discover new methods and engaging moments. Designers have to listen to what players do as much as what they say and be prepared to sacrifice our "sacred cows" when there are better ways to engage, balance, and sustain the experience.

- **Gap Analysis**: Extending from the Player Insights that have been collected, it becomes important to identify potential gaps. These can be found in the discrepancies between expected behaviour and reality revealed in game data, but often this can also be found within social posts, feedback, and ratings. Has there been a change in behaviour over time that coincides with a new update? Has the introduction of competitive or substitute games significantly impacted retention or sentiment analysis? What insights can give you clues as to what the cause was? What information or function is missing that would help us frame the activity? Do we have updates already planned to resolve that issue? Have we set any KPIs that would allow us to identify the significance of these issues? For example, if players who use a specific power-up early in the game retain better and show up as being more likely to spend – but those who do not, see significantly lower retention and conversion how can that step be better signposted? Can we fix this using an A/B test where we have a control group of players who don't see the improved changes to measure the actual impact? A/B testing is simply offering different cohorts of your audience alternative variations. This could be a trailer, or an in-game experience. Such tests can be managed via the advertising platform using deep links into the game, or in-game by isolating a selection of players based on their attribution data, some other factor or even at random. The results of such tests help us decide to create an activity which positively motivates players to try that power-up. NOTE: Prior to COVID, there were market changes including increased privacy rules and Apple's removal of the IDFA that reduced the efficacy of such A/B testing through ads. It is no longer possible to go into very fine detail with many variations, e.g. five different colours of buttons Unfortunately, this reduced accuracy makes it much more difficult to make statistically significant informed decisions. Instead, focus on discreet but meaningful variations, ideally changing just one element at a time, to get the most useful results.

- **Key Performance Indicators (KPI):** The importance of our KPIs has already been stated, but it remains the case that when we have a proposed solution, it is important to confirm that the fix actually works. This means that setting a target value for KPIs that help you confirm that you have achieved your intentional change remains vital. Setting what success in advance needs to become a muscle which you cannot ski; but which KPIs matter and how to ensure that testing is cost-effective is a balance of experimental design and the need for statistical significance. Additionally, there is a broader question about 'What Good Looks Like' for any game. The industry has a number of limitations when it comes to market data. On Mobile, there are teams like Sensor Tower[10] and Games Refinery[11] who have amazing systems, but the costs are prohibitive for anyone but the largest games teams. For PC games, there are sources like SteamDB[12] and SteamSpy[13], but these have significant issues due to the way they are hampered by the restrictions that Steam has put in place, and it's worse for console games. Whichever solution you choose in the end, the market data available is flawed at best, which means it's very hard to know if your KPIs are reasonable or not. Not having good access to general market data is risky, as it is possible to be complacent if internal data shows improvement. Was that the feature? Was that seasonal or some random fluctuation in the market? Looking for patterns in the rate of change across different KPIs can help mitigate this risk.

- **Defining an Activity**: Making recommendations on how to resolve any gap that has been identified has to realistically meet the scope available to the team. Designers with a broad remit can consider anything from building new levels, game modes, or season pass offers. Those in more specialist roles may be more limited, gameplay designers may need to tweak the parameters of a level to make one section a little easier or another a little more difficult. They may need to swap out rewards for something more narratively appropriate. For a monetisation designer, they suggest changing the packaging of a store bundle offer or increasing the discount volume of hard currency. Whatever the role, there will be a need to frame activity recommendations against the scope of the tools the designer has access to, such as regardless of the scope, by making the priority player utility, which will ground the experience in terms of value for the audience. From this, we can review Sinks/Sources, forms of exchange, and even packaging as we roll out the experience. Ask who the activity is for (cohort)? Why will they care? How will the exchange be completed? How is it being communicated? What is the unboxing experience? All of this comes down to putting player value first. A successful commercial proposition flows from that.

- **Unexpected Consequences**: Defining an activity doesn't happen in a vacuum. Each change in the payout rates for rewards, the settings for an achievement, and the challenge difficulty setting can have unintended consequences. As designers, our role is to try to predict the possible impacts as much as it is to come up with interesting concepts. In terms of balance, think about how the introduction of new elements might impact the experience wider than the intended specific activity. Any change to the availability of 'Power' or exchange has the potential for consequences beyond just whether that will increase the spend of an average player. Always consider the potential impact on engagement, retention, and conversion. Think about where the activity intersects with the playing loops and what implications that has. What contribution does it make to the supply (Source) of key utility items? Have you considered how that will impact the availability of the items or actions that require those assets (Sinks)? How will that in turn impact the power curve of the player, and of course that affects the perception of difficulty levels and progression? A common issue comes where too much supply of a utility is added into the game through seasonal rewards or offers creating inflation. Complaints from players about 'Pay To Win' are often due to this kind of mistake where the difficulty levels are overly nerfed as a result of spending, undermining the challenge of the experience. As the author is fond of saying. There is no such thing as Pay To Win... only broken games. Often the solutions to such issues can be found not in changing how the offer is presented. Remember the issue in World of Warcraft where players rejected the negative impact of 'Tiredness.' By instead presenting the very same ratio as a short-term 'Rested' bonus, this delivered the same results without the negative experience. Alternatively, try to isolate the rewards from a specific activity by giving them a 'flavour,' such as introducing a specific seasonal currency, e.g. 'Cloud Berries' which are only available in a specific Seasonal VIP package. They can only be spent on the items in that seasonal store and maybe even later converted to some form of Hard Currency at the end of the season. Perhaps the game may need an additional 'Sink' designed specifically for a specific event, e.g. a 'Buy One Get One Free' offer on health potions, combined with an event which increases damage given by the seasonal monster – requiring more health potions. It often helps to identify the unintentional consequences by turning a problem 'upside down' by switching the perspective of either the problem or the solution.

- **Testing**: Just to reinforce the point we have already made, it is important to continue testing our assumptions. Each update can be considered a mini-launch of the game and the team cannot afford to undermine the investment that has already been made. Too many games end up releasing poorly QA'd updates or changes, which end up alienating the players and this can kill the game. Whilst there should be a lot of existing information about the players' likely response, you cannot know the consequences of any changes until they encounter the player. The quote "No plan survives contact with the [Player]" applies to our proposed activities. This again shows the importance of A/B testing, User Testing (e.g. NPS tests), test marketing, and even the use of ultra-low-cost UA trailer tests could be used to confirm how appealing the proposed functions are. Always be careful of the costs and the wider impact of testing spend on the game's larger scale marketing activities.

- **Postmortem**: Too often, development teams don't have enough time to review the success and failure of their actions beyond a simple review of the commercial returns, however, this is essential for their longer-term success. This means tracking the core KPIs that were set and understanding what may have caused any variations that happened during live. It also means taking a wider look at the implications and trends against seasonal changes, and other factors that are ongoing in the industry more generally. This can be extremely challenging, especially given what has already been said about the limited access to shared market data in games. In a LiveOps postmortem, Game Designers really need to try to understand 'Event-Level Attribution'; in other words, what meaningful impact did the activity that ran most recently have on the performance of the game in terms of the following KPIs:

  - **Audience sentiment** – Social engagement and reviews referencing the event

  - **Player engagement** – Rate of change in session frequency, time between sessions, and duration

  - **Player retention** – Rate of change in longer-term play (esp. D1/D7/D30/D90)

  - **% D30 ROAS** – The proportion of the initial paid UA spend returned within the first 30 days of download (and what is the rate of change from this event)

  - **D90 LTV** – What is the average Revenue minus Cost of Acquisition of players 90 days after their download (and what is the rate of change from this event)?

  - **Resurrection Rates** – Rate of change of formerly churned (e.g. 7+/30+ days since last play)

- **Conversion Rates** – Rate of change in the percentage of players deciding to spend for the first time ever and at all within the period.

  With this quantitative data, the Postmortem can also consider the qualitative aspects of the player experience:

- What was the impact of the activity?

- What went well?

- What could have gone better?

- What can we apply to future activities?

- Have we learned something new about what players care about?

- **PreMortem**: Another important technique is to attempt to run the postmortem before you release, as a thought experiment. Think about all the variables and data points you have (and still need to find) but start with the premise that the game has failed. The team then has to consider all the possible reasons which could have caused that failure from each of their different perspectives. When that list is collated then the objective is to identify the critical control points in the flow of the delivery of the game where those issues can be optimally mitigated. This concept (and many of the approaches in this book) follows the logic of a methodology used actively in the food industry called Hazard Analysis and Critical Control Points [14] and its application is further explored in my book Games as a Service.[15]

KNOWING WHEN TO STOP (AND PIVOT)

Game development is a dynamic and iterative process that rarely follows a straight line from concept to launch. Even with a well-researched design and validation process, unforeseen challenges can arise, and player preferences may shift. The economy designer will often be the first person to have access to the information when something isn't working.

This means that the Economy Designer often becomes the 'Canary in the Coal Mine' with a responsibility to the team to be able to identify and communicate issues before they become more significant. Something which can be extremely difficult to have the awareness to do when our focus is on resolving issues as they arise. As designers, our job is not just to solve problems, sometimes it's just as important to say 'Stop'. Learning to say 'Stop' is not easy and takes bravery – it rarely helps to make friends amongst the team, leadership, or investors even when it's necessary.

Adapting and pivoting during game development or even post-launch doesn't signify failure; rather, it demonstrates a developer's ability to learn from data, respond to feedback, and optimise the game experience. Sometimes this means changing core mechanics, reworking monetisation strategies, or addressing unexpected technical issues. There are games out there which were saved from complete failure simply by changing the art style! The ability to pivot is an essential survival skill that also helps game teams stay relevant and engaging in an ever-changing environment.

Recognising the Need to Pivot

One of the most difficult aspects of game development is knowing when to pivot and when not to. Many developers, especially those deeply invested in their vision, struggle to let go of original ideas or concepts – even when the data or player feedback suggests that change is necessary. However, the ability to recognise and act on these signals can make the difference between a game that fails and one that evolves into a long-term success. This is an art, not a science, and a designer needs to be guided by the original vision, KPIs, and a fixation with player value to recognise the difference between frustration and a fundamental flaw in the delivery. For a game that has already successfully launched, there can be several key indicators that, when combined, may suggest a pivot is needed:

- **Player Engagement Drops**: If analytics show a sudden or steady drop in player engagement, it may indicate any number of things. Perhaps the players are losing interest in the current gameplay loop, or a significant replacement competitor game has been launched, or more simply that a technical issue has affected players that needs to be urgently addressed. However, check market data for other, more general changes that could explain the issue, such as the launch of a dominant game such as the next GTA or even some major international news event.

- **Players Unaffected By New Systems**: If there is no 'Rate of Change' when we introduce new elements to the game, such as a new game mode, challenges, or even new store bundles; this may signify some underlying issue. Are players actually getting to those new systems or offers and engaging with them? Consider why they failed to access those features, was there an issue with the servers? Is there too high a barrier to access that level? Poor signposting? Or perhaps the experience just does not sound compelling enough.

- **Reduced Volume of Player Feedback**: It's not just consistent negative feedback from players we need to be wary of. Ironically, that is a symptom that players care about the game. However, when feedback stops coming in, that is when we need to be concerned. This can be tested through in-game surveys, online forums, as well as the usual social media channels. Knee-jerk reactions to poor player feedback can often make matters worse, it's important to listen to all feedback and for negative feedback, to be properly considered in our planning, but we must remember that while players are great at telling you there is an issue, they are not designers, and often their proposed solutions can undermine game balance in unexpected ways.

- **Poor Repeat Monetisation**: Especially for free-to-play games, repeated monetisation is a crucial aspect of long-term sustainability. If your game is attracting a large number of players but lacks significant recurring spend from those players, your monetisation design is likely to be misaligned. The percentage of repeat spenders is a vital statistic to understand the health of the offers you are making. Players who value your game and what they buy, should be more likely to spend again (and are more cost-effective than having to recruit another paying user). Lack of recurring revenue is a sign that they aren't happy, and if there is significant churn after a purchase, then this is likely to be an extremely urgent problem.

- **Retention Pattern Changes**: Assuming you are successful at sustaining your player audience, overtime the make-up of your active player base will tend to concentrate towards the longest retained users. Some games get to the point where the level of D90 players is in the 80%+ levels. This is a potentially fantastic position to be in for any developer, as it gives significant confidence that they understand their audience needs, behaviour, and spending patterns. However, there are also has risks. Often in this situation a developer can fall into a bias towards those existing long-term players, dropping the ball when it comes to D1 users and maintaining the FTUE more generally. This is especially problematic, when the game has had additional minigames or even full game modes slapped on top of the core experience over months or years. For new players, an established game which has had a lot of updates can become extremely complicated and confusing for new or returning players. An 80% D90 userbase may be a sign that you have lost the audience refresh rate needed to sustain the game over the next year. This is why designers need to revisit the whole of the player lifecycle with the FTUE, which covered the onboaring or 'Learning' stage; the Second Time User Experience (STUE) which is all about reducinc the friction of play and building ongoing engagement; and the Lapsed Time User Experience (LTUE) which is designed to help players return to play rapidly after long periods of absence. All of these factors support building a sustainable audience over the longer term.

- **External Market Changes**: The games industry is in constant flux and it's important to think about what Political, Economic, Social, and Legal changes are likely to impact our game, teams, and distribution channels. If we fail to assess what implications these have on our audience and marketing effectiveness, we can find the game gets into trouble. Prior to the pandemic we saw significant pressure building related to privacy issues, and this was accompanied by Apple's commercial decision to remove the ID For Advertisers, as we have mentioned. The full impact of this change, and a range of other privacy-related issues that followed, was arguably hidden by the unprecedented increase in player engagement during COVID because of Lockdown. But when that ended and people went back to their normal lives, the resulting drop in games revenues, combined with increased user acquisition costs, dramatically impacted the market so mobile games saw its first decline, perhaps, ever. The introduction of the Digital Markets Act presents a range of open questions which Game Economy designers need to consider. How can we leverage this legislative change to increase the effectiveness of how we engage our most loyal players? An example of the ongoing fallout includes, at the time of writing, efforts by Apple to push back against a court order (originally handed down in 2021) that demanded Apple refrain from anti-competitive conduct and pricing and allow outside payment options in the App Store – something Apple's legal team called 'Extraordinary';[16] What does direct-to-consumer platforms mean for discovery? What could this mean for cross-platform play? etc.

These types of changes do not always make for opportunities, and we have to be prepared for changes to costs and process. We need to consider how we have to be compliant with new regulations such as the U.K.'s Age-Appropriate Design Code. Whilst this is generally a variant of the EU's GDPR regulations, there is one important differentiator which has widespread consequences. When selling to a U.K. audience you cannot assume that someone is over 18 without evidence, and a credit card transaction is insufficient. This is potentially introducing a requirement for Know Your Customer something that is understandably a requirement for gambling and banking. In itself, perfectly reasonable. However, most game developers (unless operating a direct-to-consumer offer) do not have any of this information. The platforms do. And the platforms are not being held to account – the developer is. All of this creates additional costs and process requirements, as well as barriers for smaller developers to be able to offer their games, potentially requiring the team to pivot.

Recognising the gaps in your offer and the risks that are going is not the same as recognising the need to pivot. For that, we need to go back to our original vision statements and KPIs when we considered 'What Does Good Look Like?' We need to assess if our current strategy and market approach can deliver on those KPIs or not. Don't get me wrong, if you are a low-level game designer looking at monetisation you are not responsible for managing the game team as a whole. You are just the 'Canary in the Coalmine' – an early warning system that something is not working as intended. Information you need to share with your colleagues. You also get to apply that information to your strategies and use that to propose new actions which could address those gaps at a low level. Each proposal acts as a hypothesis that you can test and gain more confidence to develop your thesis further. Something we need to do without unduly disrupting the player experience is equally important. Players are invested in the game you've created, and sudden or drastic changes can cause confusion or frustration if not handled carefully.

Pivoting within the Game Design

This book isn't about business strategy specifically, so we won't go into the wider strategic choices available to C-Suite management. From the perspective of pivoting within the game itself, there are several vectors we can apply, including:

- **Progress Flow**: Funnel analysis is a data technique where we analyse the flow of the player through the game, typically showing the percentage of players who make it through to the next stage. This helps identify moments in various progression stages in a game where we can find issues where too many players are dropping out. There may be many reasons why this is happening, but one of the simplest things to check is whether there is a failure to signpost the required steps. Making sure that progress flow is properly indicated is often a simple fix.

- **Drop Rates**: Another reason people fail to progress can come from there being a problem with the drop-rate value from success. Does this allow the player to build up their power, even when they fail and have to replay? When rewards are tied only to success, players can get stuck in a loop where progress seems unachievable, so they churn. With some reduced rewards for repeat plays (sometimes this can be done by debuffing the enemy but tends to be unsatisfying) players need to reach the point where they are strong enough to overcome the challenge. Sometimes the problem is the opposite, and instead, the rewards are disproportionate, removing all challenge and making the game meaningless. Fixing this can be as simple as adjusting the payout, but this can annoy existing players, so handle with care.

- **Difficulty/Power**: The other side of reviewing Funnel Analysis is to track the relative power of the player and the challenge they face; not just the rewards themselves. This will be less visible to the player themselves and is more tied into 'game feel' than explicit payout levels from reward boxes. Consider how flat or linear the difficulty curve is set compared to the engagement levels. If there is a problem with this being too flat, try amending the variability of difficulty to ensure more 'texture' and make the flow of the game feel more meaningful, as discussed in *Chapter 10: Balance*.

- **Narrative Framing**: Sometimes the issues identified have nothing to do with the actual numbers behind the scenes, but the way the stakes or consequences have been presented to the players. This can be fixed using narrative to change the flavour and tone of activity. Remember how we can present the game information as positive or negative reinforcement, and this has different implications despite having the same mathematical consequences. Humour and subtext play an important role in almost every game and can be used with smart writing to help avoid using too much exposition of game lore to achieve that. We can use overt methods already established in the game such as magic or advanced text to explain a boost. We can add elements to crafting or upgrade paths to explain away performance improvement or even 'an evil sweeping across the land' to explain a buff to all the enemies. We have talked about how the use of limited duration boosts or cooldown periods' effectiveness creates a different tone from the use of degrading items; but achieves the same functional benefits.

- **Resource Sinks**: Managing scarcity is a critical element in most games, and adding new sinks is often a hugely impactful way to change up the experience of your players. Simply, the exchange rate (how much of a resource is needed for an exchange) is one approach, but there are other ways to achieve the same goal. Adding a new way to use an existing resource can introduce a selection dilemma for the player. Alternatively, requiring a different resource at higher levels of progression, making the original resource redundant, removes the problem in a different way. If the rate at which such resources are sourced is restrictive, this can have unforeseen consequences, especially for early-stage players. Managing capacity can especially help with this problem, but it depends on how you manage the scaling of that system over the player lifecycle.

- **Game Modes**: Adapting the mode of play can be through the simple addition of a short-term seasonal mini-game to a fundamental change to one of the underlying loops (Core/Context/Cultural). The introduction of a minigame offer can be a charming, delightful adjustment to the playing tone (and a way to test out mechanics for future games), whilst a more fundamental gameplay pivot might be necessary if players find certain mechanics too difficult, unengaging, or repetitive. For example, a puzzle game that initially relies on time-based challenges might introduce more relaxed, strategy-focused ways to play based on player feedback or behaviour. Adding a minigame often requires considerable effort to balance and needs to remain somewhat orthogonal from the other game elements. When doing this, the designer has to decide if this is a permanent addition or, for example, a seasonal one. It is often a good exercise to introduce new modes or mini-games as part of seasonal activities, and only if they are particularly successful to integrate them more permanently. Too many systems can overcomplicate the experience.

- **Monetisation Pivot**: When a game's revenue model isn't generating the desired results, a monetisation pivot may be required. This could involve changing the pricing model, introducing new types of in-game purchases, or adjusting the balance between free and paid content. For example, a game might shift from a premium purchase model to a free-to-play model with in-game ads or microtransactions. These kinds of changes can be extremely dangerous and can risk significant player backlash. To avoid this, it is imperative to appreciate the 'sunk costs' of the existing players and how to help these players feel that we respect their prior commitment. We also must demonstrate significant additional value from this reconstructed offer. For example, introducing a 'Pioneer Pass' that would be given to all players who invested in Early Access when we originally intended it to be a pay upfront model; offering those existing players, say, 6 months of free monthly 'Battle Pass' plus some unique assets including an in-game visual marker that they are a Pioneer. Giving these players a reason to upgrade to the new subscription or in-game purchases is key, so perhaps also offer them a 20% discount during those 6 months. This can work, but only where the offer is authentic, backed up with consistent updates, and where you take the time to communicate how this will make the experience better.

- **Target Audience Pivot**: Sometimes, the players you initially designed your game for are not the ones who end up engaging with it. This is sometimes less of a pivot and more of an acceptance that your game appeals to different people than you anticipated. A target audience pivot often involves some level of rebranding or refocusing of narrative and 'Game Feel' to magnify the appeal to that different demographic but can require a complete rethink of what players value in the game economy. For example, a mid-core mobile game design with simple mechanics might be reframed to better attract a broader, more mass-market audience but needs clearer signposting in the FTUE and less 'aggressive' monetisation bundles.

- **Platform Pivot**: In some cases, developers may need to pivot from one platform to another based on market conditions or player preferences. For example, a game initially designed for PC might find greater success on mobile devices, leading to a shift in platform focus. This pivot often involves reworking the user interface, control scheme, and monetisation strategy to suit the new platform. The tools available to game developers are usually excellent for managing changes between operating systems and device controls, but the ergonomics of play and the lifestyle circumstances at the moment of play usually need careful attention. Even something as simple as switching between touch versus controller interactions can have a meaningful impact on adoption.

- **Content Pivot**: A content pivot involves changing or adding new content to keep players engaged. This might mean introducing new levels, game modes, or storylines to refresh the player experience. For example, a multiplayer shooter might add a new cooperative mode based on player requests for more team-based gameplay. These kinds of changes, whilst the most appealing to many developers, are often the most expensive and hence the most risky option to the organisation.

Each type of pivot comes with its own set of challenges, but all pivots share a common goal: improving the player experience and aligning the game with market demands.

Incorporating Player Feedback: An Iterative Process

At the heart of every successful pivot is the ability to interpret player feedback alongside data. We gather player feedback through surveys, playtesting sessions, and community interactions on social platforms. We then need to compare this with market analytics including sentiment analysis, attribution data, and gameplay behaviour. However, using all of these elements effectively is an iterative process:

- **Gather Feedback**: Use a combination of qualitative feedback (player surveys, forums) and quantitative data (analytics, retention rates) to get a full picture of how players are interacting with your game.

- **Identify Common Pain Points**: Look for patterns in the feedback. Are multiple players mentioning the same issues with difficulty, pacing, or monetisation? Identifying common pain points will help you prioritise changes that have the greatest impact on the player experience.

- **Prototype and Test Changes**: Before fully committing to a pivot, create prototypes or small updates to test potential changes. For example, if players are struggling with the game's difficulty curve, try adjusting it in a specific level and gather feedback from a small group of players. This iterative testing helps ensure that the changes you implement solve the problem without introducing new issues.

- **Implement Changes**: Once you've tested potential solutions and gathered positive feedback, it's time to implement the changes at scale. Roll out updates that address the key issues and communicate these changes clearly to your player base.

- **Monitor the Impact**: After the pivot is complete, continue to monitor player feedback and analytics to ensure that the changes are having the desired effect. Keep an eye on engagement metrics, retention rates, and revenue to measure the success of your pivot.

We all know that player feedback is incredibly valuable, and players need to know that we genuinely take it seriously, even when we decide to take a different path. There will be trolls and people with strong opinions, and these voices will usually be very loud. Which is fine, as it shows passion and engagement with the game, team, and a desire for the game to be better. As already mentioned, even negative feedback shows a level of untapped desire for the game to be better. When players see that developers are actively listening and making improvements based on their input, they usually feel more invested in the game. This builds trust and loyalty, leading to higher retention rates and a more engaged community. However, the direction for the game overall is a professional design decision, and some requests may simply not fit. Players who are willing to shout about the game will be the vocal minority. The majority who are unhappy will have already churned, so you don't get to hear their perspective at all. Frustration that a weapon is 'OP' or a character is 'Nerfed' may be hiding a wider issue related to the communication of tactical play or of rewards payout levels – perhaps the timing of a challenge type in some levels. A player's goal will be to maximise their personal utility (the stuff they value in the game), but a designer's role as economy designers is to deliver that utility in a way which maximises all of the player's engagement, retention, and that ultimately generates revenue.

Pivoting without Alienating Your Player Base

One of the biggest challenges when pivoting is maintaining your current player base. Players who have been with your game since its launch have built a connection to its original design, and sudden changes can sometimes feel jarring or alienating. To successfully pivot without losing your loyal players, it's important to communicate clearly and involve the community in the process.

Here are some strategies for pivoting without alienating your player base:

- **Transparency**: Communication is vital. Game teams need to be open with their players about why changes are being made. Explain the rationale behind the pivot, whether it's based on player feedback, market conditions, or performance data. Players are more likely to accept changes if they understand the reasoning behind them, even if they would have preferred something different. This doesn't mean teams should share every detail of the process, but players seem to be able to magically detect if the team is trying to hide things. Authenticity is important; there is no expectation for unfiltered candour.

- **Gradual Changes**: Where possible, make changes gradually rather than all at once, but make those changes unambiguously. Giving players notice and time to adjust to the new mechanics, systems, or content is positive, but make sure the team communicates those changes clearly. If you are moving from Premium to Subscription, make sure that this is clean and that the fact of the change is unambiguous; but you can still give previous players time to adjust by giving them a grace period and making genuinely valuable upgrade offers; even applying the subscription only to new users. Take another example, if you're reworking the progression system, try to roll out updates incrementally so players can see how the new system works step by step without being overwhelmed. This won't always be possible, but the intent here is to appreciate how players need care and time to adjust to system changes.

- **Beta Testing and Feedback**: Involve your community by inviting them to test new features with beta versions or special test servers where possible. This not only allows you to gather valuable feedback but also helps players feel like they're part of the development process without risking the live platform. Building a subset of the players who are deeply committed to the success of the game creates an audience of advocates; and should be highly rewarded. When players have a say in the changes being made, they are more likely to embrace those changes and take others with them. There are risks that game teams could create an exclusive clique of players and that can create a toxic culture if not handled carefully; but with strong community management, this can be avoided.

- **Reward Loyalty**: Acknowledge and reward your long-time players during any major change. Pay attention to the 'Sunk Costs' they will feel they have made, and reward that appropriately where possible. This could be in the form of exclusive in-game items, recognition, or bonuses that show your appreciation for their continued support. This does not have to be costly; indeed, it is usually better if the form of reward is something which money cannot buy such as a shout out to those players at a conference, a chance to visit the studio, or even credits in the game for the most significant individuals. For wider groups, think about exclusive options for that cohort, such as where you're introducing a major content update, offering veteran players early access or exclusive customisation options so they can show off their loyalty.

- **Maintain Core Identity**: Even during a pivot, it's important to stay true to the core identity of your game. Players were drawn to your game for a reason, and while certain aspects may need to change, it's crucial to retain the elements that made your game unique and engaging in the first place. This balance between innovation and consistency is key to executing a successful pivot. Part of this is to return to the original Vision vectors and the KPIs driving the game as a whole.

Interview

Game economies are the backbone of any engaging and sustainable game. Yet, so often, developers either treat them as an afterthought or overcomplicate them to the point of redundancy. To dig deeper into what makes an economy work – and what makes it fail – we discussed this with Tadhg Kelly,[17] a veteran designer who has worked across console, PC, and mobile, bringing a rich blend of experience from games like *The Movies* to the emerging world of hybrid-casual free-to-play models.

Kelly makes the case that game economies aren't just about virtual currencies or resource management – they're about the fundamental way players interact with the game world.

Even in games that don't have explicit in-game currencies, there are still economies of time, effort, and attention. Players constantly make decisions about how to allocate their resources, whether that's energy in a mobile game, mana in an RPG, or even guesses in a puzzle game.

> In a very, very, very real sense, all games are economic games.
> Like even Wordle actually is an economic game.

With this starting point, we explored the common mistakes in game economy design and how we might develop a framework for creating economies that don't just function but actively enrich player engagement (which in turn leads to commercial success).

A key concept kept coming up in our conversation about the importance of identifying the *possibility space* – the range of meaningful, player-influenced outcomes a system allows. For Kelly, it is vital that games have enough dimensionality and "itchiness" to compel players to act. Achieving this requires exploring interconnected systems with emergent properties rather than building redundant or isolated loops.

Early in the discussion, Kelly drove home how developers often mistake complexity for depth. When designing a game economy, the temptation is to introduce multiple layers – currencies, progression systems, crafting, rarity tiers – without considering whether they contribute meaningfully to the player's experience.

> "What I see an awful lot is developers who maybe have actually put a lot of work into setting up several systems, but not really realizing that what they've actually done is set up the same system three or four times," said Kelly.

That redundancy is dangerous. Not only does it create unnecessary development work, but it also confuses players. The best game economies present clear, meaningful choices that allow players to express themselves through play, rather than simply throwing numbers at them. Failing to pay attention to the texture and dimensionality leads too often to designers ending up just creating interchangeable resources/currencies that are dull 'denominations' of each other; really just becoming ratios of each other. Instead:

> "…there's more like a kind of a quadrant graph and that the quadrant graph is really more between say, emergence and experience or, and abstraction versus realism," said Kelly.

This is further explored on his blog post 'The Four Lenses of Game Making'.[18]

Kelly's preferred approach is to consider the possibility space, a term popularised by Will Wright and Clint Hocking, to describe the range of meaningful choices available to the player. If a game economy is well-designed, those choices will matter, and different players will find different paths through the game based on their play styles.

> I'm looking for a possibility space. So by that I mean, are there enough kind of things within how the economy of the game is set up to generate a variety of interesting outcomes?

For Kelly, this includes thinking about how to 'collapse' the possibility space, not just through monetisation, but also creating pinch points with critical choices, consequences, and moments which really focus the player's attention. Broad possibility, he states, is generally not enough for a good design. A good economy should support multiple viable strategies rather than force players into a single optimal path.

One of the most interesting concepts Kelly brought up was *itchiness*, a term he uses to describe mechanics that create a compelling drive for players to engage. If a system is *itchy*, it means that players feel an urge to interact with it repeatedly, whether that's optimising a resource, completing a challenge, or earning a reward. He often described this as the player's job, basically their functional roles in the game.

> "Calling a game itchy is mixing its hook with the job element, particularly. Whether those two things actually form together into a scenario or situation. Or that the players go like, I really want to scratch that." said Kelly.

This aligns closely with behavioural design principles. People don't just want rewards – they want to *feel* like they are working toward something significant. The best economies tap into this psychological need by carefully balancing effort, tension, and satisfaction.

> A strong example of an *itchy* economy is seen in well-balanced RPG loot systems. If everything is handed to the player too easily, the itch disappears. Conversely, if the grind is too severe, frustration sets in. The key is creating an engagement loop that players are drawn to because the act of progression itself is satisfying.

Too often, monetisation is treated as a separate problem from game design. Developers spend months (or years) refining mechanics, progression, and balance, only to later ask, "Right, now how do we make money?" That's a recipe for disaster.

This isn't about designing games just for revenue – it's about ensuring that monetisation and engagement are aligned from the start. If a game's core loop and economy are well designed, monetisation should feel like a natural extension of the gameplay, not a forced interruption.

> "[It] tends to happen an awful lot… developers who have built maybe a very cool, very interesting game …and then they try and sort of staple-on a commercial model that actually doesn't really have any business being in that game at all," says Kelly.

A prime example of what *not* to do can be found in the collapse of hyper-casual games as a dominant business model. Initially, hyper-casual games thrived on simple mechanics combined with aggressive ad monetisation. But as more developers flooded the space, player retention plummeted, and ad revenue started to collapse.

> "Because there's too many hyper-casual developers in that space all doing the same thing, you start to see collapse, cannibalization, blah blah blah blah blah, and suddenly everybody is starting to talk about hybrid casual," says Kelly.

The lesson? Sustainable monetisation strategies need to be built around long-term player engagement rather than short-term monetisation hacks or tagged-on RPG elements, which is what too many Hybrid games do.

> "I want to start building in systems that are, well, like, adding in kind of longer-term stuff, adding in IAP transactions, giving the player something to freaking do," says Kelly.

There's a common misconception that digital games can afford to be more complicated than board games when it comes to economy design. After all, the computer does all the math, so why not have multiple interlocking systems that drive deep engagement? But as Kelly pointed out, the opposite is often true:

> There is actually generally a lot less tolerance for cryptic relationships in video game economies than there is in other kinds of games.

In board games, players can see the entire system laid out in front of them, making it easier to grasp relationships between mechanics. In digital games, those relationships are often hidden behind menus, UI layers, and background calculations. If a game economy is too opaque, players won't engage with it fully, or worse – they'll disengage entirely.

Instead, clarity should be the goal. Players need to *feel* the impact of their choices. If they buy a new upgrade or unlock a new ability, that change should be immediately tangible in the gameplay experience. If they earn a new currency, its purpose should be obvious without needing to dig through a wiki.

Final Thoughts: All Games Are Economic Games

As we covered at the start of this conversation, it is Kelly's position that "All games are Economic Games."

Understanding this is critical to designing engagement systems that don't just work but thrive. Whether you're building a free-to-play mobile game, a premium single-player RPG, or a multiplayer live-service title, economy design is at the heart of how your game functions and how it connects with players.

A well-balanced economy does more than just sustain player interest – it creates *meaning*. It transforms a game from a static experience into a dynamic world where every choice matters, and every action has consequences. And that is what makes games, at their core, so compelling.

Interview

DESIGNING FOR RETENTION, EXPRESSION, AND ENGAGEMENT – AN INTERVIEW WITH ELISE TERRANOVA

In mobile game design, the term "casual" is often used to describe games that are easy to pick up and play. However, as Elise Terranova,[19] Lead Game Designer at Crazy Labs, explains, casual games do not always attract casual players. The players who engage with these games can be incredibly invested, seeking deep and meaningful interactions within these seemingly simple experiences. In our conversation, we explored the intersection of game balance, retention strategies, and player expression, particularly in fashion and lifestyle games.

> Yes, we can call them casual because they're easy to pick up and play and understand, but they can get really deep and they can get really complex. And I think the audiences that they're there for are not only interested in the top layer. There's a whole layer of complexity or layers of complexity that we can offer for these kind of players.

Elise's background in interior design provides her with a unique perspective on game mechanics and UX. Her work designing spaces with specific functions, such as hospitals, mirrors the complexity of game design, where various systems must interconnect seamlessly.

> Making games is often such a team sport. We have so many different people that we're working with all the time. I think that maybe, I don't know, a wider range of problem solving, maybe that's the... or wider understanding of how kind of things can fit together.

Designing for mobile requires a keen awareness of constraints – screen size, session length, and user expectations. For games to be engaging, they must provide a fluid experience that integrates well with players' lifestyles while still offering meaningful challenges and rewards.

Retention is one of the most critical metrics in mobile game design. Elise emphasises the importance of analysing player behaviour to identify what keeps them engaged and where new features can enhance the experience.

> I really want to double down on who the player is and what are they already enjoying in the game? So what is the thing that they come back to? What is the thing that they play the most? What is the thing that you see? Maybe they make special purchases for, and that's sort of where I look at like, what is this type of player?

For games with long-term engagement, understanding the balance between new and returning users is crucial. Retention isn't just about the first-time user experience; it also includes re-engagement strategies for mid-cycle and lapsed players.

> The last one is definitely the trickiest, especially if you're talking about gaps of play. I just think of the amount of things that they come back to if they haven't been in the game for six months, for instance.

Long gaps in play mean players may return to overwhelming UI changes, missed events, and an influx of notifications. How can developers design smoother transitions for returning users? Elise suggests that more work needs to be done in considering their onboarding journey after an absence.

In games like Glow and June's Journey, self-expression is integral to the experience. Whether it's fashion, decoration, or avatar customisation, players invest deeply in their ability to showcase their identity.

> Players like to, yes, they like to show off, but they also like to get acknowledgement. So I think there's the main drive is more so necessary than competition. I think players also like to show that they've unlocked the last thing, the hardest thing, the first thing along, so that is a progression marker as well.

Expression in games isn't just about aesthetics; it's about social belonging, identity, and even prestige. Cosmetic customisation must have stakes – if every player can obtain the same items at any time, the sense of exclusivity is lost.

One of the fascinating challenges in game design is supporting emergent play – player behaviours that developers didn't anticipate but which enhance engagement.

If they can find a different way to play a game, they will.

Players create their own subcultures and challenges within games. Whether it's subverting expected playstyles or creating their own meta-games, emergent behaviour is an opportunity for designers to foster creativity. A key example, I recalled coming from PlayStation Home, where players created unofficial competitions for the most ridiculous avatars.

In any game economy, balance is crucial to maintaining long-term player interest. This is especially true for games that monetise through cosmetics or limited-time items.

> It doesn't really matter if you're going to be able to use that item once. Players like to have something that's exclusive that they can keep.

Exclusivity drives engagement and monetisation. However, Elise cautions against re-releasing previously "exclusive" items, as this can undermine trust and devalue early adopters' investments.

A core principle of game economy design is that value is driven by the expectation of delight, not just the functionality of the reward.

> If we haven't made something feel good enough and we haven't communicated to the player that it is something that does make you feel good when you get there… then I think you've done three quarters of the job.

A well-balanced game economy ensures that all content – cosmetic or functional – feels valuable and meaningful. The best games provide opportunities for self-expression, emergent play, and status recognition, allowing players to create their own identities within the game world.

CONCLUSION: THE INTERSECTION OF ECONOMY, EXPRESSION, AND ENGAGEMENT

Elise's insights highlight that balance in game design is more than just fine-tuning numbers – it's about understanding player psychology, providing opportunities for creativity, and designing systems that keep players engaged for the long term.

> This is our fantasy realm, and whatever you want to purchase in there, if it fulfils a need… then it has value.

By integrating these principles – retention-focused design, emergent play support, thoughtful economy balancing, and self-expression mechanics – game developers can create experiences that resonate deeply with players and encourage long-term engagement.

NOTES

1 https://youtu.be/2OscBzgO2sA?feature=shared
2 www.linkedin.com/in/grahammcallister
3 https://mrbossdesign.blogspot.com/
4 https://mrbossdesign.blogspot.com/2008/09/triangle-of-weirdness.html
5 https://en.wikipedia.org/wiki/Likert_scale
6 https://ico.org.uk/for-organisations/uk-gdpr-guidance-and-resources/designing-products-that-protect-privacy/childrens-code-design-guidance/create-data-privacy-moments-maps/
7 https://goodwriterbadwriter.com/2012/05/23/the-mythbuster-philosophy-of-education-failure-is-always-an-option/
8 https://antidote.gg/
9 https://www.playtestcloud.com/
10 https://sensortower.com/
11 https://www.gamerefinery.com/
12 https://steamdb.info/
13 https://steamspy.com/
14 https://en.wikipedia.org/wiki/Hazard_Analysis_Critical_Control_Point
15 https://www.routledge.com/Games-As-A-Service-How-Free-to-Play-Design-Can-Make-Better-Games/Clark/p/book/9780415732505
16 https://www.bbc.co.uk/news/articles/c3r8rg4w2v0o#:~:text=The%20judge%20rejected%20Epic's%20monopoly,week%20was%20already%20benefitting%20consumers
17 https://www.linkedin.com/in/tadhgk/
18 https://www.whatgamesare.com/2011/12/the-four-lenses-of-game-making.html
19 https://www.linkedin.com/in/eliseterranova/

CHAPTER 12

Evolving Economies

DOI: 10.1201/9781003592471-12

AN UNDISCOVERED COUNTRY

The world of game development is constantly evolving, and with it, the way we design and manage game economies. As technology advances and player expectations shift, game economies are becoming more complex, interconnected, and innovative. Developers are exploring new ways to engage players, monetise experiences, and create ecosystems that blend virtual- and real-world value.

However, innovation is rarely a straight line, and the lessons for a designer rely on critical thinking, openness to new opportunities, and a healthy cynicism. To illustrate this, at the risk of dating the book, we will explore three trends which have been subject to enormous hype and controversy. Blockchain, Cross-Platform games, and AI up to the point of writing but with a lens of lessons to apply to consider technologies more generally.

Blockchain and NFTs

Cryptocurrency emerged in 2008 when it was introduced by a mythical figure who themselves are shrouded in controversy, Satoshi Nakamoto. It is unclear if that was a pseudonym for one person or a group, but the paper credited under that name outlines an approach for a purely peer-to-peer form of electronic money. This currency model has had a turbulent emergence into the financial world, and despite being 'trustless' or better stated needing not a trusted centralised authority, it has been wild with criminal exploitation, not least the notable collapse of the Crypto Exchange FTX, which has been likened to a Ponzi scheme and led to Sam Bankman-Fried being sentenced to 25 years imprisonment.[1]

In the gaming industry, there have been a series of innovators looking to integrate aspects of blockchain technology through the concept of Non-Fungible Tokens (NFTs). The idea being that blockchain, with its ability to create decentralised game economies, means that a player can, theoretically at least, truly own their in-game assets and even trade or sell them outside of the game's ecosystem. An NFT becomes a truly unique digital asset, and the concept of 'smart tokens' can conceivably continue to evolve in every game in which they are used.

In online games, without blockchain, players don't realistically "own" the in-game assets in a meaningful way. Should the game shut down or make changes to its terms of service, players could essentially lose access to their purchases. Blockchain theoretically changes this by giving players true ownership over their in-game assets. Once an item is minted as an

NFT on the blockchain, it exists independently of the game, and players can trade or sell it on external platforms. For example, a rare weapon or cosmetic skin in a blockchain-based game could be bought, sold, or transferred across different games or even real-world marketplaces. This creates new opportunities for player-driven economies where value is determined not just by in-game demand but also by broader market trends. However, integrating blockchain into games comes with challenges:

- **Environmental Impact**: Blockchain technology relies on high-power GPU technology to run the enormous levels of calculations, and 'proof-of-work' systems. This has been considerably reduced for transactional processes using 'side chains'; but the underlying energy costs remain a concern.

- **Ownership**: The process of creating an NFT or minting can be applied to any asset in principle but there is no proof of original ownership intrinsic in the initial creation of the asset itself. This has led to appropriation, and even outright theft, of creative assets that undermine the core benefit that blockchains have to trace any transactions and changes applied to that asset. To make that worse, the protective status of that asset is questionable, especially where the asset, e.g. Bored Ape, is a computer-generated image, but as copyright at the time of writing only applies where a person created it, not an AI, so is that asset protectable? The 'Monkey Selfie' copyright dispute[2] engrained in law the principle that the owner of a camera didn't have copyright over an image created by a 'non-person'. Add to that the disturbing scale of commercial exploitation of other people's images by minting images into NFTs which has left a lot of creators and consumers antagonistic to the concept. When an NFT is essentially little more than the contents of a URL which could potentially be altered this further undermines the concept of what you actually own. There is a Metaverse Standards Forum[3] attempting to alleviate some of the issues related to interoperability, but at the time of writing, there seems little appetite for games-industry teams to offer open access to assets from different games.

- **Regulation**: The mainstream economy remains likely to rely on 'fiat' currency and associated regulatory frameworks that protect international trade, day-to-day contractual processes and that attempt to prevent fraud and money laundering. The various Financial Services bodies are still coming to terms with how to manage such electronic currencies and their application as NFTs. This is made more complicated by the anonymous nature of transactions and innovative exploits, such as where systems designed to speed up transactional speeds exposed some platforms to 51% attacks, allowing fraudulent transactions to take place.

- **Complexity**: The process to acquire and use crypto is fundamentally opaque to new users, and the market changes, delisting, and processes are so changeable that for most people it's simply not worth the effort. Every transaction can feel overwhelming with risk, and in the end, the dream of ownership of in-game is rarely relevant, as in order for you to use an item in another game requires more than just ownership of the asset.

As developers, we need to make a call about whether we want to be early adopters, fast movers, or laggards (even rejectors) when it comes to blockchain. Are we convinced that the technology will reach widespread adoption, and that the consumer perception of the technology is advantageous to the game brand? But most of all, is the technology being used for its intended application?

For full disclosure, in 2019 I worked on the design of Reality Clash,[4] a blockchain game with tokens (predating the current NFT format). The concept included design elements which would leverage smart contract history, that would support other games leveraging the assets and indeed where the setting for the items (combinations of gun types and cosmetic skins) had inherent scarcity and usable scores inspired by collectable-card game style mechanics. Whilst the game was not a success in itself, it was the first blockchain game approved by the Apple App Store. Since that time, I would argue that only a few examples of blockchain games have actually attempted to leverage the intrinsic benefits that come from a peer-authenticated economic system, but games like The Sandbox[5] and Decentraland[6] have attempted to demonstrate the potential to facilitate shared creative experiences.

Cross-Platform Economies

The dream of playing the same game seamlessly across multiple devices first became a reality in 2001 when Capcom vs. SNK 2 was released with cross play for PlayStation 2 and Dreamcast.[7] Despite that starting over 24 years ago, it's only recently that this has become commonplace and the release of Nintendo Switch 2 including 'cross-play' as one of the key improvements. We aren't quite there that we can assume cross-platform play will be available for games, but the development barriers are gradually being removed. Games tend to remain discrete for each platform because there is additional development effort required, but there are still some disparities in the levels of support and terms for device-specific platforms. This has improved considerably, but developing systems to maintain in-game progress, currency, and ownership of items between different platforms requires a level of experience and technical development to create the tools and manage the associated security requirements, including protecting privacy and managing commercial transitions via each platform. With the introduction of the Digital Markets Act and the rise of direct-to-consumer experience, will we see an evolution of this?

One of the issues with this approach has always been how the ergonomics of the game match the lifestyle mode of use of the player with the specific devices. Whilst theoretically a player can play almost any game on any device, the combination of controls, immersion, pace, and the risk of interruption all play a significant part in the suitability of a given game to have such a cross-play experience – even if the developers have the technical skills and infrastructure capability to deliver it. There are significant costs to porting a game to a new platform (even if these have reduced significantly over time), but the management of the player account between platforms is a separate beast. If you require a player to repurchase items for each platform, that can be additional revenue for the team, if they get all the assets they have unlocked to date, where is the upsell for the game? On the flip side, if players can engage with an experience across more devices, that can create more moments to engage, build deeper retention, and longer-term revenue as a direct result. As always, consider whether the costs and implications of the development requirements can be offset by the potential revenue and retention benefits.

If the changes to the competitive landscape triggered by legislation like the Digital Markets Act have the impact some have predicted, there may be considerable opportunity to engage your players on all devices through one window. However, attempts by EA, Ubisoft, and others to create rival experiences to Steam, through their own launchers and stores, have never really worked. The 'Discovery' benefits of having content from multiple developers in one place, so that I can look for what I want as a consumer, not a subset of that content which is being offered by each specific provider on each of their own bespoke platforms. Look at the explosion of channels offering streaming video services at an additional premium. Consumers simply don't have the appetite to pay a subscription to more than a small number of services, and when content discovery becomes too complicated consumer/players simply give up and find something else to do. There was a reason Napster had such an impact on the music industry in the early '00s.[8] It was not just that the content was free, the barriers to access were gone! Spotify's rise can be traced directly to the simplicity and ease of access to content for consumers, but music artists will have a different perspective, of course. With regulation likely to lead to an increase in direct-to-consumer experiences used it will be essential to consider player simplicity, choice, and how developers can build deeper relationships with their most engaged players. However, that won't eliminate the need to work with the mainstream channels, even if they do evolve from technology platforms to content markets. For example, conceivably, PlayStation could start offering content to many devices at some point, not just on their bespoke technology – especially given their technology is little more than a bespoke PC build currently. Xbox Live already does this, and Epic Games Store has announced plans to do the same.

Player-Driven Content and Economies

As gaming communities grow and become more active participants in the development process, player-driven content is emerging as a powerful trend. In many games, players are not just consumers – they are creators, contributing to the in-game economy by designing content, crafting items, or influencing the market.

EVE Online

A pivotal game that has been online since 2003 and arguably demonstrates the ultimate player-driven economy. At a basic level, players can mine for resources, sell those resources, acquire technologies, skills, and vessels, and use that to explore and exploit regions of space. This is a game where 'Death' matters, and the destruction of assets is a critical factor that drives the game economy. When you play EVE, you are going to lose your ship. Indeed, this is so common that as Daniel Ramotowski, Senior Designer on EVE has stated, players think of their ships as 'Ammunition'. Players have formed huge corporations, conducted economic warfare, committed fraud and scammed other players within the context of the game. All of this is permitted in the game. This can make the experience a tough one to get involved with, but it has sparked a curious reaction. The fact that the game is hard is the point. It makes the game exponentially more meaningful for the players. Add to that, given players and what they can do are the actual practical limited resource, recruiting and helping new players becomes an essential factor in the success of player groups, known as Corporations. Some of which have over 40,000 active members! This approach has led to unique design and balance challenges which have consequences in terms of simulation which are even being studied by real-world economists and which allow us to make insights which have a broader impact on society than you might have expected from a game. In 2014, The Battle of B-R5RB was an enormous conflict in EVE Online with an estimated loss of US$300k–330k. This is part of the game economy. The same year, a notorious player, "Scooter McCabe" as part of a notorious group known as Goonswarm, scammed and dismantled an entire corporation, something which in context was seen as 'part of the game' by CCP. Taking this truly laissez-faire attitude is not without its challenges and is definitely not for any game, but for EVE, it has created experiences which are arguably cultural milestones in how humans engage in virtual worlds as well as helping us understand more about the function of economics in games. The introduction of free to play mechanics into EVE illustrates some of the challenges of maintaining the economy. Talking to some long-term players who had been highly active, each running many multiple accounts at a time, changes to game balance, combined with the introduction of new commercial items, can have unintended consequences – in the case of EVE, this includes the concentration of power into the hands of the largest corporations and a focus on enormous headline-grabbing conflicts.

User-Generated Content (UGC)

User-generated content (UGC) is not a new concept in gaming, but its role in shaping game economies is expanding. Games like *Minecraft*, *Roblox*, LittleBigPlanet, and *Fortnite* have shown the potential of UGC to drive player engagement and create vibrant in-game economies. Players who create and share their own maps, skins, levels, or even game modes contribute to the overall ecosystem, often generating additional revenue for the developers through sales or microtransactions.

UGC adds value to a game by giving players more control over their experience and offering a virtually limitless supply of new content. For developers, UGC can extend the lifespan of a game by allowing the community to contribute to its ongoing evolution. In some cases, UGC creators are even able to monetise their content, either through in-game marketplaces or by partnering with the developers.

However, it would be a mistake to see UGC as a cheap or easy way to add more value into your game.

First, for vanity content to work at all, players need a reason to care about that. As has been said before: Vanity goods require a vanity 'loop.' Without the space for players to engage and care with some form of customised experience, you won't see widespread adoption of UGC in your game.

Secondly, there is the 'TTP' problem – you can imagine what that acronym stands for given that it is the time it takes for someone on social platforms to create offensive content, usually the drawing of male genitalia; and usually measured in seconds.

Thirdly, most content developed by players will not be good. Creating good-looking assets requires a dedication to both the tools and the skills and creativity of the player. Framing the scope of assets increases the likelihood of content looking good (the Nintendo's Mii Avatars are incredibly simplistic) but in turn this limits the scope and marketability of such items. Developers typically estimate that just something like 10% of players will even engage with UGC tools more than once, and that less than 10% of the content those players produce will even be interesting to other players. This leads to a major discovery problem: How do you find the content that isn't dull or even terrible? And most of the content produced will be junk! Add to this the question of whether you charge for using the tools? Or consuming the content? If you can't do either, how can you demonstrate that the engagement, cultural impact, and marketing power delivered by the existence of such content offsets the costs of tools, technology, and testing involved? UGC can be amazing to drive success. Minecraft, Roblox, Fortnite, and NetEase[9] have all demonstrated incredible success built as much from the creativity of players as the game itself. However, this is a complicated feat to pull off, and many development teams have fallen when trying to implement it in their games.

As a rule of thumb, UGC usually works best when the creation of assets is deeply connected to the gameplay, and where personal expression and creativity are intrinsic to the game's identity and player utility.

Secondary Markets

In some games, virtual items have real-world value due to their rarity or desirability. This has led to secondary markets, often counter to the terms and conditions of the game licence. EverQuest[10] was famous for a rise in Gold Farming, where people would create multiple accounts solely for the purpose of collecting and selling in-game currency and character accounts for real money. A practice allegedly taken up by criminal gangs, allegedly commonly in China, to launder money. This had a significant impact on the game economy and couldn't be ignored due to the scale of the interactions. Eventually, the developers decided to offer currency for retail within the game. A lot of the lessons applied in free-to-play arguably come from observation of this phenomenon.

Other games have embraced the role of such external markets, for example, the trading of rare cosmetic skins or in-game items in games like *Counter-Strike: Global Offensive* or *Dota 2* that can be sold for hundreds or even thousands of dollars in online marketplaces (including some crypto ones). This tie to real-world markets, where players buy, sell, and trade in-game assets for real money, has implications for game balance, and we need to understand the implications on the elements of reward in gameplay, what we offer commercially, and indeed how we support or constrain such purchases.

Blockchain technology has been raised as having the potential to enable a secure, decentralised way of trading in-game assets; but as outlined above, this has not yet delivered an ideal solution. Games like The Sandbox use the technology not just as an exchange mechanism but to trace the creation path so that players are credited for the materials they create. This could help allow players to maintain ownership and value of their creations outside the game's ecosystem, but there remain complications to the approach, as discussed above.

Competitive Gaming and Esports

The rise of esports has created new opportunities for players to monetise their gaming skills through competitive tournaments and events. Players can earn real money by competing in organised events, whether as part of a professional team or through individual competitions. This has led to the creation of entire ecosystems around competitive gaming, where sponsorships, streaming, and merchandise sales generate significant revenue.

For developers, supporting competitive gaming can enhance player engagement and drive long-term loyalty. Games that become popular in the esports scene often benefit from increased visibility, community support, and revenue opportunities.

However, the reality is that very few games have ever made it as esports. Just as it is the audience who decides if your game will have the long-term longevity as a LiveOps experience, it is the players who will decide if your game will end up as an esport.

Physical Merchandise

Some games capture the cultural zeitgeist to such an extent that the audience wants to wear your logo/brand as a personal identifier. Just like in the music industry where t-shirts, posters, and other physical objects have become a major revenue model, the same can be said for some games. However, not all games can pull this off. Only games which have had a cultural impact are likely to have the scope to benefit from the economy of scale necessary to profit from the production warehousing, wholesale, and retail distribution necessary for physical goods. There are platforms which help smaller brands exploit their IP in this way, and it can be a great way to extend visibility amongst your most loyal players (your tribe), but of course, they take a significant cut to do that. Rovio's Angry Birds was the first mobile game to develop 'plushy' toys from their characters, and these can still be found in international airports for sale. The point is that this can be done and has secondary value for building up your engagement with your audience and helping encourage word of mouth. However, in doing this, ensure that the objects have intrinsic value and that their quality matches expectations for the game. There are lots of hidden costs that need to be considered from design, tooling (setting up factory equipment to make the designs such as preparing art for screen printing or creating bespoke die-cut tools), minimum quantities, material sourcing, supply logistics, storage, and of course, distribution.

If your game is successful, other people will exploit your brand. This might be directly (in breach of your copyright and trademarks) or indirectly through parody and reference, and whilst you can engage legally support, this is costly and in the case of references or parody, there is often nothing you can do. Judging the point where you can successfully offer either a limited line or a sustainable physical goods portfolio requires its own level of expertise. In the meantime, protect what you can through copyright (which is generally automatic for western territories) and by registering your trademarks.

It should be noted that as we mentioned in *Chapter 8 Functions of Exchange,* the Digital Markets Act and recent anti-competitive legislation against Apple's prohibition of using external stores may act as a significant boost to physical merchandise; assuming that tariffs make this commercially impractical.

AI as Tools or Tyrants?

No book written in 2026 can ignore the potential role of AI. The idea of AI in games was historically about the rules used to control the movement and actions of NPCs and other forms of Mobs (mobile objects). As machine learning has developed, it has allowed game economy designers to get a deeper understanding of patterns of usage and helped with predictions of adoption, retention, and conversion. In my professional life I have been working on ways to leverage this kind of data at an 'Event Level' for LiveOps games to help teams plan more effectively for the longer-term development of their games.[11] In the R&D phase we explored the use of ML and large language model generative AI (GenAI) to review the performance of events by tag against the effort/costs required to deliver those elements and provide 'nudges' to help teams improve their performance over time. This kind of modelling uses game data anonymously, ethically separating operational performance from private information. Tools like this all every user to benefit from deeper learning, without putting any commercial information at risk (when well designed!). AI could potentially be used to dynamically optimise the games' FTUE or even reward/power curves, perhaps even adapting at an individual player level. This is quite a challenging area and has been the cause of some disputes amongst both players and designers, as when handled badly or unethically it carryies risks of breaking the 'social contract' in the game. Other forms of GenAI open even deeper ethical conundrums. Whilst there are considerable opportunities to improve the speed and efficiency of delivering new, interesting asset using visual GenAI through Midjourney[12] and OpenAI's Sora[13] but where have the core materials been obtained. There have been cased that show that unlicenced materials have been used in training some AI models – with the Getty Watermark appearing on some AI creations resulting in a legal case against Stability AI.[14] In May 2025 Fortnite featured an AI Darth Vader which used AI to provide unique interactive voice conversations for each player in the game, leading to the Screen Actors Guild – American Federation of Television and Radio Artists (SAG-AFTRA) filing charges against Epic Games.[15] Where games leverage AI tools to increase the efficiency of creating concept art or monthly update assets, is that necessarily unethical or exploitative? The controversy of these issues directly affects the livelihood of many creative people, not least as some management types seems to have made the mistake (IMHO) that GenAI's role is to replace these teams. As clever as AI it is currently, our view that they can only be tools that need to be directed by talent and creative minds. AI is not creating something new, but rather using predictive models to develop images from source materials it has trained on. The question remains how we can best navigate the implications this technology has on our industry and wider culture. For the avoidance of doubt, we have explored how we could use AI tools during the process of making this book. However, whilst we see the potential that AI offers as a useful tool to speed up the effectiveness and delivery for individuals, we also note that it has its limitations, not least as it does seem to "revert to the mean". In the end, a large language model AI is a prediction engine; even if a highly sophisticated tool able to do incredible things very fast, that requires clear guidance, and often having to reset this represents the equivalent of the 'uncanny valley'[16] which has held up 3D humans in video games and movies, even to today, and as a result completed. We get a sense of unease looking at AI images and animations still. But that may not last if it did in video games. There is a long way to go before we see how legislation, commercial terms, and equitable distribution of its returns take to catch up with this revolution and I am glad to see folks standing up for human creativity, even whilst experimenting with the tools myself. This is a wild west, and until it's fully resolved, it will remain an ethical minefield.

Regulation Changes

At the time of writing the regulatory framework has started to get ever more complex. Regional governments have started to enforce more overt restrictions, rather than leaving the industry to self-regulate. This is arguably our own fault as an industry as we still fail to share market data commonly shared in other industries and we have the habit of 'reinventing the wheel'. This has led to a series of bad practice events. The use of what has now become called 'Dark Patterns' that illustrate a failure of appreciating the implications or more malicious intent. Either way regulations such as The Online Safety Act in the UK, Digital Markets Act and the (upcoming at the time of writing) Digital Fairness Act in the EU all seem to be increasingly restrictive on games and game design. Unfortunately, the regulatory language has also been written in ways which the author considers unlikely to make any consumer safer. The acts/bills seem to place the responsibility on the developer to adapt, manage and deliver the solutions; rather than the platforms. At best this is likely to increase the barrier to entry for smaller developers and at worst leave players more vulnerable to cyberattacks and phishing exercises. The Digital Fairness Act is likely to more directly affect game design and seems intent to restrict the application of virtual currencies in games. The specifics won't be finalised by the time of publication, but they are likely to require developers to state a real money value for currencies, even if they are earned through play.

In a similar vein, at the time of writing Google and Epic are discussing a two tier charging mechanism, with 20% on game affecting items but only 9% for cosmetic items. That may sound reasonable on the surface, but a) who will decide? and b) is this just an arbitrary tax on game affecting items? The unintended consequences from both store policy changes and regulation are yet to be fully understood (and they have yet to be confirmed).

Looking Ahead

Whatever happens Game Designers will have to adapt to the regulations in intelligent ways to defend the player experience and ensure that this complies with the framework we are required to operate within. For example if virtual currencies are explicitly banned, we need to not panic, instead to understand why such currency mechanisms make the player experience better and how they allow us to deliver purpose, progression and consumable reward. We then need to adapt our approach ensuring that any currency we do offer makes sense within the new rules, and new solutions which can be appropriately distanced from the old forms of currency.

Game markets and economic techniques do not remain static. We need to understand what best practice looks like and where there is potential for innovation. We do not have to be first movers. Knowing what is working and being able to apply the lessons to our games is vital. Better to be 'Fast Followers' who learn from those who have led the way, but who apply the lessons whilst avoiding the pitfalls. Those organisations who can adapt to changing conditions strategically without being caught in their past approaches will survive and often are the very organisations who come out on top. In my career I have been lucky enough to have had the opportunity to take the first steps in many of the models which are taken for granted today. Whilst this has not led to vast riches personally, it has given me a perspective on how to leverage new technologies and commercial models and, without this experience, I would not have been able to write a book like this.

Game economies have become more interconnected, blending value on platforms, in-game, and in the real world. New devices and approaches will continue to appear and our access to global markets may change, not least with the return of tariffs being introduced by the USA in 2025. As game economy designers, we need to ensure that we observe and learn and find ways to apply these lessons to ensure the life of our games and how we deliver value to our players.

Interview

UNDERSTANDING THE EVE ECONOMY –
AN INTERVIEW WITH DANIEL RAMOTOWSKI

In this deep dive into the mechanics and philosophy behind *EVE Online*, Daniel Ramotowski[1] shares how the long-running MMO has developed one of the most fascinating and socially complex virtual economies in gaming history. His insights reveal not only how a functioning game economy works at scale, but also how those systems are shaped by – and shape – the behaviour of players over time.

While many developers define game economies in terms of progression or monetisation, Ramotowski sees a deeper function: player interaction. Not necessarily synchronous, combat-style interaction – but the kind of asynchronous exchange that defines human behaviour in persistent online spaces.

> Essentially, economy to me is a way for players to interact with each other. Like that's my perspective on the economy in games, especially like asynchronous interaction, right? Because for synchronous interaction I usually think about combat and things like that. But when you think about asynchronous interaction, then economy is that thing to me.

This frame sets the tone for understanding *EVE's* market systems not as bolt-ons, but as integral to how the game communicates meaning between players. Items aren't just loot – they're social artefacts, and the economy is the language players use to translate their efforts into value for others.

A core insight Ramotowski offers is that exchange doesn't begin with the presence of a market – it begins with the presence of differing value perceptions. Once players possess something that's more valuable to someone else than to themselves, trade is inevitable – even without formal systems.

> "Players will try to find a form of exchange themselves if they end up having something that is more valuable to someone else than for them. And I think that's the foundation of how economies work," Said Ramotowski.

This natural emergence of trade is what makes player-driven economies feel alive. Instead of setting static prices or supply chains, CCP creates the conditions for exchange and allows players to determine what happens next.

Ramotowski explains that value in games is highly contextual. What one player sees as essential, another might ignore. And those perceptions change as the player progresses – not just in-game levels, but also in understanding the systems.

> "The value [players place] can be tied to progression… At the start, you are not very worried about how much money you have, but rather whether you have a basic axe to cut a tree," Said Ramotowski.

He emphasises that players mature through gameplay – not just in skill, but in how they assign value to different items and strategies. *EVE* even has its own version of Maslow's hierarchy of needs: first, survive and replace losses; later, aspire to prestige and luxury. With *EVE's* scale and player-driven systems, fundamental economic principles apply: supply, demand, scarcity, specialisation, and even vertical integration. And yes – having a background in real-world economics or trading can give you a tangible advantage.

> "One of the most successful traders talks about the economy in EVE extensively [on their Twitch channel]. In his daily job, he's an economics analyst." said Ramotowski.

Players who understand economies of scale or how to avoid intermediary taxes by vertically integrating production chains find themselves thriving. What's remarkable is not just that these systems exist, but that *EVE* rewards real-world knowledge in practical, meaningful ways.

One of Ramotowski's most striking revelations is how he uses market prices – set entirely by players – as balancing signals when working on game design. In most games, designers set the prices. In *EVE*, prices reflect actual utility and scarcity, offering valuable data for design decisions.

> "One of the attributes that I looked at for each module was its market price, which is 100% dictated by players." Said Ramotowski.

This makes *EVE* one of the few games where the economy not only reflects player behaviour but also actively shapes how the game is tuned over time.

In *EVE*, nothing is safe – not even your prized ship. The game's ethos of meaningful risk creates a constant tension between gain and potential loss. Players calculate everything: how often they'll lose a ship, how long it takes to earn enough to replace it, and whether the effort is worth the risk.

> "Your ships are your ammo... if you acquire a new ship, you will lose it. Just be okay with that," said Ramotowski.

This commitment to consequence shapes every decision. It's not just that items have a cost – it's that loss is real, and players have to factor that into their strategy.

The balance between sourcing and sinking resources is at the heart of any sustainable game economy. In *EVE*, scarcity is real – and sometimes CCP has had to step in to correct imbalances. Ramotowski describes the impact of a single mining ship, the Rorqual, which disrupted the economy by introducing vast resource oversupply.

> "We even have a period in the history of EVE that we call the Rorqual era... it wasn't very healthy in the end." Said Ramotowski.

To restore balance, CCP began a multi-year period of economic adjustment, dubbed the "Scarcity Era," where the availability of resources was deliberately reduced. The community's reaction was mixed – but for CCP, the long-term stability of the economy had to take precedence.

Large-scale economic management isn't done in isolation. *EVE* has its own democratically elected

Council of Stellar Management (CSM), where representatives of major in-game organisations provide feedback to CCP, particularly on high-level economic concerns.

> "If you have someone... with influence over a group of 40,000 players, they can give you perspective that you cannot acquire otherwise," said Ramotowski.

This blend of community feedback and developer oversight creates a unique governance layer within the game – almost a model of distributed leadership.

Despite the risks, wealth in *EVE* does accumulate. But rather than locking out new players, it often fuels support systems. Veteran-run corporations invest in newcomers, providing ships, training, and guidance.

> "Those groups use that wealth accumulated by previous generations... to prop up the new members." Said Ramotowski.

This cycle mimics real-world organisational behaviour: capital investment in human resources to ensure future productivity. The incentive? New players are the most valuable resource in the game – human capital is the only thing that creates value at scale.

Finally, Ramotowski reflects on the nature of difficulty and connection in multiplayer games. *EVE* is famously punishing – but that's part of what forges its strongest communities.

> "EVE is hard, is very harsh… and that kind of by accident made it so that players have to collaborate." Said Ramotowski.

The challenge builds bonds. Difficulty creates depth. And while CCP continues to work on onboarding and accessibility, they remain committed to the core idea that meaning requires consequence.

> "The game should reward effort, right? But more precisely, it should reward well-placed effort," concludes Ramotowski.

NOTE

1 https://www.linkedin.com/in/daniel-r-6615534/

Interview

EVE ONLINE'S ECONOMY FROM THE PLAYER PERSPECTIVE – AN INTERVIEW WITH SIMON ROMANOS AND BRIAN MAIR

EVE Online has long been recognised for its complex, player-driven economy. Unlike many games where economies are curated and heavily moderated by developers, EVE's economy thrives on player interaction, scarcity, and real-time decision-making. Following the conversation with Daniel Ramotowski, we interviewed Simon Romanos and Brian Mair, veteran EVE players for nearly 20 years. Their reflections offer a different perspective on games as a service and the impact on broader economy designs.

Simon, who began playing in 2006, describes the core appeal:

> For me, the beauty of the game wasn't mining – it was extracting assets from other players.

This sentiment underscores a foundational principle of EVE's economy: risk and reward are tightly interwoven. Players can build fortunes by outsmarting others, but that wealth is never secure. Destructible resources mean that everything has inherent risk.

> "The more power you have, the more you have at stake," said Romanos.

> "When I started, it was all about mining and learning the basics. Eventually, we expanded into escorting miners, PvP, and trading. It was a vast world where you could dabble in various roles," Mair added.

This variety allowed players to find their niche, fostering long-term engagement.

While EVE's economy thrives on player agency, this freedom has its downsides. Mair recounts how large player corporations consolidated power:

> These massive groups controlled vast regions, gating essential resources. If you weren't part of them, you were effectively locked out of large parts of the game.

This concentration of power mirrors real-world economic monopolies. This could be compared to late 19th-century 'Robber Barrons' who had sufficient control over resources that they could almost manipulate markets at will. Such monopolisation creates functional barriers, especially for new or casual players.

> "You might want to dabble in building or fighting, but certain materials were moved to high-risk zones controlled by dominant factions. You either risked everything by venturing out or faced an impossible grind buying materials on the market," Mair explained.

In an attempt to broaden its player base, CCP Games introduced significant changes to the new player experience. While the influx of new players was notable it did not come without consequence.

> "…they simplified things so much that players could only use basic ships and capped skill points. It was easy to get bored quickly. This means that a well-intentioned approach inadvertently funnelled newcomers into large corporations, accelerating the concentration of power," said Romanos.

Mair elaborated on this:

> New players would join 'alpha-friendly' corps, but their growth was capped with those groups. Without meaningful progression paths, retention suffered.

The balance between accessibility and depth is delicate and there is always the risk that oversimplification can undermine long-term engagement.

One of the most polarising changes discussed was the introduction of skill injectors – items purchasable with real money that fast-track character progression.

> "Players could buy skill injectors, skip months of training, and immediately pilot advanced ships," said Mair.

While this seems advantageous, it introduced unforeseen consequences. Romanos highlights the issue:

> People would buy shiny ships without understanding how to use them, lose them quickly, and either get frustrated or spend even more money.

This dynamic undermines the organic learning curve that previously fostered mastery and meaningful progression. From a monetisation perspective, selling skill points seems lucrative. But if players can bypass the anchor of progression, there is a risk of eroding the very sense of achievement that drives engagement.

It is important to note that this feedback is coming from the perspective of two veteran players, both of whom already have considerable experience in the game, and a large amount of sunk cost in the previous design. So, their interpretation of the changes may not reflect the wider impact on the game, particularly for newer players. As we have said before Players are not designers and we need to remember the differences in these lenses. However, from Romano's and Mair's perspective, the ease of obtaining skills that these changes introduced clashed with what they felt was the game's foundational principle of earning one's place through effort and risk.

We cannot complete a discussion on EVE without addressing perhaps its most controversial aspect – the acceptance of in-game scamming.

> "One of my friends plays solely to scam people. The bigger the con, the more satisfying it is for him," said Romanos.

While this might seem unethical to the uninitiated, EVE's design treats deception as a legitimate strategy, adding layers of psychological warfare. This makes EVE a fascinating sandbox for players to take on behaviour they would never consider in the real world and create truly emergent gameplay. Not one without risk however, and this set-up can alienate any players expecting to encounter a fair playing field. Striking a balance between freedom and fairness is crucial but as EVE demonstrates the stance you take helps define the game feel and the choice to make the game difficult and uncompromising is a significant part of what makes the experience matter so much for its players.

Discussing EVE Online's economy with both veteran players and one of the senior designers shows the pivotal lessons that this game offers any game economy designer – perhaps even anyone interested in real-world economics as well!

These lessons include:

- **Destruction Matters**: Destructible assets and high-stakes gameplay create tension and deepen investment in the game. However, it will deter many players especially if it is not a foundational part of the game.

- **Beware of Monopolisation**: Without checks, player-driven economies can mirror real-world inequities, discouraging newcomers and casual players. However, in EVE this is arguably a feature not a bug.

- **Progression Should Feel Earned**: Fast-tracking through purchases can undermine long-term engagement unless carefully balanced with learning curves.

- **Emergent Gameplay Needs Boundaries**: While scamming adds depth, it risks alienating players seeking fair competition.

- **Metrics Can Be Misleading**: Tracking genuine engagement versus inflated account numbers is vital for understanding player behaviour

EVE's economy remains a masterclass in complexity that brings one of the ultimate realistic simulations, but it is an experience which can be demanding on its players. Probably, why so many have been playing it for decades!

"It's a simulation of economies done remarkably well – it's just not always pleasant to play." Concluded Mair, a 20-year veteran player.

NOTES

1 https://www.investopedia.com/what-went-wrong-with-ftx-6828447
2 https://en.wikipedia.org/wiki/Monkey_selfie_copyright_dispute
3 https://metaverse-standards.org/
4 https://realityclash.com/blog/reality-clash-game/about/
5 https://blockchaingames.fun/games/the-sandbox/
6 https://blockchaingames.fun/games/decentraland/
7 https://en.wikipedia.org/wiki/Capcom_vs._SNK_2
8 https://iu.pressbooks.pub/perspectives3/chapter/napster-the-black-market-that-publicly-dominated-the-music-industry/#:~:text=Without%20the%20legal%20rights%20to,was%20fueled%20by%20its%20popularity
9 https://naavik.co/deep-dives/the-state-of-ugc-games-2025-deep-dive/
10 https://everquest.allakhazam.com/wiki/Gold_Farming_%28WoW%29
11 https://arcanix.ai/
12 https://www.midjourney.com/
13 https://openai.com/index/sora/
14 https://www.judiciary.uk/wp-content/uploads/2025/01/Getty-Images-and-others-v-Stability-AI-14.01.25.pdf
15 https://www.sportskeeda.com/fortnite/news-fortnite-darth-vader-ai-voice-causes-legal-trouble-sag-aftra-files-charges
16 https://en.wikipedia.org/wiki/Uncanny_valley

CHAPTER 13

Sustainability and Ethical Design

DOI: 10.1201/9781003592471-13

WHAT DO ETHICS HAVE TO DO WITH GAME DESIGN?

Game design doesn't happen in isolation. As we have hopefully shown in the other chapters, game developers create our experiences in an ever-changing environment. Whether that is in the form of regulation, market conditions, or political changes, game developers have to adapt. That games have grown to have such an impact on culture as the single largest form of digital entertainment on the planet has consequences. When more than 40% of the population of the planet play computer games[1] with 48% of US gamers being female. This ultimately means the tone, conduct, and narrative elements have a vital cultural impact. More than 85%[2] of games' revenue comes from live-service or 'Free-To-Play' games in an industry projected to be worth over $580 billions[3] worldwide by 2030. That puts the design decisions of game economy designers under an intense spotlight. It is essential to consider the ethical implications of our designs or risk damaging the industry as a whole. This is no speculative risk. This has already happened on multiple occasions, just consider how data has been mishandled. loot crates, and the mishandling of in-app purchases, all of which have led directly to regulatory changes. The industry only recently shook off the completely baseless allegations that games were to blame for adolescent violence[4] and still bad actors and poorly considered designs continue to damage our reputation. Add to this, the controversies that surround character representation, AI, Blockchain, power consumption of hosting servers, and it is not possible to avoid wider cultural questions, whether that means politics, climate change, or diversity issues. We don't all have to carry a torch, but it is dangerous to ignore the shadow we cast.

Balancing monetisation, player engagement, and environmental sustainability is crucial in ensuring that game economies remain fair, transparent, and responsible. Getting this right is a commercial necessity, and it is naïve short-termism to pretend otherwise.

The future of game economies is full of exciting possibilities. New technologies and player-driven innovations are creating opportunities for developers to rethink how they design and manage in-game economies. By staying ahead of these trends and adopting a forward-thinking approach to game design, developers can create economies that not only meet the needs of today's players but also anticipate the demands of the future. But there are pitfalls that must be considered.

PITFALLS IN GAME ECONOMY DESIGN

Designing a successful game economy is a delicate balancing act. When done well, a game economy can enhance player engagement, drive long-term retention, and generate sustainable revenue. However, there are many potential pitfalls that can undermine these goals. From failing to connect price with player value to overusing manipulative monetisation tactics, poor economy design can lead to player frustration, early churn, and long-term damage to both the game and the broader industry.

In this chapter, we'll explore the most common mistakes in game economy design and explain why these errors are not only harmful in the short term but also detrimental to the long-term health of the gaming ecosystem. This includes exploring how developers might avoid such pitfalls by focusing on what some mistakenly think of as soft factors like fairness, transparency, and player value. These principles are difficult, exacting, and supported by evidence to help ensure that games remain engaging and profitable over the longer term. And make no mistake we have a legal responsibility as well, we are offering of consumer goods and have to comply with relevant regulation.

Failing to Connect Price with Player Value

One of the most critical aspects of game economy design is aligning the price of in-game purchases with the value players perceive from them. When the price of an item, currency, or upgrade doesn't match the value that players attach to it, players are less likely to make purchases, and they may even feel alienated by the game's economy.

Players need to feel that their money is well-spent when making in-game purchases; and given the hot/cold empathy gap (*see Chapter 2: Defining an Economy*), how we introduce the payment matters. Post-purchase remorse is a critical factor we ignore at our own risk. If a high price is attached to an item that offers little utility or aesthetic appeal, players may view the purchase as unfair or exploitative. For example, if cosmetic skins are priced too high according to general perception against the associated visual/social impact, or if premium currency doesn't offer a meaningful advantage to the exchange process, players will feel like they're being overcharged. This creates friction between the player and the game, which can lead to dissatisfaction, reduced spending, and eventually churn. So much of this is subjective. Pricing in mobile apps tends to be rated against the price of a high-street coffee, but PC/console items often command higher value expectations – regardless of the effort or exclusivity of the item. Is an $80 price for a Switch 2 'pay upfront' game sustainable? What about paying that same $80 over 8 months for a 'LiveOps' game?

On the other hand, when prices are aligned with what players value – whether that's cosmetic appeal, gameplay enhancements, or exclusive content – players are more likely to make purchases, and they will feel satisfied with their investment. This is why it's essential to conduct research, compare with similar titles on the market, and to gather player feedback on what players value most in your game, ensuring that prices reflect this understanding. Happy spenders tend to be more likely to spend again, and this starts having an impact that resembles 'Compound Interest' for the game maker, creating a sustainable, more predictable revenue stream which builds ever more value the longer the player stays playing.

Examples of Mispricing and Its Consequences

There are numerous examples of games that have failed to properly connect price with player value:

- **Overpriced Cosmetic Items**: Some free-to-play games offer cosmetic items at prices that players find unreasonable. While cosmetic items are often a popular source of revenue, setting the price too high relative to the item's appeal can result in poor sales and player frustration. For example, charging the equivalent of $20 for a simple character skin with no special features might alienate casual players who expect a more reasonable price. Note that being exclusive can command higher prices, but the price itself is rarely sufficient to justify that.

- **Paywalls for Essential Progression**: Some games make the mistake of locking essential gameplay elements, such as new characters or abilities, behind a steep paywall. If these items are necessary for progression or success in the game, players may feel forced to spend money to continue playing. This leads to dissatisfaction, particularly among free players, who may view the game as pay-to-win. Often, these barriers are introduced as an unintended consequence, and designers need to be alert to them.

- **Dropping Price without Notice**: Players can often react badly when a price change happens without some notice. Reducing the price is great for the player getting the benefit, but for the player who has just made that purchase at the higher price, they will feel robbed. Additionally, once the price is reduced, it is likely that you will see the willingness to pay full price plummet! Which is why Steam is so sales-focused. Pricing generally can only go down – rarely up.

The consequence of mispricing is twofold: it not only reduces the likelihood of purchase but also damages player trust. Once players believe that the game is trying to extract more money than the experience is worth, they may stop spending entirely, or worse, quit the game. Maintaining trust by aligning price with perceived value is essential for long-term success.

Disconnect with Utility: Failing to Provide Meaningful Rewards

Another common pitfall in game economy design is failing to ensure that the items or rewards players earn or purchase have meaningful utility within the game. If players feel that the items they acquire – whether through in-game currency or real-money purchases – don't contribute to their progression or experience, they are unlikely to stay engaged.

As discussed in *Chapter 7: Understanding Utility*, Utility is the measure of how useful or impactful an item is within the context of the game – including culturally. If an item is purely cosmetic but offers no gameplay advantage, it can still hold some value (i.e., Social Capital) for players seeking to express themselves. However, if an item is intended to improve gameplay (such as an upgrade, weapon, or ability) but has minimal obvious impact, players may feel that their investment was wasted; and if it has a lot of obvious impact, other players may consider it 'broken' or 'pay-to-win' – even if that is far from the case.

In games that rely on progression systems, the rewards players earn should meaningfully enhance their gameplay experience and still leave them wanting more. If players grind through difficult challenges only to receive uninspiring, low-value, or low-impact items, they may become frustrated and lose interest. This can lead to early churn, especially in games where progression is tied to resource scarcity or complex upgrade systems.

In trying to monetise a game economy, it can be tempting to focus on the revenue aspects rather than player utility. This can lead to aggressive pricing, or a dependency on fear of missing out rather than the value proposition for the player. It can lead to an overemphasis on conversion metrics at the expense of Lifetime Value – especially in the 'Learning' Lifestage, where players have yet to decide whether the game fits into their routine. Don't misinterpret this statement. Conversion is critical, but repeat purchase is possibly the most effective measurement to understand if players value what is being sold to them. However, don't ignore other data points; for example, if there is a drop in the number of sessions or session duration after a spend, there may be other problems in the game.

OVERUSE OF DARK PATTERNS: EXPLOITATIVE MONETISATION PRACTICES

It has become popular for journalists and players to talk about 'Dark Patterns' when it comes to game monetisation. This refers to the design practices allegedly used by 'Bad Actors' to manipulate players into making purchases or engaging with the game in ways that benefit the developer at the expense of the player. In practice, intentional 'bad acting' is (somewhat) less prevalent than is perceived; rather, a lack of understanding or care over the consequences of a monetisation design is more commonly the cause. Or indeed, targets being set that focus on the speed to Return on Advertising Spend or more general short-termist revenue targets.

Regardless of intention, there is a point where legitimate design models can become exploitative; but this is self-destructive, eroding player trust, and damaging the game's reputation. There is always a cost in LTV.

- **Pay-to-Win Mechanics**: Perhaps the most notorious dark pattern is the use of pay-to-win mechanics, which has been discussed across the book. Where players can spend money directly to gain a significant advantage over non-paying players, this generally has a negative impact on the game. This is because it creates an unfair dynamic, especially in competitive games, where paying players can dominate free players through sheer financial power. While this might generate revenue in the short term, it often leads to player churn as non-paying players become frustrated and leave. However, what is Pay-To-Win for some players (particularly in Western markets) may not be an issue at all in other markets (especially in Asia). Indeed, the ability to show off wealth and to 'Front-Load' your game to gain a competitive advantage can be part of the experience. Looking at this through the lens of player value and the 'unintended consequences' of items helps us focus on the experience without ignoring commercially valid offers.

- **Time-Limited Offers and FOMO (Fear of Missing Out)**: Another commonly quoted 'dark pattern' is the overuse of time-limited offers that prey on players' fear of missing out. Flash sales, limited-time events, and exclusive offers can create an artificial sense of urgency or scarcity, pushing players to make impulse purchases. While these tactics can boost revenue, they also create anxiety and regret among players who feel manipulated into spending money. This tactic relies heavily on the principle of the 'Hot/Cold Empathy gap'. Relying on player engagement at the time of presenting those offers to seduce them into making decisions based on emotion rather than analysis. Players tend to attempt to justify such expenditure, but where it becomes overwhelming, they will churn, often angrily, which inevitably leads to very negative reviews. That doesn't mean that offers are intrinsically bad, in fact, they are necessary. Players need a reason to make a purchase now, rather than to put it off indefinitely. This is not a games thing, this is a retail thing, something profoundly human. There is no issue with creating a reason, but this requires balance and sensitivity to the player's experiences and a respect for their time and commitment to the game. Creating unreasonable pressure is not just wrong, but explicitly prohibited by Advertising Standards[5] and EU Consumer Protection regulations.[6]

- **Energy Mechanics and Progression Blockers**: Some games use energy systems that limit how much players can progress in a single session, often requiring them to wait for their energy to refill or purchase more to continue. While energy mechanics can create a sense of scarcity, they can also frustrate players if they feel they are being unfairly blocked from progressing unless they spend money. Not all barriers are immediately obvious and can arise out of a series of interconnected systems – sometimes even unintentional. The analogy for understanding this for the author is to think of this as a form of momentum. Each time you are in a flow and hit a stop, it takes energy away. If you keep hitting those barriers before getting refreshed (unlocking positive rewards or resting from the game), you will lose all momentum and churn from the game. Fixing this issue is harder to resolve than other design issues as you need to track the whole path of player engagement, not just the last activity where they churned. Remember, though, this pattern is also an essential aspect of design; managing player progression is essential to ensuring that actions feel meaningful and that the game is 'worth playing.'

- **Randomness Manipulation**: Some games will leverage randomness in the delivery of items making the specific rewards unlocked by a reward or 'Loot Crate' subject to chance. When done positively it can add a sense of excitement and uncertainty which can be engaging; as well as providing a reason to acquire (through play or purchase) that item again and again. However, there are numerous risks associated with this approach. If there is true randomness, there remains the risk that players will never get the item they want, if using pseudo randomness, can the game avoid this being seen as manipulation? If players get material benefit from those items, what makes this different from a lottery or slot machine? Such risks are minimised where the player cannot 'cash out' the item, but sensitivity to this area, and its blurring of the lines, make people wrongly equate such methods with 'Gambling'. It's essential (and required by some platforms/ markets) to communicate the payout rates and to ensure that the value a player unlocks is equivalent even if not identical each time it is opened. In 2012, the practice of compounding multiple layers of randomisation (e.g. you have to unlock something to have a chance to unlock other rarer items, etc.) was made illegal in Japan and since then the practice has largely disappeared. Whilst the gambling comparison is often made, there is potentially more significant issue when it comes to randomisation, the Illusion of Control.[7] Suzanne C. Thompson wrote about this under the title 'How we overestimate our personal influence'[8] and how personal involvement, familiarity, and foreknowledge of the desired outcome can lead players to falsely believe they have more control of the outcome than they actually do in practice. When rolling a set of dice, does that feel like we have any agency over the outcome; is that agency weaker if someone else rolls those dice? Despite the reality it certainly can feel like it is. The same applies if a player is already deeply familiar with the process, or where they know that they might unlock a 'special seasonal skin' from a lootbox this time; even after failing three times before. These circumstances can give players a baseless illusion that they will get the result they want from the randomised item 'this time!'. This is a very human response, even when the participants are logically aware of the effect, they can find themselves falling for it and this can open them up to risk of manipulation. But take a different perspective for a moment. these very factors can feel immersive and engaging, they also can help the player feel more deeply engaged with the reward process; it can be part of what makes the reward personal, even special! Randomness is a tool that designers can use authentically to intensify the fun when applied authentically; but, if misused it can become very problematic.

Dark patterns clearly exist, but they are often the result of misunderstanding, not just intentional manipulation by bad actors. The systems described as 'Evil,' 'Dark,' or 'Manipulative' are usually either poorly designed or misguided attempts to use normal economic levers in a game. What truly makes them Dark is in the intention of the designer. The measure of this however, is how the player perceives the systems, not just what was intended. A game that feels 'manipulative' will be negatively affected whether it is intended or not. Another game, using the exact same tools, but where contextually appropriate, may simply not feel 'manipulative'. Games like Monopoly GO! from Scopely are hugely successful, the model is valid, but when the same monetisation design is used in other games, often this appears overly aggressive and even arguably manipulative. It all comes down to understanding Player Utility that the game is addressing, and Monopoly GO! has been enormously successful, dominating the charts. What is considered 'Dark' is subjective and always in context with the game, something which regulatory intervention is rarely good at handling.

To be effective, designers need to focus on how to deliver player value in balance with both short- and long-term financial goals. In the end, games need systems which are sustainable and that also generate revenue now. It is not just a question of ethics, although having an ethical, authentic, player-focused mindset absolutely helps avoid many of these potential issues. Players who feel exploited by what they see as manipulative tactics will lose trust with the game and/or the developer. That will affect retention, revenue, and reviews (i.e., adoption) and ultimately the core measure of success, LTV.

Unfortunately, overuse of 'dark patterns' continues to damage the broader gaming industry by contributing to a negative perception of free-to-play and monetised games. Players have become increasingly wary of in-game purchases, associating them with predatory practices rather than meaningful value. This erosion of trust can make it harder for developers – especially in the free-to-play market – to create games that are both profitable and player-friendly. The impact of this has already led to an increase in regulation related to Online Privacy, Online Safety, and 'Loot Crates'; and with the UK's Online Safety Act, the EUs Digital Markets Act and upcoming (at time of writing) Digital Fairness Act we are seeing the attitude of governments around the world hardening against the games industry. These legislative changes create artificial barriers that disproportionately affect smaller, independent teams and that in turn impacts the very creativity that helped make games this cultural phenomenon. We only have to look at regulation around 'Cookie's' to see the risk of the unexpected consequences of regulators who don't understand what they are trying to regulate.

A healthy game economy should generally offer players multiple paths to progression. Players should feel that they are making meaningful progress whether they are spending money or not. This can be achieved by designing a progression system that rewards skill, time investment, and strategic decision-making. Free players should be able to enjoy the game and progress without feeling punished, while paying players should feel that their purchases offer convenience, customisation, or unique experiences maximising their experience without giving them an unfair competitive advantage.

Developers should pay attention to the unintended consequences so they can avoid manipulative monetisation practices, such as pay-to-win mechanics, loot boxes with hidden odds, or time-limited offers that pressure players into making impulsive purchases. This is increasingly being regulated, but will lead to further, more restrictive, regulation if we don't put a stop to bad practice. Instead, they should focus on creating monetisation models that are transparent, ethical, and aligned with player expectations. Players actively appreciate knowing exactly what they are paying for and feeling in control of their purchases. Providing clear information about how items and currencies are priced and ensuring that players feel they are getting good value for their money fosters long-term loyalty and repeat transactions. Directly manipulative techniques, such as not revealing the price until the last minute, actively reduces conversion and additionally, longer term willingness to spend. Putting pricing upfront and clear rather than abstracting the costs was an early lesson and a contributing factor to 3UK mobile games offer being so successful, relative to other Java MIDP games platforms at the time (2006).

Finally, successful developers are those who actively engage with player feedback and adapt their economy design based on player needs and preferences. Creating open channels of communication through forums, surveys, and social media allows developers to understand how players perceive the economy and where improvements can be made.

Regularly reviewing feedback, analysing in-game data, and making data-driven adjustments to pricing, progression, or rewards can help developers course-correct before dissatisfaction grows. Players appreciate when their voices are heard, and responsive developers who are willing to pivot based on feedback are more likely to maintain a dedicated, loyal community. That does not mean that developers should do exactly what players say they want! Players are rarely good at designing solutions, but they are great at identifying problems.

A sustainable, player-first economy is one that respects player investment, provides meaningful rewards, and fosters trust through ethical monetisation practices. By avoiding exploitative tactics and ensuring that every aspect of the economy is designed with the player's experience in mind, developers can create games that not only generate revenue but also build lasting communities and positive player relationships.

The long-term health of the gaming industry depends on developers embracing fair, transparent, and value-driven economy designs. By focusing on player satisfaction and creating economies that reward engagement and loyalty, developers can contribute to a healthier, more vibrant gaming ecosystem that benefits players and developers alike.

Interview

GAME ECONOMY INSIGHTS – A CONVERSATION WITH CHRIS KACZMARCZYK-SMITH

Game economies are complex, requiring a deep understanding of resource flows, player incentives, and long-term sustainability. To explore this further, I spoke with Chris Kaczmarczyk-Smith,[9] a game economist specialising in economic modelling, progression systems, and live-service economy management. Our discussion ranged from foundational economic principles in gaming to strategies for balancing player behaviour, resource availability, and monetisation.

Kaczmarczyk-Smith initially pursued economics without the intention of working in the games industry. However, a research paper he wrote about the in-game economy of *EVE Online* – examining whether supply and demand functioned in virtual environments – became the first step toward his career as a game economist. Over time, his background in labour economics and data analysis led him to apply economic theory to large-scale MMO economies, where scarcity, pricing, and specialisation all play crucial roles.

> People experience economics the same way, whether they're in a video game or at the market buying fruit.

The significance of economy sinks and sources (drains and faucets) – those mechanisms that regulate resource flow to maintain balance:

> In Eve Online, I think the most common item in that economy is called Tritanium. Player 1 comes in and she starts mining up a bunch of Tritanium, and she ends up accruing 100,000 units. We should have some sort of sink, that's burning that. She can go and continue doing this over and over over again, but there should be some natural sink in the economy.

The items which provide that balance need not be a simple one-to-one exchange, and Kaczmarczyk-Smith provides an example:

> ...like a tax built natively into the game, such that everything you do is going to cost you a little bit of fuel. You have to compensate

for that fuel consumption with production. I think of classic sinks and faucets.

He stresses that trade should emerge naturally through specialisation. If every player can do everything, trade loses its value. Instead, economies thrive when players have unique advantages based on their location, skill set, or access to specific resources.

> In Econ 101. They call it the Robinson Crusoe economy. One guy is better at making sticks, and one guy is better at making rocks. One guy is better at catching fish, and one's better at making shelter. What's the trade there? …If there's trade, that means specialization is happening. Players must rely on each other to fill gaps, making the economy more engaging.

In a game all resources are digital, so without any true scarcity. This can lead to resource or currency inflation, which rapidly undermines the value of the rewards and, as a result, the effort the players put into the game. This is where a Sink (a method to reduce the volume of a type of asset) becomes critical, often as a method of exchange for power, progression, or cosmetics. However, how we handle this has other consequences, Kaczmarczyk-Smith states:

> Let's say I want less of a material in the economy. I can do one of two things. At the very, very high level, I can increase the burns [effort], so it's more costly to acquire that thing or it's more difficult, or you can decrease the [rate or release of the] faucet/source. …both ultimately result in the same thing, but people are less reactive to an increase in cost than they are to a decrease in the initial benefit.

Modelling player behaviour in aggregate is more effective than trying to create overcomplicated systems with hyper-detailed simulations, Kaczmarczyk-Smith argues:

> People in aggregate will behave a certain way. So with a few simplifying assumptions, I'm able to abstract away from all of that complexity and create what I call the foundations of the economy. And this is basically how much material is in this economy. How quickly can it be extracted from the economy? How fast does stuff move from point A to point B?

This approach helps avoid unnecessary complexity while allowing the economy to function dynamically as players optimise their strategies. The fundamental goal is ensuring that resource scarcity and abundance are balanced to create meaningful progression. However, to do that, we need to understand something about the players.

> I've got to balance this economy to somebody. In other words, how hard is it to create an engine in this game? How many hours does it take? Well, when you're asking that question, you also have to ask what type of player are we talking about?

He highlights that the game economy, particularly for multiplayer games, can shine when we embrace these player specialisations.

> Variety and trade are what make a good game economy. If people are trading back and forth and there's variety, I think it's a good thing.

Kaczmarczyk-Smith tracks this behaviour using a toolkit of metrics that he feels are fundamental to how to look at the economy. For example, he looks at the quantity of stuff traded divided by the quantity of stuff produced, what he refers to as the "production to trade" ratio. The health of the game economy is measured against that metric.

> In my economy, for some assets, that's a two to one ratio of traded to produced, which is really cool because that tells me that every unit that's produced has changed hands twice.

He also refers to the "production to consumption" ratio which is similar, but relates to items which are removed from the economy and combined with an analysis of pricing, it helps us understand more about what is happening in the economy.

Monetisation, he says, should also focus on long-term engagement rather than short-term gains:

> Over-monetization burns out players. If you push too hard for revenue today, you're sacrificing long-term value. The best monetization makes players want to invest because they enjoy the experience.

Kaczmarczyk-Smith admires companies like Supercell, which implement monetisation in a way that enhances, rather than detracts from, the player experience.

Balancing economic progression involves setting clear reference points. Kaczmarczyk-Smith uses a 'North Star' material – an essential resource that acts as a benchmark for balancing other assets. This ensures that fluctuations in resource availability or price align with the game's intended difficulty curve.

> Prices are actually just a ratio of quantities. That's what a price is. It just so happens we've come up with this handy-dandy thing called a currency that allows us to more easily figure those ratios out. So in a single-player game, even if there's no trade at all, there's still a ratio.

Additionally, price elasticity plays a crucial role in game economy design. Kaczmarczyk-Smith describes a scenario where an item's price remained static despite player complaints of scarcity:

> Players said it was rare, but its price wasn't rising. Increasing supply didn't change the price either. The issue wasn't scarcity – it was a lack of meaningful uses for that item. Adding more sinks resolved the imbalance.

This illustrates how price signals reveal deeper issues within an economy, guiding necessary adjustments.

Contrary to the pursuit of perfect balance, Kaczmarczyk-Smith argues that *intentional imbalance* is a crucial driver of engagement:

> I think that good imbalance, which maybe is a weird word, is one of the coolest things that you can have in an economy. Perfect balance is B.S. It's an impossibility, first of all. And second of all, the second you get it, if you were to get it, five minutes later, it's going to be gone.

He argues that imbalance, such as regional resource disparity creates an inherent dynamic, driving behaviour and engagement in the game.

> [There are] types of emergent phenomenon that come from physical games that use really complex physics engines, I think there's an analogy in economic systems, and that's why think economic systems should be as open as possible.

This philosophy aligns with Tadhg Kelly's concept of *possibility spaces* – open-ended environments where player choices drive emergent gameplay. By ensuring that certain resources or strategies are more viable in specific contexts, developers can create dynamic economies that adapt over time.

Key Takeaways for Game Economy Design

Kaczmarczyk-Smith offers several guiding principles for game economy design:

- **Keep it simple**. Overcomplicating systems leads to unnecessary challenges and often unintended exploits.

- **Use prices, use metrics** to drive decision-making about the actual economy once it's running

- **Appreciate the long term**, the long view, what kind of experience are you trying to curate? Tapping money today is costing us potentially money in the future.

By adopting these principles, developers can create game economies that drive engagement, support meaningful player progression, and remain commercially sustainable in the long run.

Kaczmarczyk-Smith continues to share his insights through his blog and podcast,[10] where he discusses game economy topics with other industry professionals. His expertise demonstrates the importance of understanding economic fundamentals when designing systems that keep players invested for years.

NOTES

1 https://academyofanimatedart.com/gaming-statistics
2 https://www.wepc.com/news/video-game-statistics/
3 https://www.grandviewresearch.com/press-release/global-video-game-market
4 https://www.ox.ac.uk/news/2019-02-13-violent-video-games-are-not-associated-adolescent-aggression-new-study-finds-0
5 https://www.asa.org.uk/resource/guidance-on-advertising-in-game-purchases.html
6 https://www.twobirds.com/en/insights/2025/european-move-towards-protecting-users-from-harmful-practices-in-video-games-eu-consumer-protection
7 https://www.taylorfrancis.com/chapters/edit/10.4324/9781315696935-10/illusions-control-suzanne-thompson
8 https://www.jstor.org/stable/20182602
9 www.linkedin.com/in/christopher-kaczmarczyk-smith-2557b7224
10 https://chriseconomics.substack.com/

CHAPTER 14

Game Design Principles in Other Industries

DOI: 10.1201/9781003592471-14

IS GAME ECONOMY DESIGN RELEVANT FOR OTHER INDUSTRIES?

Game economy design at its heart speaks to human behaviour and how we apply the communication of ideas, incentives, and rewards into satisfying, sustaining experiences. Any commercial organisation which has a collective audience that needs to be sustained over the longer term, can benefit from understanding how game systems function.

Game economy designers model experiences and adapt to player/user choices within a context. This might be a narrative world in a game, but users have their own experience journeys when engaging with Education, Banking, Fitness, and, of course, other forms of entertainment content. The same underlying psychological motivations for players to retain within a game can generally be applied to the 'real world.' Just look at how influential the Eve Online Economy has become and how it has been used to help model real-world economies.

Designers create systems which are all about keeping our players (users) invested, motivated, and continuously engaged through carefully orchestrated cycles. These cycles consist of start conditions, challenges, resolutions, and rewards, the logic of which can be applied to any organisation seeking to build engagement, foster loyalty, and increase long-term participation. By understanding these dynamics and adapting them to other contexts, almost any business can transform its audience interactions and create sustainable ecosystems of value exchange.

THE CORE LOOP CYCLE

In a typical game, the Core Loop cycle rolls through a **Start Condition**, **Challenge**, **Resolution,** and **Reward**, where the player is introduced and then led through a task or objective with an outcome which sets them up to reinvest in the experience and repeat that activity. The same concept applies when engaging any consumer with a brand, team, or even charity. When someone tries to learn a new topic or how to use an online application, game mechanics are extremely effective. Where are they in their journey, what set-up do we need to convey, and how do we develop a sense of anticipation? And how do we keep them engaged?

Start Condition

The start condition in games sets the stage for the player's journey. It could be as simple as presenting a new level to explore or a mission to complete. Outside of gaming, the start condition represents the initial interaction or touchpoint a customer has with a business. This could be browsing a website, entering a store, downloading an app, or subscribing to a service.

Organisations can optimise these start conditions by focusing on user experience, ensuring that first impressions are smooth, intuitive, and inviting. It can be expressed through brand design, the consistency of marketing materials and messaging, and of course in the points of sale/contact such as websites or social channels. For e-commerce, for example, a seamless and visually appealing homepage with clear calls to action can deliver an effective start condition. For a healthcare app, onboarding that introduces the user to the value of the platform and introduces them to set initial goals may serve a similar function.

To design an effective start condition, businesses should ask:

- What motivates users to begin interacting with our product or service?

- How can we remove barriers to entry and provide a frictionless start to their experience?

- How to make users feel comfortable and aspire to engage with the brand?

Challenge

Challenges are central to game design – they create obstacles that test a player's skills or knowledge, keeping them engaged and giving them a reason to continue. In non-gaming industries, challenges are the tasks, goals, or milestones customers need to achieve to derive value from a product or service.

For example, in fitness apps, the challenge might be completing a workout or reaching a specific step count. In education, it could be mastering a new concept or passing a quiz. Retail companies may present challenges through limited-time offers or loyalty programmes, where customers are encouraged to make purchases to unlock better value or even bonus rewards.

Effective challenges are designed to:

- Be achievable but still require effort, creating a sense of progression and accomplishment.

- Increase in complexity as the user becomes more familiar with the product or service, ensuring continued engagement without overwhelming them.

Resolution

In games, the resolution is the outcome of the challenge, and it's not always a victory. Whether the player succeeds or fails, the resolution is a critical moment of feedback that tells the player how they performed and what they could do differently. This feedback loop is vital in non-gaming industries as well.

In a fitness app, the resolution is the feedback the user receives after completing a workout – whether they met their target or need improvement. In a retail experience, it could be a purchase or for a charity, a donation. In a subscription-based service, the resolution might occur after a trial period when the customer decides whether to continue using the product based on their experience.

Businesses need to ensure that their resolutions are clear, immediate, and meaningful. Feedback should reinforce progress and guide users toward future success. For instance, a customer service platform can provide instant notifications that reward customers for resolving an issue on their own or give pointers on how to improve next time.

Reward

Rewards are the cornerstone of keeping players engaged in games, and they function in much the same way in other industries. Rewards can take many forms, from tangible benefits like discounts or points in loyalty programmes to intangible benefits such as the satisfaction of completing a task or achieving a personal goal. However, it can also be driven from sharing the journey of the project with the audience. This is particularly the case with charity organisations, where after getting the donation we follow up and demonstrate what has been done with that money – authentically demonstrating the contribution from the individual. This leaves the door open for re-engagement and developing further opportunity for repeat donations. Thinking about your consumers as an audience transforms the relationship, building anticipation, and desire, as well as FOMO – even if they don't spend money on the initial engagement. Authentically building that relationship through making them feel your brand is part of their tribal identity creates momentum that will pay off down the line. And of course, if they are rewarded for their membership (purchase behaviour), this can reinforce the reasons to tell others and, importantly, do it again.

Crucially, rewards need to feel valuable, aligned with the user's effort, and foreshadow value from doing it again. For example, a customer who completes a loyalty challenge to earn points in a retail app expects that these points will lead to meaningful discounts or exclusive offers, and you can also offer them further opportunities down the line. In educational platforms, rewards can be badges, certificates, unlocking new areas for study, or simply the sense of accomplishment that comes from mastering new skills.

Rewards should be:

- **Timely**: Delivered soon after the resolution to reinforce the desired behaviour.

- **Relevant**: Tailored to the user's preferences and aligned with their motivations.

- **Variable**: Adjusted to maintain excitement and avoid predictability, much like how games vary rewards to keep players intrigued.

Context and Cultural Loops

This way of thinking is not limited to the Core Loop. Industries which are seeking to sustain longer-term engagement with their audience can also look to the Context and Cultural loops.

The context aspects are all around understanding the consumer's purpose and sense of progression they attain from engaging with your organisation. Rather than resorting to superficial loyalty schemes, consider how the consumer can evolve their relationship with you, and what optimisation they can develop through that engagement. How does the business offering support their longer-term goals and help them more, when they engage with the business? Even more than that, can the business create a narrative of that journey, positive stories of engagement that they want to share with others, further reinforcing their engagement with the brand and the value that brand brings.

This leads swiftly into the cultural loop where teams can consider the conditions that their consumers find themselves in at the point they engage with the business. What form of social engagement do they have with the offer, and why, importantly, would they tell others about their positive experiences?

Thinking about the emotional transitions of your consumer in your industry need not be as detailed as within a game, but asking the same questions about "Why they should care?" and how to deliver utility is fundamental to successful retention and growth.

APPLYING THE LOOP CYCLE ACROSS INDUSTRIES
Retail and E-commerce

The application of game economy principles in retail is already well underway, particularly in loyalty programmes, limited-time challenges, and reward structures that mimic gaming loops. For instance, many brands offer tiered loyalty programmes where customers can progress through levels based on their spending. Each level unlocks additional rewards or perks, akin to how players advance through game levels. This approach keeps customers motivated to spend more, as they feel a sense of achievement and progression.

However, some of these loyalty schemes are soulless and overly simplistic points generators that fail to reinforce why the consumer should care or even aspire to more points. For example, Avios, the reward program used by the team at British Airways uses point. However, access to using them has become so constrained by the need for a second more temporary currency of 'tier points'; and a different pricing valuation which affects the taxable of the acquired ticket. This additional complexity has rendered left-over Avios essentially worthless – the author has over 200,000 Avios, but trying to spend them on a flight seems to always end up costing more in 'taxes' than buying the same ticket as a standard economy flight.

Challenges in retail can also come in the form of flash sales or limited-edition product drops, where the scarcity and time-limited nature of the offer create a sense of urgency. Customers are more likely to engage with these challenges when they know that a valuable reward, such as a discount or exclusive item, awaits them.

So how does this thinking actually apply outside of games? Here are a few examples:

Fitness and Wellness

The fitness industry has embraced the loop cycle model through the use of gamification in apps and wearable technology. Apps like Fitbit or Strava engage users by setting daily challenges (e.g. achieving a certain number of steps or completing a workout) and providing real-time feedback (resolution) on their performance.

Users are rewarded with badges, rankings, or personal progress data, all of which motivate them to continue engaging with the platform.

The start condition here is simple: users begin with the intention of improving their health or fitness. As they interact with the app, the challenges become progressively more difficult, pushing them toward their goals. The resolution phase offers critical feedback, often accompanied by motivational messages, and the rewards reinforce the effort – be it virtual medals, personal bests, or social recognition.

Education and Skill Development

In education, particularly with online learning platforms, game economy design principles have reshaped how users engage with content.[1] Platforms like Duolingo or Khan Academy use the loop cycle to keep learners coming back. A learner starts with a goal (start condition), completes lessons or quizzes (challenge), receives feedback (resolution), and is rewarded with points, badges, or access to new levels (reward).

These platforms carefully balance difficulty to ensure that users feel challenged but not overwhelmed. The use of variable rewards, where learners don't always know what they'll receive for completing a task, keeps the experience fresh and exciting.

Subscription Models and Digital Services

For businesses operating subscription models, maintaining user engagement over time is critical to reducing churn. The loop cycle can be applied by offering customers ongoing challenges, such as new content releases or personalised recommendations, based on their usage patterns.

For instance, a streaming service might encourage users to explore new genres (challenge), and upon completion of watching a show, provide tailored suggestions or access to exclusive content (reward). The resolution in this context involves immediate feedback in the form of user ratings or personalised feedback on viewing preferences, which helps shape future recommendations.

Subscription models, which have no opportunity for upsell, will always be particularly vulnerable as this will impact the ability to strategically invest in new innovation, and that will damage the longevity and scalability of the offering. Some entertainment platforms have tried to offset that by offering ad-supported content or charging content creators for listing positioning; however, adding material value-added offers is usually necessary to deliver the innovation required to sustain audiences and to fight off new entrants in the longer term.

Financial Services and Savings Programmes

The loop cycle can also be applied to financial services, particularly in savings programmes or financial wellness platforms. Here, the start condition could be the user's decision to save or invest money. The challenge is maintaining consistent contributions or reaching specific financial milestones, while the resolution is the progress made toward these goals, often tracked via visual indicators or personalised feedback.

The reward could be as tangible as achieving a savings goal or as abstract as the peace of mind that comes with financial security. Platforms like Acorns[2] or Oportun (formerly called Digit)[3] have already adopted this approach, using gamified elements to make saving money feel like a rewarding and engaging challenge.

CONCLUSION

The loop cycle of start condition, challenge, resolution, and reward is a powerful framework that extends beyond the boundaries of game economy design. By incorporating these principles, industries ranging from retail and fitness to education and financial services can create more engaging and satisfying user experiences. At the heart of this approach is the ability to motivate users to continuously participate, fostering a deeper connection with the brand or service. In an era where attention is the most valuable currency, applying game economy design principles can help organisations build lasting engagement and loyalty with their audiences.

Interview

DESIGN AS A BRIDGE BETWEEN BRANDING AND GAMES – AN INTERVIEW WITH MONIKA MONKO

Design, at its core, is about fulfilling a purpose. Whether in branding, game design, or product packaging, good design ensures that the user's journey is seamless, engaging, and rewarding. Monika Monko,[4] a design project manager at Kraft Heinz, brings a wealth of experience spanning graphic design, UX, branding, and packaging. Her insights help bridge the gap between these seemingly different industries by emphasising the common thread of function and user experience.

> In the simplest way I can think of it, it's when things that are made to do, made to fulfil some purpose, do that exactly without obstructions.

Whether it's a well-designed ketchup bottle that allows for smooth dispensing or a video game that intuitively guides the player through challenges, design exists to remove friction and enhance the experience. Monko highlights that while many people think of design purely as aesthetics, it is, in fact, deeply rooted in functionality.

Many consumers take for granted the iterative processes that go into designing everyday products. From ideation to prototyping, testing, and refinement, the journey of a product to market is filled with deliberate design choices.

> Previously, I was involved with ice cream, and there were samples delivered from the R&D department that would just come in little boxes with a simple label written in pen… And we were testing if it tastes OK, if it's going to sell, if the balance of flavours is right.

This process mirrors game design in many ways. Just as a food product undergoes iterative testing to ensure it meets consumer expectations, games go through playtesting, balancing, and refinement before they reach the public. Early access in games provides a similar opportunity to assess what works and what doesn't, though Monko points out the risk of staying in early access indefinitely or failing to act on collected feedback.

> I participate myself, and if it's games I'm passionate about, then I really do my best to participate, to report any bugs, any feedback whatsoever. But there's also been games that have been in early access for years or never left early access or left early access and were immediately abandoned.

This highlights the importance of clear objectives and a structured approach to design, whether in consumer goods or digital experiences.

Scarcity plays a crucial role in both branding and game economies. Limited-edition food products create hype and exclusivity, much like rare in-game items or time-limited content in live service games. However, Monko notes that major consumer brands often struggle to use scarcity effectively due to production constraints.

> Nowadays I see it more as a one-off thing, which is designed to go viral on social media, and then it's really limited… Some people managed to get their hands on this exclusive product. It's never happening again.

This tactic is reminiscent of how game developers create urgency with seasonal content or battle passes. The difference, however, is that digital scarcity can be manufactured at no additional cost, whereas physical products require costly production adjustments.

One of the biggest challenges in large-scale consumer branding and game development is maintaining a global identity while catering to regional preferences. Brands like Kraft Heinz maintain localised variations of their products while ensuring their overarching identity remains intact.

> There's a few global brands that you will see being almost identical products in all the countries where you can buy them, which Heinz is the best example of it. And there is lots of regional, very local brands… that essentially back in the day were all smaller companies and in time would be bought over by FMCG giants.

This mirrors the localisation challenges in gaming. A game might have a universal gameplay loop but needs significant adaptation in its visual, textual, and even mechanical elements to resonate with different audiences.

Monko underscores how early-stage risk assessment is critical in ensuring a successful product launch. The same applies to game development – understanding the potential roadblocks before full-scale production prevents costly mistakes.

> Honestly, years of experiencing this not being done… The more risks they consider, the more unexpected things and different sides, different faces to a project they consider early on, the higher the chances are that they will actually launch something successful and usable.

Game designers often approach projects with a problem-solving mindset, identifying potential player experience issues before the game is in players' hands. This concept is echoed in branding and packaging, where usability testing ensures that consumers can engage with a product as intended.

Accessibility is another critical factor that applies to both branding and game design. Good design benefits everyone, not just those with specific disabilities or limitations.

> If you design for those with different needs from able-bodied persons, everyone benefits.

This principle is evident in video games that incorporate customisable UI, colourblind-friendly palettes, and alternative control schemes. Similarly, in branding and packaging, legibility, contrast, and physical ergonomics play a major role in making products usable for a diverse audience.

> There is some standards that have to be adhered by, such as the minimum font size required by the European Union. Anything below that value will not be legible, so it can't be printed in that form.

This standardisation ensures that crucial information – whether in-game tooltips or ingredient lists on packaging – is accessible to as many users as possible.

A brand's visual identity is often subject to change, just as a game may evolve through updates or sequels. However, these changes need to be informed by audience expectations.

> Lots of companies think they can solve fundamental problems… by redesigning their whole brand without any sort of research, any sort of groundwork, any foundation where they don't actually know what they stand for.

This cautionary note applies equally to games. Franchises that stray too far from their original appeal can alienate their core audience, much like brands that fail to recognise what their consumers value.

Thoughtful, Purpose-Driven Design

Design – whether in consumer branding or game development – should always begin with a deep understanding of the user's needs, potential risks, and a clear definition of the problem being solved. Monko's insights highlight that good design transcends industry boundaries and shares fundamental principles across different disciplines.

> The earlier you think about what could potentially go wrong… the easier it will be later on. It's really a lot of work up front, but if you don't invest, if you don't do that work up front, you end up with so many bottlenecks along the way and so many unsuccessful launches.

For game designers, brand strategists, and UX professionals alike, this serves as a reminder that thoughtful, intentional design leads to products that are both functional and meaningful to their users.

NOTES

1 https://pmc.ncbi.nlm.nih.gov/articles/PMC8150082/
2 https://www.acorns.com/
3 https://oportun.com/savings/
4 www.linkedin.com/in/mmonko

CHAPTER 15

Conclusions

IS THIS EVERYTHING?

Commercial Game Design is not just about making money. But money is inevitably a factor which affects how we look at any design.

Thinking about why we play and why we pay has profound consequences for how we understand how humans behave, and I feel it can do more to help how we look at life.

I want to encourage you to think about how we can motivate people to engage more deeply in the experiences we create, and how that can help us sustain their interest by thinking about their core, context, and cultural experiences.

Remember that Engagement = Retention = Revenue.

Perhaps it's too cliché, but I do hope the commercially minded find in this book a reason to care about the player experience and what our audience values. But equally, I hope the creatively minded can see how the structures and processes of professional economy design, and importantly, "system thinking" can offer meaning as well as sustainability for your projects.

However, the most important lesson I hope comes from the realisation that there are many different views on what drives good design, what drives monetisation, and that this industry is constantly evolving. At the time of writing, we had just come out of the most significant downturn I have ever seen in nearly 30 years of my career. An event that arose out of an unprecedented event in modern times, the global COVID lockdowns that ironically spurred the industry to even greater heights.

DOI: 10.1201/9781003592471-15

The framework in this book outlines what I consider when I look at building a game economy and the tools I use to help try to rescue or to decide to recommend killing games. I hope that it provides you with some tools and ways to think that perhaps can help you to go on to make even better games.

Index

Note: *Italic* page numbers refer to figures.

For Product Safety Concerns and Information please contact our EU
representative GPSR@taylorandfrancis.com
Taylor & Francis Verlag GmbH, Kaufingerstraße 24, 80331 München, Germany